Make that Grade
Irish Tort Law

Second Edition

Make that Grade
Irish Tort Law

Second Edition

Kathleen Moore Walsh

Gill & Macmillan

Gill & Macmillan Ltd
Hume Avenue
Park West
Dublin 12
with associated companies throughout the world
www.gillmacmillan.ie

© Kathleen Moore Walsh 2006
ISBN-13: 978 0 7171 4026 8
ISBN-10: 0 7171 4026 1

Print origination in Ireland by Carole Lynch

The paper used in this book comes from the wood pulp
of managed forests. For every tree felled, at least one tree
is planted, thereby renewing natural resources.

A catalogue record is available for this book
from the British Library.

CONTENTS

INTRODUCTION

I. Historical background

*A. Tort comes from the **Latin word tortus,** meaning twisted.* **[1]**

    1. Tort is found in the French language and means *wrong*.
    2. At one time tort was used in the English language as another word for wrong.
       a. Similarly, the word 'wrong' is said to be derived from 'wrung'.
       b. After the word 'tort' left common English speech, it continued to be used in the law.

B. Early torts **[2]**

    1. Generally in the early English common law, remedies for wrongs depended on the issuance of writs to bring a defendant into court. The procedures were rigidly prescribed, and only two writs were available for tortious acts:
       a. **Trespass;**
       b. **Trespass on the case** or action on the case.
    2. **Trespass** first emerged in the thirteenth century and was criminal in character.
       a. Directed at serious and forcible breaches of the peace.
       b. Courts were primarily concerned with punishment.
       c. If convicted, a defendant was fined and imprisoned if the fine was not paid. This is how damages first became awarded to an injured plaintiff.
       d. **Remedy** for all *forcible, direct* and *immediate injuries,* whether to persons or property.
    3. **Trespass on the case** is sometimes referred to as action on the case, and developed as a supplement to trespass. It was designed to afford a remedy for obviously wrongful conduct resulting in indirect injuries.
    4. **Distinction** between **trespass** and **trespass on the case:** **[3]**

Trespass	Trespass on the case
Developed around the thirteenth century.	Developed around the fourteenth century.
Criminal in character.	Developed as a supplement to trespass.
Directed at serious and forcible breaches of peace. (Direct injuries)	Directed at injuries caused by some obvious and secondary causes. (Indirect injuries)
Liability imposed without regard to fault. Requires no proof of any actual damage. (Actionable per se)	Liability only imposed with proof of wrongful intent or negligence. (**Not** actionable per se)

5. Distinction between direct and indirect injuries is found in the classic case of *Reynolds v Clarke* (1725) 1 Stra 634. Fortescue J. explained that if a log is thrown into the highway, if a person is struck when it is being thrown, that person could maintain trespass against the thrower. The injury is direct. If a person is injured because the log was tripped over as it lay in the highway, the injured person could only bring a trespass on the case action. The injury is indirect.

II. Modern tort law

A. The historical classifications of injuries as direct or indirect is being abandoned.   [4]

1. **Focus** is now on the intent or fault (negligence) of the wrongdoer.
2. Old common law action of *trespass* has given rise to some modern tort actions.
   a. All may be maintained without proof of damages.
   b. **Examples:**
      (1) Battery   (5) Trespass to chattels
      (2) Assault   (6) Conversion
      (3) False imprisonment   (7) Detinue
      (4) Trespass to land
3. Likewise, *trespass on the case* has given rise to some modern torts where damage is the basis of the action.
   a. **Examples:**
      (1) Intentional infliction of emotional distress
      (2) Negligence
      (3) Deceit

B. *Definition of tort* [5]

1. Generally, academics have difficulty in defining tort. However, all definitions of tort refer to the unreasonable interference with the interests of others.
2. Various definitions of tort include:
   a. A tort is a civil wrong (other than a breach of contract or a breach of trust) for which the normal remedy is an action for unliquidated damages. McMahan citing, *Secretary of State for War v Studdert* [1902] 1 I.R. 375 (H.L.), aff'g [1902] 1 I.R. 240 (C.A.).
      (1) Unliquidated damages are damages determined by the court.
   b. A tort is a civil wrong, other than breach of contract, for which the court will provide a remedy in the form of an action for damages. (Prosser)
   c. Tortious liability arises from the breach of a duty primarily fixed by law; this duty is towards persons generally and its breach is redressable by an action for unliquidated damages. (Winfield)
   d. A civil wrong for which the remedy is a common law action for unliquidated damages, and which is not exclusively the breach of contract, or the breach of a trust, or other merely equitable obligation. (Salmond)

C. *Function of modern tort law* [6]

1. The protection of interests.
   a. **Examples**:
      (1) Defamation protects good name;
      (2) Nuisance protects use and enjoyment of land; and
      (3) Battery protects bodily integrity.

D. *Goals of modern tort law* [7]

1. Compensation for injuries to interests.
2. Loss distribution for injuries.
3. Punishment of wrongdoers.
4. Deterrence against future injuries and retaliation.

E. *Modern tort liability* [8]

1. Is generally divided into three main areas.
   a. Intentional torts

    b. Fault-based torts
    c. Strict liability
  2. Not all torts fall within just one of the three main areas.

F. Distinction between tort and criminal wrongs [9]

Tort	Crime
Private dispute between individuals.	Public dispute between an individual and society.
Primary goal is to compensate for harm suffered.	Primary goal is to punish wrongdoer.
Plaintiff brings the action (case).	The state (through DPP) brings the action.

G. Distinction between tort and breach of contract [10]

Tort	Breach of contract
Breach of duty fixed by law.	Breach of duty fixed by parties themselves.
Duties owed to people in general.	Duties only owed to parties in contract.
Primary goal to compensate for harm suffered.	Primary goal to enforce terms (promises) in contract.
Unliquidated damages – damages may be of any amount.	Liquidated damages – the limits of liability, i.e. damages, are fixed by the parties to the contract.

III. List of abbreviations of commonly cited tort works [11]

A. Irish

  1. McMahon   McMahon and Binchy, *Irish Law of Torts*, 3rd ed., Dublin: Butterworths 2000.
  2. Quill   Quill, *Torts in Ireland*, 2nd ed., Dublin: Gill & Macmillan 2004.
  3. Burke   Burke and Corbett, *Essential Law of Torts*, Dublin: Round Hall 2003.

B. Other

1. Salmond — Salmond and Heuston, *Salmond and Heuston of the Law of Torts*, 21st ed., London: Sweet and Maxwell 1996. (English and Irish)

2. Street — Street, *The Law of Torts*, 10th ed., London: Butterworths 1999. (English)

3. Winfield — Winfield and Jolowicz, *Winfield and Jolowicz on Tort*, 15th ed., London: Sweet and Maxwell 1998. (English)

4. Prosser — Prosser and Keeton, *Prosser and Keeton on the Law of Torts*, 5th ed., St. Paul: West 1984. (American)

5. Restatement — American Law Institute, *Restatement (Second) Tort*, St. Paul: American Law Institute Publishers 1990 (American).

Review Questions

1. What is the primary function of modern tort law?
2. Distinguish between torts and criminal wrongs.
3. Distinguish between tort and contract law.
4. Distinguish between the ancient writs of trespass and trespass on the case.

SECTION I:
INTENTIONAL LIABILITY

INTENTIONAL TORTS
TO THE PERSON

Chapter Synopsis

I.   Trespass to the person
     Battery
     Assault
     False imprisonment
II. Intentional infliction of emotional distress
III. Defences to intentional torts of the person

I. Trespass to the person [12]

A. **Definition**: *Direct and intentional acts of interference by the defendant with the person of the plaintiff.*

B. *There are three modern torts to the person that flow from the ancient principles of trespass.*

   1. Battery
   2. Assault
   3. False imprisonment
      a. All three are crimes as well as torts. [13]
         (1) Tort – does *not* require the mental element of *mens rea*.
         (2) Criminal cases can often be used in tort as authority, but always note the different context of the decisions.

C. *Common characteristics: All three trespasses to the person have the following three* common *characteristics.* [14]

   1. **Voluntary act by the defendant.**
      a. Voluntary meaning under defendant's *conscious control.*
         (1) **Example**: A person who strikes another while suffering an epileptic seizure did not act voluntarily, i.e. act with conscious control.

    (2) **Classic case**: *Scott v Shepherd* (1573) 96 ER 525. Persons in a busy market who were throwing fireworks away from themselves were not acting voluntarily because they were acting in self-defence after a person had thrown the fireworks toward them.

  b. The defendant's act must be *intentional* or *negligent*.   **[15]**

    (1) It is not necessary for the plaintiff to prove that the defendant intended to injure the plaintiff.

    (2) However, it is necessary to prove that the defendant intended the acts which led to the plaintiff's injury.

    (3) **Example**: As a romantic gesture, if Tarzan swept Jane off her feet, but dropped her, causing Jane to break her wrist, Tarzan did not intend the injury, but he did intend the act.

  c. **No transferred intent**: The intent to commit a tort against one victim *cannot* be transferred to another victim.   **[16]**

    (1) Historically, transferred intent applied to the five intentional torts of battery, assault, false imprisonment, trespass to chattels and trespass to land.

    (2) Legal commentators appear to agree that transferred intent should *not* be applied in a civil case (although the concept is accepted in criminal law).

    (3) **Note**: Negligence may apply. A person is always deemed to intend the natural and probable consequences of their actions.

      (a) **Example**: Sally and Greg are in a crowded pub. Sally is annoyed with Greg and intends to throw her glass of red wine on him. If Sally misses and hits Danny with the wine, she has committed a battery to Danny although she did not intend to hit him with the wine.

2. **Direct injury to plaintiff**. See [3] for difference between direct/indirect.   **[17]**

  a. Injury can be a mere *contact* or *impact* to plaintiff's person, property or rights (such as freedom).

  b. **Actionable per se**: No proof of damages is required to maintain an action.

3. **Causation**: The injury to the plaintiff must be caused by the defendant's voluntary act or some force set in motion by the defendant's act.   **[18]**

   a. **Burden of proof**
      (1) The plaintiff must prove that the defendant's conduct caused the injury, contact or impact.
      (2) The onus then shifts to the defendant to prove that the injury, contact or impact was not intentional or negligent.

Battery

> **Definition**: The direct application of physical contact upon the person of another without consent. *Dullaghen v Hillen* [1957] IR Jur Rep 10, 13.   **[19]**
>
> **Required Elements of Battery**   **[20]**
> A. Voluntary act by the defendant
> B. Physical contact (or impact) to the plaintiff
> C. Intention or negligence
> D. Causation
> E. No consent

A. *Voluntary act by the defendant*   **[21]**

   1. Voluntary meaning under defendant's conscious control.
      a. **Example**: A person who strikes another while suffering an epileptic seizure did not act voluntarily, i.e. act with conscious control.
      b. **Classic case**: *Scott v Shepherd* (1573) 96 ER 525. See [14].
   2. Force is *not* required.   **[22]**
      a. A hostile intent is *not* necessary for a battery.
         (1) **Examples**: Caressing or kissing the plaintiff.
      b. However, the least touching of another in anger is a battery. *Cole v Turner* (1704) 90 ER 958.
         (1) **Examples**: Hitting, striking, pinching or spitting on the plaintiff.
   3. Mere passive obstruction is not a battery.   **[23]**
      a. **Example**: John is standing in the doorway of the shop, and Mary wishes to enter the shop. John has not committed a battery even if Mary brushes against him.

B. *Physical contact (or impact) to the plaintiff*   **[24]**

   1. **No harm or injury required.**
      a. The plaintiff is not required to suffer any harm or injury such as bruising, cuts or broken bones from the contact.

b. The contact (or impact) is enough. *Rationale*: Battery protects bodily integrity.

2. **Physical contact** [25]

a. Extends to *any* part of the plaintiff's body that is touched,

b. Or to anything, which is *attached* to the plaintiff's body and practically, identified with it. **Examples**:

(1) Removing an orange lily from a lady's coat by a policeman was held to be battery. *Humphries v Connor* [1864] 17 IR CLR 1 (QB 1864).

(2) Striking the horse plaintiff was riding *Dodwell v Burford*, (1669) 86 ER 703.

(3) Pulling out the chair upon which a person was going to sit.

(4) Grabbing a plate out of a person's hand or knocking a hat off the plaintiff's head. [26]

3. **Impact**: No actual contact between the defendant and the plaintiff is required.

a. **Example**: If Fred hits Barney with a brick, Fred has committed a battery even though he did not actually touch Barney himself.

C. *Intention or negligence* [27]

1. **Intent**

a. It is not necessary for the plaintiff to prove that the defendant intended to injure or harm.

b. The plaintiff must show that the defendant intended the act(s) that constitute the battery.

2. **Negligence** [28]

a. **Natural and probable consequences**: Everyone is deemed to intend the natural and probable consequences of their actions.

b. **Example**: If Kitty hits a customer while practising her golf swing in a crowded sports shop, the contact with the customer would be a natural and probable consequence of Kitty's actions. Kitty owes a duty of care to the customer to act as a reasonable person (see [335] *et seq*). It is not reasonable to swing a golf club in a crowded sports store. Kitty has acted negligently.

D. *Causation* [29]

1. Direct application.

The contact (or impact) to the plaintiff must have *directly* resulted from the defendant's act(s). *Leame v Bray* (1803) 3 East 593. See causation [530].

2. Note: The intention to do the act disposes of any question of remoteness of damages. *Quinn v Leathan* [1901] AC 495. See remoteness [558].
   a. Proof of damages: Is not an issue because trespass is actionable per se.
3. Onus shifts: Once the plaintiff has proven a direct injury, i.e. contact or impact to the plaintiff's body, the onus or burden shifts onto the defendant to show that he did not act intentionally or negligently.

E. No consent (see defences [72])   [30]

1. **Express consent**: A verbal or written agreement to the physical contact.
   a. **Example**: A written consent form for surgery to be performed.
2. **Implied consent**: A presumed agreement to the physical contact based on the plaintiff's acts.
   a. **Example**: Rolling up sleeve and offering arm to doctor for blood to be drawn.
3. **Exceeding consent**: If consent, either express or implied, is exceeded, a battery occurs.   [31]
   a. **Example**: *Nash v Sheen* [1953] CLY 3726. The defendant hairdresser caused a skin complaint when she gave the plaintiff an unwanted hair dye when the plaintiff had requested a perm. The plaintiff's consent to physical contact had been exceeded, therefore the defendant was liable for battery.

Legal dilemma   [32]
1. Practical jokes and other contacts of modern life have caused difficulties.
   a. **Example**: It is technically a battery to slap someone's shoulder in congratulations or to bump into another on a crowded footpath.
2. **Implied consent fiction**: Some jurisdictions have skirted the problems associated with contacts of modern life by finding implied consent for the contact.
   a. By going out onto a crowded footpath, a person by her conduct consents to the normal bumps and impacts of walking on a crowded footpath.
3. **English approach**: Appears to reject the implied consent fiction and appears to view such contacts as battery if the contact is **hostile**.   [33]

a. Leading case: *Wilson v Pringle* [1987] QB 237; [1986] 2 All ER 440. A schoolboy was injured when another boy pulled his shoulder bag roughly.

b. **Hostility requirement**: Was rejected by Lord Goff in *F v West Berkshire Health Authority* [1989] 2 All ER 545, 564.

4. **American approach**: Rejects the implied consent fiction. Battery in the US has been restricted to harmful or offensive contact. [34]

a. Incidents of modern life, such as patting someone on the back, is not harmful or offensive, and thus not a battery in the US.

b. However, an unwanted kiss would be offensive.

c. Intentionally blowing cigar smoke into the plaintiff's face for the purpose of causing physical discomfort, humiliation and distress was found to be a battery. *Leichtman Communications v WLW Jacor*, 634 N.E.2d 697 (OH 1994).

Assault

> **Definition**: An act by the defendant that places the plaintiff in reasonable apprehension of an immediate battery. *Dullaghan v Hillen* [1957] IR Jur Rep 10. [35]
>
> **Required elements of assault** [36]
> A. Voluntary act by the defendant
> B. Apprehension by the plaintiff
> C. Intent or negligence
> D. Causation

A. *Voluntary act by the defendant* [37]

1. **Voluntary: Simply means under the defendant's conscious control**.

a. See [21].

b. **Assault example**: Mr Magoo is tired of pedestrians walking in the roadway instead of on the footpath. In an effort to teach Paul the pedestrian a lesson, Mr Magoo drives straight for Paul, only turning away at the last minute. Paul is frightened and thinks that he is going to be hit by the automobile. Mr Magoo performed a voluntary act, i.e. driving toward Paul. However, if Mr Magoo had passed out and his automobile veered toward Paul, causing Paul to think that the automobile was going to hit him, Mr Magoo has not performed a voluntary act.

2. **Words as the voluntary act**   **[38]**
   a. **General rule**: Words alone, no matter how harsh, lying, insulting and provocative, can never amount to an assault.
      (1) 'Sticks and stones may break your bones, but words will never harm you…no matter how harsh, lying, insulting, and provocative they may be…', Fawsitt J. in *Dullaghan v Hillen* [1957] IR Jur Rep 10.
   b. **Exception**: In a particular context, words alone may be an assault if the words induce a reasonable apprehension of an immediate battery. *Dullaghan v Hillen* [1957] IR Jur Rep 10.
      (1) **Example of exception**: In a dark, secluded alley a man whispers to a young girl, 'Don't move or I'll hurt you!'
   c. **Circumstances**: Under certain circumstances, words alone may render some conduct harmless that would otherwise constitute an assault.   **[39]**
      (1) **Classic case**: *Tuberville v Savage* [1669] 86 ER 684. Defendant, with his hand on his sword, said to the plaintiff: '[i]f it were not Assize time, I would not take such language from you.' (In earlier times, courts only sat at infrequent intervals, referred to as Assize time. In other words, the defendant was saying that because the courts were in session, he would ignore your remarks.) Held not to be an assault.

3. **Silence as the voluntary act**   **[40]**
   a. Legal commentators are divided over whether repeated harassing *silent phone calls* can amount to an assault.
   b. In two criminal cases, *R. v Ireland*; *R. v Burstow* [1998] AC 147, the defendant's silence was found to be capable of being a criminal assault. The defendant made repeated silent harassing phone calls to his victim.
      (1) These decisions have been criticised, as they do not fit nicely within the required elements of the tort of assault, i.e. how could a person be in reasonable apprehension of an immediate battery by a silent phone call if that person is home alone behind a locked door?
      (2) To deal with stalking and harassment that did not fit into criminal assault or the tort of assault, many jurisdictions have enacted anti-stalking and anti-harassment legislation.

　c. **Irish approach**: Section 10 of the Non-Fatal Offences
　　Against the Person Act 1997 makes it a criminal offence to by
　　any means including the telephone harass another by persis-
　　tently following, watching, pestering, besetting or communi-
　　cating with the victim.
　d. **English approach**: Protection from Harassment Act 1997.
　　(1) Introduced the tort of harassment into English law.
　　(2) Section 1 prohibits a person from pursuing a course of
　　　conduct that he or she knows or should know amounts
　　　to harassment of another.
4. **Passive obstruction**　　　　　　　　　　　　　　　　　　[41]
　a. **General rule**: Mere passive obstruction is *not* an assault.
　　(1) **Example**: *Innes v Wylie* (1844) 1 Car and K 257. A
　　　police officer stood still and barred the plaintiff's way.
　　　Held not to be an assault.
　b. **Exception to general rule**: If the defendant takes active steps
　　to block or obstruct the plaintiff, this may be an assault.
　　(1) **Example**: *Bruce v Dyer* (1966) OR 705 (Canadian). A
　　　driver parked his vehicle on the roadway to block anoth-
　　　er driver. This was held to be an assault.

B. *Apprehension by the plaintiff*　　　　　　　　　　　　　　[42]

1. **Assault**
　a. Said to be a *touching* of the *mind*, not the body.
　b. *Protects* against purely mental disturbances.
　c. No contact or impact to the plaintiff's person is required.
　　(1) An assault may occur without a battery.
　　(2) A battery may occur without an assault.
2. **Apprehension**　　　　　　　　　　　　　　　　　　　　　[43]
　a. Is *not* fear.
　　(1) Reasonable apprehension does *not* require the plaintiff to
　　　be in fear. The plaintiff must realise or perceive that a
　　　battery is imminent.
　b. Must be reasonable.
　　(1) A reasonable person would have the belief that a battery
　　　was imminent based upon the defendant's act(s) and the
　　　surrounding circumstances.
3. **Imminent battery required**　　　　　　　　　　　　　　　[44]
　a. Threats of future harm are generally *not* considered an assault.
　　(1) **Example**: *Thomas v National Union of Mineworkers*
　　　[1985] 2 All ER. The plaintiff, a miner, refused to join his

co-workers on strike. The plaintiff was brought to the pit on a bus through the picket lines. The striking miners made violent gestures to the occupants of the bus. These gestures of violence were held not to be an assault. The police held back the striking miners and the plaintiff was on the bus, therefore the plaintiff had no reasonable grounds that an immediate violent act was going to occur.

C. Intent or negligence   [45]

1. **Intent** see [15].
    a. **General rule**: An assault is *not* dependent on the defendant's intentions:
        (1)   Toward the plaintiff, or
            (a)   **Example**: Henry is throwing stones at his enemy Malachi while Malachi is talking to Sue. If Sue is placed in a reasonable apprehension of an immediate battery (being hit by a stone), Henry has committed an assault to Sue even though he did not intend to do so and had no quarrel with her.
        (2)   To carry out his threat.
            (a)   **Example**: If Conor points a gun in a threatening manner at Michael, it does not matter whether the gun is loaded or even able to fire; an assault has occurred if Michael is in reasonable apprehension of being shot. However, there would be no assault if Michael also knew that the gun was not loaded. *R. v St. George* (1840) C and P 483.

2. **Negligence**   [46]
    a. Natural and probable consequences: Everyone is deemed to intend the natural and probable consequences of their actions, so if the defendant negligently acts so as to cause the plaintiff to believe that a battery is imminent, he is liable for an assault.

D. Causation   [47]

1. **The plaintiff's reasonable apprehension must have *directly* resulted from the defendant's act(s).** See [29].
2. Onus shifts: Once the plaintiff has proven a direct injury (the act(s) of the defendant placed the plaintiff in a reasonable apprehension of an immediate battery), the onus shifts onto the defendant to show that he did not act intentionally or negligently.

False Imprisonment

> **Definition**: The unlawful and total restraint of the personal liberty of another. *Dullaghan v Hillen* [1957] Ir Jur 10. **[48]**
>
> **Street's definition**: Any act by the defendant which directly or intentionally or negligently causes the confinement of the plaintiff within an area delimited by the defendant. (Definition preferred by most legal commentators.)
>
> **Required elements of false imprisonment** **[49]**
> A. Voluntary act by the defendant
> B. Confinement of the plaintiff
> C. Causation
> D. No consent

A. Voluntary act by the defendant **[50]**

1. **Voluntary**: Meaning under the defendant's conscious control. See [21] and [37].
2. **Acts** may include the defendant:
   a. *Constraining* the plaintiff;
   b. *Compelling* the plaintiff to go to a particular place;
   c. *Confining* the plaintiff; or
   d. *Detaining* the plaintiff against his or her will.
3. **Physical contact** with the plaintiff's person is *not* required. **[51]**
4. **Words** alone may be a sufficient act for false imprisonment. **[52]**
   Examples:
   a. Threats of force: 'If you leave that chair I'll make you sorry you were ever born.'
   b. Asserting authority: 'You are under arrest. Don't move.'
5. **No act** **[53]**
   Failure to release: If the plaintiff becomes imprisoned on the defendant's land, there is *no* false imprisonment if the defendant did not place or induce the plaintiff to become imprisoned.

B. Confinement of the plaintiff **[54]**

1. **Requires *total restraint* of the plaintiff.**
   a. The inability of the plaintiff to go in *any* direction.
      (1) Including back the way the plaintiff came.
      (2) However, if the plaintiff is only prevented from going in

a certain direction, i.e. north, this is not a total restraint. *Bird v Jones* (1845) 115 ER 668.

2. Does *not* require the plaintiff to risk: **[55]**
   a. Injury; *Sayers v Harlow UDC* (1958) 1 WLR 623;
   b. Humiliation; or
   c. Property damage.
      (1) **Example**: Brutus stood in the only door into Oliveoil's office and demanded a kiss or he would not allow her to leave the office. The office is located on the third floor of the Spinach Exchange Building. Oliveoil is falsely imprisoned because she is totally restrained. The law does not require her to endure a humiliation (Brutus's kiss) to escape or to risk injury or damage to her clothing by climbing out the window onto an adjoining roof.   **[56]**

3. **Overt surveillance** is *not* a detention. *Kane v Gov of Mountjoy Prison* [1988] IR 757 (SC). So long as the person is free to go where she or he wants.

4. **Imprisonment**   **[57]**
   a. A sentence of imprisonment is *not* a false imprisonment.
   b. Continuation of imprisonment: A person who helps to continue a wrongful detention commits false imprisonment. This is true even if the person is not responsible for the original detention.

5. **Consciousness of confinement** is not required.   **[58]**
   a. False imprisonment may take place without the plaintiff being aware of being confined.
   b. **Examples**:
      (1) A sleeping or unconscious person.
      (2) A child.
      (3) A mentally handicapped person.

C. Causation   **[59]**

1. The defendant's act(s) must be the cause of the plaintiff's false imprisonment. See causation [29].
2. Onus shifts: Once the plaintiff shows that the act(s) of the defendant caused the plaintiff to be confined, then the onus shifts onto the defendant to prove that he did not act intentionally or negligently.

D. No consent (see defences [72]). **[60]**

II. Intentional infliction of emotional distress

Definition: Conduct by the defendant that intentionally or recklessly inflicts severe emotional distress to the plaintiff. **[61]**

Birth of Tort **[62]**
1. *Wilkinson v Downton* [1895-9] All ER 267. The defendant told the plaintiff that her husband had been seriously injured in a road accident. He further told the plaintiff that her husband wanted to come home. The plaintiff sent a servant and her son to bring the injured man home. Later, she learned that the story was not true. The story had been intended as a practical joke. The plaintiff suffered trauma to the extent that she suffered serious physical injury with lasting effects.
   a. The defendant in *Wilkenson v Downton* had not committed a recognised trespass to the plaintiff's person (battery, assault, false imprisonment).
2. **Distinguished from trespass.** **[63]**
   a. Intentional infliction of emotional distress flows from the ancient principles of trespass to the case rather than trespass.
   b. **Proof of injury** *is* necessary to maintain a cause of action, therefore intentional infliction of emotional distress is *not* actionable per se.
Required elements of intentional infliction of emotional distress **[64]**
   A. Voluntary act by the defendant
   B. Severe emotional distress to the plaintiff
   C. Intent or recklessness
   D. Causation

A. Voluntary act by the defendant **[65]**
1. **Voluntary**: Means under the defendant's conscious control. See [21] and [37].
   a. **Words**: Unlike assault, words may be sufficient as the required voluntary act.
   b. **Example**: *Janvier v Sweeney* [1919] 2KB 316. The plaintiff was deceived by a private investigator who misrepresented

himself as being a policeman. He threatened the plaintiff with criminal proceedings if she did not give him letters that were kept in the house where she worked as a servant. This caused the plaintiff to become ill with 'shock, neurasthenia, and shingles'. The Court allowed her claim for intentional infliction of emotional distress.

B. *Severe emotional distress to the plaintiff*   [66]

1. **Proof of injury** to the plaintiff is required.
   a. Plaintiff *must* suffer severe emotional distress.
   b. No physical manifestation of the emotional distress is required.
      (1) **Traditionally**: A physical injury was required to ensure against fraud.
      (2) **Modern approach**: In most jurisdictions, a demonstrable physical injury is not required. **Rationale**: There is now a better understanding of mental diseases and illness. Fraud is less of an issue. See nervous shock [482].

C. *Intent or recklessness*   [67]

1. **Intent**: The defendant must have intended to cause severe emotional distress to the plaintiff.
2. **Recklessness**: The defendant must have acted in disregard of a high probability that his actions would cause severe emotional distress to the plaintiff.

D. *Causation*   [68]

1. The defendant's act(s) ***must*** be the cause of the plaintiff's injury. See [29] and [530].
2. No onus shift: Intentional infliction of emotional distress is not actionable per se, therefore the plaintiff must prove that the defendant acted intentionally or negligently. The burden of proof does not shift onto the defendant.

No Irish cases reported
1. **English approach**   [69]
   a. McMahon believes that the tort may have been usurped by the statutory tort of harassment.
2. **American approach**   [70]

a. Tort applies to intentional or reckless infliction of emotional distress through extreme or outrageous conduct.
b. *Extreme or outrageous conduct required.*
   (1) No objective standard, but mere rude or offensive behaviour is not sufficient. Restatement 2d, section 46 describes it as exceeding all bounds of decent behaviour.
   (2) **Example:** *B.N. v K.K.* (1988) 538 A.2d 1175 (Maryland). The defendant doctor had sexual relations with his nurse, knowing that he had an active case of herpes. The defendant, as a doctor, was aware that the disease was painful and incurable. The defendant was found liable to the plaintiff for the intentional infliction of emotional distress. Note: The plaintiff could not plead battery because she had consented to the contact.

III. Defences to intentional torts to the person [71]

Defences to intentional torts to the person
A. Consent
B. Necessity
C. Inevitable accident
D. Parental authority
E. Statutory authority
F. Defence of self and/or property

A. Consent [72]

1. **General rule**: The plaintiff's consent to the defendant's contact or conduct renders the contact or conduct lawful.
   a. **Examples:**
      (1) *Hegarty v Shine* (1878) 4 LR Ir 288. No battery was found to have been committed against a woman who had been infected with a venereal disease by her partner. The woman had consented to sexual relations with her partner.
      (2) *R. v Linekar* [1995] 3 All ER 69. The defendant agreed to pay a prostitute £25 for sex. After, he refused to pay her. The defendant was charged with rape because the prostitute had consented to the contact for the promise of payment. **Held**: No rape. The prostitute had consented to the act.

2. **May be expressed or implied.**   **[73]**
   a. **Express consent**: A verbal or written agreement to the phys-
      ical contact or actions of the defendant.
      (1) **Examples**:
         (a) (Verbal) 'Please cut my hair.'
         (b) (Written) Signing a consent for surgery form.
   b. **Implied consent**: Consent is implied by the plaintiff's con-
      duct or act(s).
      (1) **Example**: Sitting in a barber's chair implies consent to a
          haircut.   **[74]**
      (2) **Test for implied consent** is objective.
         (a) **Reasonable**: From the plaintiff's conduct, was it
             reasonable for the defendant to think that the plain-
             tiff was consenting?
3. **Invalid consent** is consent obtained by fraud or deceit.   **[75]**
   a. **Exception**: The general rule regarding the defence of consent
      will *not* apply if the defendant obtained the plaintiff's consent
      by fraud or deceit.
      (1) *R. v Case*, 1 Den CC 580. A man told a young girl that
          the sexual acts that he perpetrated upon her was a surgi-
          cal operation.
      (2) *R. v Flattery* (1877) 2 QBD 410. A young girl was told
          that sexual acts would cure her asthma.
      (3) *R. v Williams* (1922) All ER Rep 433. A young girl was
          told by her singing teacher that his acts (sex) would
          improve her singing voice by making an air passage.
   b. **Note**: To invalidate the plaintiff's consent, the defendant's
      fraud or deceit *must* go to the nature of the act.
      Examples: **[76]**
      (1) **Not to the act**: Joey tells Monica that his name is
          Chandler, and later he asks Monica for a kiss. If Monica
          consents to the kiss, i.e. the act, Joey's fraud or deceit, i.e.
          lying about his name, does not invalidate Monica's con-
          sent to the kiss.
      (2) **To the act**: However, the fraud or deceit would go to the
          nature of the act if Joey asked Monica if he could whis-
          per a secret in her ear, but when she leaned toward him
          he grabbed and kissed her. Joey's deceit, i.e. lying about
          his act, invalidates Monica's consent (to allow Joey to
          whisper in her ear).

4. **Involuntary consent** [77]
   a. **Undue influence** may occur where there is an imbalance of power between the parties, rendering the consent involuntary.
   b. **Example**: *Norberg v Wyannib* (1993) 2 LRC 409 (Canadian). A doctor was engaging in sexual conduct with a patient in exchange for drugs for her addiction. The court held that her consent to the doctor's acts was not voluntary, and therefore invalid.
5. **Consent to medical treatment** [78]
   a. **General rule**: It is a battery to perform any medical treatment or procedures on a patient *without* the patient's consent. *Walsh v Family Planning Services Ltd* [1992] 1 IR 469. (SC) *obiter*.
      (1) **Example**: *Potts v N.W. Regional Health Authority* (1983) (unrep. Eng.). The plaintiff was given a long-acting contraceptive without her consent. Held to be a battery.
   b. **Informed consent** occurs where a patient consented to treatment but: [79]
      (1) His *consent was exceeded,* **or**
      (2) He was *not fully advised* of the risks of the treatment.
         (a) **Negligence is the proper tort** (not battery). *Walsh v Family Planning Services Ltd* [1992] 1 IR 469. *obiter*
         (b) See [365] *et seq*.
   c. **Consent of minor patient** [80]
      (1) **Non-Fatal Offences Against the Person Act 1997, section 23** enables minors aged 16 or older to legally consent to any surgical, medical or dental treatment.
   d. **Right to refuse treatment** [81]
      (1) **Nutrition**: An adult of sound mind has a specific right to refuse food and water. *Sec. of State for the Home Dept. v Robb* [1995] Fam 12.
      (2) **Medical treatment**: An adult of sound mind has the right to refuse medical treatment, even if her foetus would die. *St. George's Healthcare NHS Trust v S.* [1999] Fam 26.
         (a) **Note**: *St. George's* is an English case, therefore Article 40.3.3 regarding the right to life did not apply.
6. **Sporting events** [82]
   a. **Players**
      (1) **General rule**: Players *consent* to physical contact inherent in the particular sport.

    (a) *Simms v Leigh Rugby Football Club* [1969] 2 All ER 923. The plaintiff suffered a broken leg when tackled and thrown against the wall. The game had been played according to the rules and the defence of consent was held to be valid.

  (2) **Exception to general rule**: A player's consent may be *invalidated* by flagrant, intentional breaches of the game rules resulting in physical injury to the player. *McNamara v Duncan* (1971) 26 ALR 584.   **[83]**

    (a) *Smolden v Whitworth* [1996] unrep. CA. The defence of consent did not apply where the referee was sued under negligence for failing to apply anti-injury rules in a rugby match.

7. **Spectators**   **[84]**
  a. **General rule**: Spectators voluntarily assume the risk of harm caused by players, so long as the harm does not result from intentional or reckless behaviour. *Wooldrige v Summer* [1963] 2 QB 43.

B. *Necessity*   **[85]**

1. **Definition**: The intentional commission of a tortious act to prevent some greater evil where there is no reasonable alternative.
  a. Legal commentators wonder if the defence is still valid today.
  b. McMahon notes that the cases are very old, controversial or not on point.

2. **Reasonable alternative**   **[86]**
  a. *Lynch v Fitzgerald* [1938] IR 382 (SC). The plaintiff claimed damages for the death of his son who was killed by the police when they fired into a mob. It was held that necessity was not a good defence, since shooting could only be a *last resort* to protect lives or property.

C. *Inevitable accident*   **[87]**

1. **Definition**: An inevitable accident is defined as when the consequences complained of as a wrong were not intended by the defendant and could not have been foreseen and avoided by the exercise of reasonable care and skill. *McBride v Stitt* [1944] NI 7, 10.

2. A person will not be liable for an event over which he had *no* control, and could not have avoided using even the highest skill and care.

a. **Example**: *Stanley v Powell* (1891) 1 QB 86. A bullet rico-
cheted off of a tree and injured the plaintiff. The injury was
held to have been an inevitable accident.
3. **Note**: Many legal commentators believe that inevitable accident
has no useful function, 'and it is doubtful whether much advantage is gained by the continued use of the phrase'. (Winfield)

D. *Parental authority* [88]

1. **General rule**: Parents may exercise *reasonable* restraint or chastisement on their children without committing intentional torts
to the person.
   a. **Example**: If a parent disciplines a child by sending the child
   to his room for a period of time, the parent has not committed false imprisonment.
   b. **Exception to general rule**: Art. 3 of the European Convention.
      (1) *A v United Kingdom* [1998] 2 FLR 959. The European
      Court of Human Rights (ECHR) found that English law
      violated Art. 3 of the European Convention that prohibits
      torture, inhumane or degrading treatment or punishment.
      Facts: The stepfather of a 9-year-old hit the boy several
      times with a garden cane, causing bruises. He was
      charged with causing actual bodily harm to the boy, but
      a jury acquitted him. The boy appealed to the ECHR,
      arguing that the English law failed to protect him.
2. *Loco parentis*: Acting as a substitute parent, i.e. a guardian or
teacher. [89]
   a. **General rule**: A person acting in *loco parentis* may exercise
   reasonable disciplinary measures.
   b. **Exception to general rule: Non-Fatal Offences Against the
   Person Act 1997, section 24** abolished the criminal immunity teachers had for physical punishment of students.

E. *Statutory authority* [90]

1. Some statutes authorise acts that would otherwise be the commission of an intentional tort to the person.
2. **Lawful arrest**
   a. **Criminal Law Act 1997, section 4**: Arrest without a warrant.
      (1) Reasonable cause: Where the police have reasonable cause
      to suspect an arrestable offence has been committed, they
      may arrest without a warrant any person reasonably
      believed to be guilty.

    (2) Arrestable offence: An offence that is punishable for five or more years' imprisonment.

    (3) **Citizen's arrest**: Any person has the right to arrest another person for any arrestable offence where: **[91]**

        (a) The arresting person has reasonable cause to believe the person arrested is in the act of committing an arrestable offence.

        (b) An actual crime must have been committed.

        (c) The arresting person must reasonably suspect that the person arrested was avoiding or likely to avoid arrest by the police.

        (d) Any person arrested by a citizen must be transferred to the police.

  b. **Non-Fatal Offences Against the Person Act 1997, section 19(1)** allows the use of reasonable force by an individual to make a lawful arrest.

    (1) **NFOAPA 1997, section 19(3)**: Whether or not the arrest is lawful will be judged according to the circumstances as the person making the arrest believed them to be.

3. Lawful detention   **[92]**

  a. A sentence of imprisonment is *not* a false imprisonment.

  b. Medical exams and tests

    (1) Health Act 1947, section 38 authorises the detention and isolation of persons believed to be the probable source of infectious diseases.

    (2) Medical Treatment Act 1945 authorises the protective confinement of mentally ill persons.

    (3) Mental Health Act 2001 authorises the involuntary admission of mentally ill persons to approved treatment centres.   **[93]**

  c. Protective custody (unlawful): The protective custody for non-medical purposes, such as for a child witness, is not lawful even where it was argued that the child's life was in danger. *Connors v Pearson* [1921] 2 IR 51.

F. Defence of self and/or property   **[94]**

1. Self-defence

  a. **Common law**: A person may use *reasonable force* to protect himself or to protect another person.

    (1) The degree of force must be balanced against the seriousness of the attack.

(2) **Example**: *Ross v Curtin* (1989) unrep. (HC). A shop-keeper awoke one night when three men broke into his premises to rob him. When confronted, the three men advanced toward the shopkeeper. He fired a warning shot into the air, but one of the intruders was struck in the head by the shot. It was held that the shopkeeper had acted reasonably in the circumstances to defend himself.

b. **Criminal statutory reform** [95]

  (1) **Non-Fatal Offences Against the Person Act 1997,** sections 18–20 mostly restate the common law.

    (a) **Example**: Section 18(1). *Justifiable use of force*: Provides that the only *reasonable force* may be used for the protection of oneself or another from injury, assault or detention that is caused by a criminal act.

    (b) **Note**: NFOAPA 1997 does *not* apply to fatalities, only to non-fatal offences. Thus, if the defendant defends himself or another person and kills the attacker, the defendant must rely upon the common law.

  (2) **NFOAPA 1997, section 18(1)(b)** allows a person to use reasonable force to protect himself or herself from a trespass to his or her person.

  (3) **NFOAPA 1997, section 18(e)** allows the use of reasonable force to prevent a crime or a breach of the peace.

2. **Defence of property** [96]

a. **Land**

  (1) **Common law**

    (a) **Right to eject trespassers**: An occupier may use no more force than is reasonably necessary to evict a trespasser. *Green v Goddard* (1798) 91 ER 540.

    Example: *MacKnight v Extravision* (1991) unrep. CC. The plaintiff was preventing the defendants' access to their premises. The defendants were entitled to lay hands on the plaintiff to move him aside. When this failed, they sought the help of a boxer to remove the plaintiff. Excessive force was used, rendering the plaintiff unable to work for several weeks.

    (b) If the entrant's entry was *without force* he *must* be requested to leave before force may be used. *Green v Goddard* (1798) 91 ER 540.

(2) **Criminal statutory reform**　　　　　　**[97]**
　(a) **Criminal Justice (Public Order) Act 1994, section 13(1)** provides that an occupier may, after a reasonable time, using reasonable force, eject the person who fails or refuses to leave.
　(b) **NFOAPA 1997**, section 18(1)(c) allows a person to use reasonable force to protect his or her property. Section 18(1)(d) allows the use of reasonable force to protect the property of another.
　　(1) Under section 1 of the Act, property is defined as property of a tangible nature, whether real or person, including money.

b. **Chattels**　　　　　　**[98]**
　(1) **Common law**: A person could use *reasonable force* to defend one's chattels or the chattels of another.
　　(a) Chattels are generally goods and personal property such as furniture, jewellery, pets, livestock and vehicles.
　　(b) **Example**: A person could use reasonable force to stop a pickpocket from taking his watch.　**[99]**
　(2) **Criminal Statutory Reform: NFOAPA 1997** restates the common law.
　　(a) NFOAPA 1997, section 18 (1)(c) allows a person to use reasonable force to protect his or her property.
　　(b) Section 18(1)(d) allows the use of reasonable force to protect the property of another.
　　(c) Under section 1 of the NFOAPA 1997, property is defined as property of a tangible nature, whether real or person, including money.

Chapter 1 Questions

1. Conor told the drunken man that was annoying him in the pub, 'If it weren't for your grey hair, I would tear your heart out.' Name the tort.
2. Goliath the Giant noticed David approaching, swinging his slingshot, preparing to fight Goliath. Goliath was not afraid. Name the tort.
3. Sam Spade, a private detective, followed Veronica everywhere she went for two weeks. Veronica became afraid and refused to leave her home. Name the tort.
4. Anthony's girlfriend, Bertha, was angry when she learned that

Anthony was seeing another woman. Bertha cornered Anthony in the local pub and sat on his lap until he agreed to give up his other woman. Name the torts.

5. Peter seduced Anne by telling her that he is a millionaire. Peter is an unemployed actor, and Anne states that she would not have consented to sex with Peter had she known the truth. Will Anne's consent to the sexual conduct be a valid defence for Peter if Anne sues him for battery?

6. Captain Blackbeard agreed to take Grainne in his rowboat, named the QE 1/2, across the River Suir. Once Grainne got into the rowboat, Blackbeard rowed to the middle of the river and told Grainne to 'put out or get out'.
   (a) Has Blackbeard committed a battery?
   (b) If Grainne is a strong swimmer, is this a case of false imprisonment?

7. Little Rotten Ralphie was being very naughty in school. His teacher told him to stand in the corner, where he continued to make rude noises. The teacher raised a book as if he was going to hit Rotten Ralphie with it, but decided not to do so. Later, the other students told Rotten Ralphie about the book.
   (a) Has Ralphie been falsely imprisoned?
   (b) Did the teacher commit an assault when he raised the book?

8. Oliver, an osteopath, was treating Sinead, a keen sportswoman, for whiplash. Oliver told Sinead that he could cure her condition by 'nerve block tests' which consisted of Oliver spanking Sinead very hard on the buttocks. Sinead agreed to the treatment and attended several sessions until her coach noticed her severe bruising and called the authorities. Medical experts believe that Oliver was spanking Sinead for his own sexual excitement. Sinead is humiliated and seriously upset.
   (a) Will Sinead's consent to the treatment be a good defence for Oliver if Sinead brings an action for battery against Oliver?
   (b) What other trespass to the person, if any, could Sinead bring against Oliver?

9. Helen was seated next to an elderly gentleman on a transatlantic flight. Helen reminded the elderly gent of his dearly departed wife, Jo. During the flight they both fell asleep. However, Helen was rudely awakened when the elderly gent groped her, murmuring in his sleep, 'Oh Jo!' Can Helen maintain a cause of action for battery against the elderly gentleman if she was asleep when he touched her?

10. Lulu saved until she could afford to have plastic surgery. She went to Dr Quack and he agreed to operate to repair her nose, which had been broken in a field hockey accident. While Dr Quack was operating, he decided to try out a new technique for removing lines from around the eyes. Although her nose turned out perfect, Lulu is upset that she has two black eyes. Can Lulu bring an action for battery against Dr Quack?

11. When Santa tried to slide down Liam's chimney on Christmas Eve, he got stuck. Santa could not go up, nor could he go down. Has Liam falsely imprisoned Santa?

12. Mike snatched an elderly lady's handbag from her arm and ran away. Ken saw the incident and chased Mike. As Mike was trying to escape over a wall, Ken caught him by the leg. Mike lost his grip and fell onto Bob, an innocent bystander.
    (a) Identify all the possible intentional torts to the person in the problem.
    (b) Are there any valid defences to these torts?

13. Ronan wanted to win a 'reality' video contest, so he placed a baby in a pram, then had one friend push the pram into the path of a car driven by another friend. Ronan filmed the reaction of the shocked onlookers. Unfortunately, Mrs O'Grady suffered a heart attack after seeing the car strike the pram.
    (a) Can Mrs O'Grady maintain an action for assault against Ronan and his friends?
    (b) Can Mrs O'Grady maintain an action for any other tort against Ronan?

14. Liz was out celebrating her birthday and had a little too much to drink. She went into the toilet and fell asleep. When Steve was closing the pub, he entered the toilets to turn off the lights, but did not check the stalls. When Liz awoke at 4 am she was locked into the empty pub. Name the tort, if any.

15. Silly Millie was chasing butterflies when she fell into Finbar's unused slurry pit. Luckily, Millie was not injured in the fall, but because of the height of the pit she could not get out. Finbar is tired of Silly Millie entering his land and protesting against the live export of cattle, so when he saw her in his old slurry pit, he just smiled and continued on his way to town. Will Millie be able to maintain an action for false imprisonment against Finbar?

16. Eve was a great distance away from Adam when she threw an apple at Adam and hit him. Eve is shocked that she hit Adam, and experts are in agreement that it was highly unlikely that Eve could

hit Adam at that distance with an apple. Can Adam maintain an action for battery against Eve under the circumstances?

17. Kate was absentmindedly tossing pebbles into the river, and Spenser was sailing by in his boat. Because he was watching Kate, Spenser sailed his boat into a piling and was injured when he hit his head against the wheelhouse. Spenser wants to sue Kate for battery.

    (a) Was Kate performing a voluntary act?
    (b) Was there a physical impact or contact with Spenser?
    (c) Did Kate intend her acts of tossing pebbles or did she perform the act negligently?
    (d) Was the contact or impact to Spenser causally linked to Kate's acts?

2

INTENTIONAL TORTS
TO PROPERTY

Chapter synopsis

I. Trespass to land
    (Modern) trespass to land
    Defences to trespass to land
    Remedies for trespass to land
II. Intentional torts to chattels
    Trespass to chattels
    (Modern) trespass to chattels
    Conversion
    Detinue
    Defences to intentional torts to chattels

I. Trespass to land

A. Historical background to common law trespass to land   **[100]**

1. **General rules**:
    a. Recovery required an invasion which:
        (1) **Interfered** with the right of *exclusive possession* of the land, and
        (2) Was a *direct* result of some *act* committed by the defendant.
            (a) Dealt with *direct* or *forcible invasions* to land.
            (b) **Examples**: Throwing a stone onto the land of another, or forcing your way into the building of another.
    b. Trespass was actionable per se. (No proof of damages required.)
2. **Trespass to land legal principles**   **[101]**
    a. Were *strict* and *severe* for the common law action of trespass.
    b. Have survived until modern times.

(1) Until recently, this resulted in an *unreasonable* distinction between injuries to persons and injuries to property.

(2) **Example**: If a tram jumped its tracks and struck a pedestrian on the footpath before destroying a shop front, the pedestrian could only bring an action for negligence. On the other hand, the owners of the tram were absolutely liable to the owner of the damaged shop.

B. *Trespass on the case (action on the case)* [102]

1. **General rule**:
   a. Dealt with *indirect* invasions, and
   b. *Required* proof of negligence or intent as well as substantial damage.
   c. Example of indirect invasion: Obstructing or diverting a stream so that water ultimately flowed into a neighbour's premises.
2. **Direct/indirect distinction** between trespass to land and trespass on the case has been largely abandoned.
   a. **Example**: Under the common law, if a person failed to remove personal property at the end of an agreed period of time from the plaintiff's land, an action had to be brought on the case as there was no forcible invasion to sustain an action for trespass to land. *Winterbourne v Morgan* [1809] 103 ER 1056. Today, the same situation is simply trespass to land.
   b. **Note**: Directness does distinguish *trespass* and *nuisance*. See [114] and [122].

C. *What is land?* [103]

1. Under the common law maxim **quicquid plantatur solo solo cedit**, whatever is affixed to the land belongs to the owner of that land and is regarded as land. **Examples**: Fences, trees, buildings, gates are regarded as land.
2. The common law maxim: **Cujus est solum ejus est usque ad coelum**.
   a. Roughly translated: 'He who has the soil owns upward unto heaven, and by analogy, downward to hell.' [104]
   b. *Hannabalson v Sessions* 116 Iowa 457 (1902), '[T]he title of the owner of the soil extends not only downward to the centre of the earth, but upward *usque ad coelum*, although it is, perhaps, doubtful whether owners as quarrelsome as the

parties in this case will ever enjoy the usufruct of their property in the latter direction.'

3. **Exception**: The right to things under the surface of land was
qualified.   **[105]**
   a. **Treasure trove**: If an item made of gold or silver was deliberately
   concealed on land and subsequently found, and its true owner
   could not be located, at common law the Crown was entitled to
   the item under the royal prerogative of treasure trove.
      (1) Originally, items were melted down to make coins.
      (2) Eventually became a means of securing and preserving
      artefacts of archaeological significance.

(Modern) trespass to land

Definition: The intentional or negligent entering or remaining
on or remaining or directly causing anything to come into contact with land
in the possession of another, without lawful justification. (Street)
                                                              [106]

Required elements of trespass to land   **[107]**
A. Voluntary act by the defendant
B. Intent or negligence
C. Invasion of land
D. Plaintiff in possession or entitled to possession of land
E. Causation
F. No lawful authority

A. Voluntary act by the defendant   **[108]**

1. The defendant *must* have voluntarily acted. See [14] and [21].
   a. **Example**: It is not a trespass to be carried onto the land of
   another.
2. **Trespass to land is actionable per se.**   **[109]**
   a. Even most *trivial acts* of trespass are actionable.
3. **No damages required to the land**: The plaintiff is *not* required
to show or prove any damage.
   a. Illustrates importance attached from ancient times to protection of the possession of land.
   b. **Note**: To recover substantial damages, the plaintiff must show
   an appreciable loss.

4. Acts include: **[110]**
   a. **Entering on land**
      (1) Slightest crossing of boundary of land will constitute trespass.
      (2) Not necessary to cross boundary.
      (3) Physical contact with land is enough. **Examples**:
         (a) Striking door with intention of breaking it. *Whelan v Madigan* [1978] ILRM 136.
         (b) Leaning a ladder against a wall. *Westripp v Baldock* [1939] 2 All ER 799.
      (4) **Abuse of right of entry** may constitute trespass if the purpose for the entry is outside the scope of authority granted for the entry. **[111]**
         (a) **Example**: *DPP v McMahon* [1987] ILRM 87. Police entered a licensed premise and committed trespass. They had entered without a warrant to investigate possible breaches of the Gaming and Lotteries Act 1956. Section 39 of the Act required a warrant. The police could not claim that they had a public right of entry because they were not there to buy food, etc. and they did not have statutory authority to enter.
   b. **Remaining on the land** **[112]**
      (1) **Lawfully entered and remained**
         (a) Where a person has lawfully entered land in the possession of another, he will commit a trespass if he remains there after his right to stay has terminated. *Wood v Leadbitter* (1845) 153 ER 351.
         (b) Or by failing to remove property at the end of the agreed time period.
      (2) **Refusal to leave**: It is trespass to refuse or fail to leave after being requested to do so.
      (3) **Reasonable force**: The occupier, after a reasonable time using reasonable force, may eject the person who fails or refuses to leave. See defences [95]–[97].
   c. **Placing things on land** **[113]**
      (1) **General rule**: It is a trespass for a person to *place* any chattel on the land of another or to *cause* any object or substance to directly cross the boundary of another person's land, or even to *reach* the boundary. **Examples**:
         (a) Animals chased onto the land of another person.

(b) Tossing litter onto the land of another.

(c) Placing manure against a boundary wall belonging to a neighbour.

(d) Causing a third person to enter land; by carrying the third person by force, or by leading the third person to enter by making false representations, such as saying, 'You may hunt in that field.'

(2) **Invasion must be direct**: To constitute an actionable trespass for placing things on land, the *invasion must be direct* rather than consequential.   **[114]**

(a) **Note**: *Direct* invasions tend to be classified as trespass and *indirect or consequential* invasions tend to be classified as nuisance. See [122].

(1) **Example**: Fred Flintstone operates a quarry. During recent blasting, his neighbours' land has been invaded by hurled stones and dust. Stones invading the neighbours' airspace and landing on the ground are direct invasions, i.e. trespass. The dust is purely transitory particles, and if it does not accumulate results in an indirect invasion, i.e. nuisance.

B. Intent or negligence   **[115]**

1. It is not necessary for the plaintiff to prove that the defendant intended to invade, injure or harm the plaintiff's land.

a. **Example**: If Goldilocks enters the house of the three bears because she believes it to be her own, she has trespassed even though she did not intend to do so.

2. The defendant must have intended the act(s) that caused the invasion.

a. **Example**: Gary loves to garden. Noticing a healthy crop of weeds in a corner of his garden, Gary begins to pull the weeds and tosses them over his shoulder. He thinks that the weeds are landing in a pile in his garden. Unfortunately, most of the weeds are landing in Grainne's garden. Gary intended the act, i.e. tossing the weeds over his shoulder, that caused the invasion, although he did not intend to invade Grainne's garden. Gary was also negligent in how he carried out his act.

C. *Invasion of land*

1. **Land** [116]
   a. **Modern statutory provisions**: Generally follow common law approach.
      (1) Whatever is affixed to the land is land. See [103].
         (a) **Example**: Paragraph 14 of the Schedule to the Interpretation Act 1937 provides that the word 'land', when used in an Act of the Oireachtas, includes 'messuages, tenements, and hereditaments, houses and buildings, or any tenure' unless there is an indication of a contrary intention.
      (2) Land stretches 'from heaven to hell'. See [103] *et seq.*
2. **Direct invasions**: Include anything of substance coming into contact with land.
   a. **Air space above land** [117]
      (1) An encroachment or intrusion into the air space above land constitutes a trespass to the land even though there is no contact with the surface of the land. **Examples**:
         (a) An advertising sign affixed to an adjoining building that overhangs the plaintiff's roof.
         (b) The arm of a crane swinging over the plaintiff's land.
      (2) **Common law encroachments** for *social necessity* and the *common good* have been recognised for: [118]
         (a) Communication satellites; and
         (b) Air travel.
            (1) **Example**: *Lord Beirnstein of Leigh v Skyviews and General Ltd* [1978] QB 479. It was held that a balance has to be struck between the rights of an owner to enjoy the use of his land and the interests of the general public in utilising air space. *The balance was achieved by restricting the rights of an owner in the air space above the land to such height as is necessary for the ordinary use and enjoyment of the structures on it.* Above that height, the owner has no greater rights in the air space than any other member of the public. The defendant had flown over the plaintiff's land taking aerial photographs.
      (3) **Statutory qualification**: Section 55 of the Air Navigation and Transport Act 1936, as amended by section 47(1) of

the Air Navigation and Transport Act 1988, provides that no action in trespass or nuisance will lie by reason only of any flight of any aircraft over any property at a height above the ground which, having regard to the wind, weather and all the circumstances of the case, is reasonable.

b. **Under the surface of land**   **[119]**
  (1) An intrusion into the soil under the surface of land is a trespass, but this rule is qualified.
    (a) **Antiquities of importance**: *Webb v Ireland* [1988] IR 353 (SC). Prerogative of the Crown (treasure trove, see [105]) did not survive the establishment of the Free State in 1922. However, under the 1937 Constitution, with its express reference to the historical origins of the state and the common good, the Supreme Court held that this carried with it a right of the state to ownership where antiquities of importance are discovered and there is no known owner. Majority relied upon Article 10, while the minority relied upon Article 5 of the Constitution.
                                                                    [120]
    (b) ***Webb v Ireland* facts**: The plaintiffs were trespassing and found the 'Derrynaflan Hoard'. A dispute arose as to who had the better claim – the plaintiffs as the finders, or the land owners.
  (2) **Statutes**: The Minerals Development Act 1979, section 12 gives the Minister for Energy the exclusive right to work minerals, irrespective of who happens to own the land on which they are located. (Part II of the Act gives the owner of the land a right to compensation.)   **[121]**
  (3) **Social necessity and the common good** may develop in the future for such things as underground mass transit. (This has been recognised in other jurisdictions.)
    (a) **Example**: *Boehringer v Montalto*, 254 NYS 276 (1931). A sewer located 150 feet below the surface of the plaintiff's land was held not to invade the surface owner's rights.

c. **Directness distinguishes trespass from nuisance.**   **[122]**
  (1) **Nuisance** applies where the invasion or entry on property is **indirect. Examples:**
    (a) Where smoke or fumes drift onto neighbouring land; or

    (b) Tree roots or branches encroach onto neighbouring land.

(2) **Trespass** applies where the invasion is *direct*. **Examples**:
    (a) Throwing coins in a farmer's stream; or
    (b) Walking across another person's field.

(3) US approach: Trespass is an invasion of the plaintiff's interest in the exclusive possession of his land, while nuisance is an interference with the use and enjoyment of it.

D. *Plaintiff in possession or entitled to possession of land*   [123]

1. **General rule**: The plaintiff *must* be in possession of the land invaded.
   a. **Note**: Trespass protects *possession* rather than *ownership*.[124]
   b. **De facto possession**
      (1) Any person in de facto possession can sue anyone who does not have an immediate right to recover possession of the property.
         (a) **Example**: *Petrie v Owners of SS Rostrevor* [1898] 2 IR 556. The plaintiff had no legal entitlement to the foreshore, but he placed oysters on it to begin a business. The defendant's boat ran aground, damaging the plaintiff's oysters. The court held that the placing of chattels (oysters) on the land allowed the plaintiff to become possessed of it de facto. The defendant only escaped liability because he had authority from the owners of the foreshore.

2. **Occupiers v owners**   [125]
   a. **General rule**: If the owner exceeds his lawful authority, the occupier may maintain a trespass action against the owner.
   Example: *Whelan v Madigan* [1978] 1 IR 136. The landlord committed trespass against his tenants by damaging the land, i.e. doors and letterbox.
   b. **Exception: Rented rooms**   [126]
      (1) **Lodgers or hotel guests** do *not have possession* of the room to maintain an action for trespass. **Examples**:
         (a) Lodger: *Allan v Liverpool Overseers* (1874) LR 9 QB 180.
         (b) Hotel guests: *Larkin v Porter* (1828) 1 Hud and Br 524.

E. Causation   [127]

1. The defendant's act(s) must have caused the invasion of the plaintiff's land.
2. Onus shift: Once the plaintiff shows that the act(s) of the defendant caused the invasion of the plaintiff's land, the onus shifts onto the defendant to prove that he or she did not act intentionally or negligently. See [29].

F. No lawful authority   [128]

1. The defendant must not have had a legal right to invade the plaintiff's land. See rights of entry in defences [132] and [133].

Defences to trespass to land   [129]

> A. License or consent of the plaintiff
> B. Common law right of entry
> C. Statutory rights of entry: Trespass *ab initio*
> D. Necessity
> E. Not a defence: *Jus tertii*

A. License or consent of the plaintiff   [130]

1. **Definition**: A license is consent from the person in possession to enter land or premises. A license prevents an entry from being unlawful.
   a. **A bare license** is one not supported by consideration.
      (1) Consideration could be the price for entering the premises.
      (2) A bare license can be withdrawn at any time.
      (3) **Examples**: Shopper in department store or visitor in a hospital.
   b. **License with an interest** is a license with consideration or price for entering or remaining on the land. Person can only be removed in accordance with the terms of the license.   [131]
      (1) **Examples**: Swimming pool patron has a right to remain in the pool until the swimming period expires. Cinema patron has a right to remain in the cinema until the film is finished.

B. Common law right of entry   [132]

1. People are permitted to enter land in the possession of another in certain circumstances.

2. **Example**: The privilege of abatement of a nuisance by self-help is of ancient origin.

C. *Statutory rights of entry: Trespass* ab initio [133]

1. **Statutes allowing entry**: Various statutes grant a number of public officials and others a right of entry onto the land or premises of another.
   a. **Examples**:
      (1) Control of Bulls for Breeding Act 1985; and
      (2) Misuse of Drugs Act 1977 and 1984.
   b. **The Criminal Law Act 1997** allows the: [134]
      (1) **Entry without warrant**: Section 6 gives police extensive powers to enter dwellings to arrest with or without a warrant (or committal order).
      (2) **Note**: Constitutional Protection: Article 40.5 provides that '[t]he dwelling of every citizen is inviolable and shall not be forcibly entered save in accordance with law.'
   c. **Abuse of right of entry** may constitute trespass if the purpose of the entry is outside the scope of the authority granted for the entry. See [111].
2. **Doctrine of trespass *ab initio*** [135]
   a. **Common law procedural device**
      (1) **History of doctrine**: Trespass *ab initio* is said to have been first articulated in the *Six Carpenters Case* (1610) 77 ER 695. This case involved the refusal of the six defendants to pay for a quart of wine and a penny worth of bread that they had ordered and consumed in the plaintiff's inn. The court held that the six were not trespassers *ab intitio* (trespassers from entry).
      (2) The doctrine was designed to circumvent the general rule that an action for trespass under the common law could not be brought if the original entry was lawful.
   b. **Modern definition**: [136]
      (1) Where a person enters land *under authority of law* and he later abuses or exceeds that authority, he is deemed to become a trespasser *ab initito*, or trespasser from the entry.
         (a) Doctrine usually arises in the exercise of police powers.
         (b) Doctrine also protects chattels and persons.
      (2) **Requirements**: [137]
         (a) An act of *positive misfeasance* (wrongful act).
         (b) A mere nonfeasance, such as a failure to pay for

goods or services, is **not** trespass *ab initio*.

(c) **Misfeasance** includes remaining on land longer than is necessary for the purpose of entry.

c. **Independent reason for entry** [138]

(1) Where an abuse takes place after entry, there is no trespass *ab initio* if there remains an independent ground or reason for the entry.

(a) In other words, a wrongful act will only render the original entry unlawful where it takes away the entire basis of the lawful entry.

(2) **Example**: *Elias v Pasmore* [1934] 2KB 164. Police officers lawfully entered property to arrest a man, but then wrongfully seized documents. It was held that the police were trespassers only as to the goods (papers) and not trespassers *ab initio*.

d. **Criticism** [139]

(1) English approach

(a) In *Chic Fashions (West Wales) Ltd v Jones* [1968] 2 QB 299, the English Court of Appeal criticised the very existence of the doctrine. **Rationale**: A subsequent event cannot make an act unlawful if it was lawful when originally performed.

(b) Criticism ignored: In later cases, such as *Cinnamond v British Airports Authority* (1980) 1 WLR 582.

(2) American approach: The 2nd Restatement rejects the doctrine in all situations.

(3) Many legal commentators believe that with modern rules of evidence, there is no longer a need for trespass *ab initio*.

D. *Necessity* [140]

1. **Definition**: The intentional commission of a tortious act to prevent a greater evil where there is no reasonable alternative.

2. **General rule**: To avail of defence it must be shown that:

a. The trespass was *necessary*; and

b. The defendant was ***not*** *negligent*.

(1) **Example**: *Rigby v Chief Constable of Northhamptonshire* [1985] 2 All ER 985. The defence of necessity was successfully used when defendant caused a fire by firing tear gas into plaintiff's shop in an attempt to eject a dangerous criminal suspect.

3. Defence probably only applies when there is a *threat* to life or property.
   a. **Example**: *Cope v Sharpe* [1912] 1 KB 496. The defendant, a gamekeeper, set fire to heather on the plaintiff's land to act as a firebreak to stop the threatened spread of a fire on plaintiff's land onto the land of his employer. The defendant was sued for trespass, but necessity was held to be a good defence. There was a real threat of fire and defendant was held to have acted reasonably.
4. **Note**: The defence only applies if the defendant did not cause the greater evil or peril to life or property.

E. Not a defence: Jus tertii [141]

1. **General rule**: *Jus tertii* is generally not a valid defence to trespass to land.
   a. *Jus tertii* is where the defendant is sued for trespass and alleges that the plaintiff has no right to possession of the land because the right (*jus*) is vested in a third person (*tertii*).
   b. **Example**: Paul finds David cutting firewood in the field next to Paul's home. Paul has occupied the field for several years, but is not the legal owner. If David alleges that Paul does not have the right to possession of the field, this is not a good defence to trespass onto the land.
2. **Exception**: *Jus tertii* may be a valid defence where the defendant has entered the land with the authority of the person with the true right to possession.
   a. **Example**: Assume George owns the field next to Paul's home. If George authorised David to cut firewood in the field, David may allege *jus tertii* as a defence to Paul's charge of trespass.

Remedies for trespass to land [142]

A. Injunction
B. Action for recovery of land
C. Re-entry
D. Action for mesne profits
E. Distress damage feasant
F. Damages

A. Injunction [143]

1. Available where trespass is threatened, or
2. Where a trespass is of a continuing nature.

B. Action for recovery of land [144]

1. A lawsuit may be brought seeking possession of land to the exclusion of others.

C. Re-entry [145]

1. A common law remedy of self-help.
   a. **Note**: All common law self-help actions are fraught with difficulties.
2. **Example**: A possessor of land may re-enter land and expel a trespasser using reasonable force if necessary.

D. Action for mesne profits [146]

1. Enables the plaintiff to claim:
   a. The profits taken by the defendant during his occupancy;
   b. Damages for deterioration; and
   c. The reasonable costs of acquiring possession.

E. Distress damage feasant [147]

1. Allows any occupier of land to *seize* any chattels which are *unlawfully* on the land and have done or are doing *damage*.
2. The occupier may *detain* the chattels until the payment of compensation has been made.
3. Originally applied to animals, but now *extends* to all chattels.
   a. **Example**: *Ambergate Ry. v Midland Ry.* (1853) 23 LJQB 17. The plaintiff railway was held entitled to seize and detain the defendant railway's locomotive engine, which was wrongfully trespassing on plaintiff's line.

F. Damages [148]

1. **Trivial trespasses**
   a. Damages will be nominal.
2. Beneficial use of land
   a. Where a trespass involves some beneficial use of land, the plaintiff is entitled to a reasonable remuneration (payment) for the use of land.

b. The value is determined as if made by agreement in a contract, i.e. fair market value for the use of the land.

II. Intentional torts to chattels

A. In general   [149]

1. There are three torts recognised today.
   a. **Trespass to chattels**: The direct interference with the chattels of another.
   b. **Conversion**: The wrongful assertion of dominion (ownership) over the chattels of another.
   c. **Detinue**: Withholding the chattels of another from the person entitled to their immediate possession.
2. All three protect personal property and goods.   [150]
   a. **Note**: The same act(s) could give rise to more than one of the torts.
   b. **Example**: *British Wagon Co. Ltd v Shortt* [1961] IR 164. A machine under a hire purchase agreement was 'sold' to the defendant. The defendant was not aware of the hire purchase agreement and performed repairs on the machine. The owner sought the return of the machine under theories of detinue and conversion. The defendant refused to return the machine unless compensated for the repairs. It was held that the owner was entitled to succeed on either claim.
3. *Distinction* **between conversion and detinue**   [151]
   a. **Conversion** is a *denial* of title by the defendant.
      (1) Conversion is a single act of denial of title.
      (2) Damages are usually awarded to compensate the owner for the loss.   [152]
   b. **Detinue** is the *retention* of the chattel(s) by the defendant.
      (1) Detinue is a continual denial of possession.
      (2) The central issue is the return of the chattels.
4. *Distinction* **between conversion and trespass to chattels**
                                                                    [153]
   a. **Conversion** is an *indirect* interference with the chattels.
   b. **Trespass** is a *direct* interference with the chattels.

Trespass to chattels

Historical background [154]

A. *Developed from the ancient* trespass de bonis asportatis.

1. *Trespass de bonis asportatis* applied to cases where chattels were asported (carried off).
2. Later extended to include chattels damaged but not taken. **Examples**:
   a. Animals killed. *Wright v Ramscot* (1668) 85 ER 93.
   b. Animals beaten. *Slater v Swann* (1730) 93 ER 906.
3. Eventually extended to include any *direct* and *immediate intentional interference* with a chattel in the possession of another.
   a. Direct and forcible interference required (*Covell v Laming* (1808) 170 ER 1034), otherwise trespass on the case. See [3].
   b. In possession: The plaintiff had to be in possession of the chattel at the time of the interference.
      (1) Rule relaxed to include plaintiffs entitled to possession.
   c. As *trespass de bonis asportatis* evolved, various remedies developed, such as detinue, replevin and trover, to deal with other types of interference to chattels.
   d. Over the centuries, the various evolving torts dealing with chattels became confused and overlapped.

B. *Modern tort of trespass to chattels* [155]

1. **Lacks clarity**
   a. Generally, commentators agree that the modern tort of trespass to chattels lacks clarity and consistency in Ireland.
2. Statutory reform: In England, there has been some reform with the enactment of the Torts (Interference with Goods) Act 1977.
   a. However, commentators agree that further reform is needed.

(Modern) trespass to chattels [156]

Definition: The intentional, direct and unlawful injury to, or interference with, chattels in the possession of another.
Required elements for trespass to chattels
A. Voluntary act by the defendant
B. Intent to deal with the chattel
C. Injury or interference
D. Plaintiff in possession or entitled to immediate possession
E. Causation

A. Voluntary act by the defendant   [157]

1. **Voluntary,** i.e. within the defendant's control. See [14].
2. **Note**: Actual physical contact with the chattel is not required.
   a. **Example**: Tony chased Helen's hen out of Helen's hen house.

B. Intent to deal with the chattel   [158]

1. Traditionally, as with trespass to land, the *interference* or injury must have been *legally caused* by the defendant's act or a force set in motion by his act.
   a. At common law, all trespass had to be intentional or wilful.
   b. **Example**: *McMullan v Bradshaw* (1916) 50 ILTR 205. The defendant's deliberate use of a chattel, believing it to be his own, was held to be a trespass.
2. Present status: The injury or interference must be *wilful* or *negligent*.
   a. In Ireland, relying on some English cases decided before the Tort (Interference with Goods) Act 1977, negligence has crept into the traditional intentional torts.   [159]
   b. **Example**: *ESB v Hastings and Co. Ltd* [1965] IR Jur Rep 51. Liability under trespass to chattels was imposed on the negligent acts of the defendants. While resurfacing a road, the defendants allowed their digger to damage a high-tension electrical cable in the possession of the plaintiffs. The plaintiffs warned the defendants about the presence of the cable.
   c. Some commentators argue that trespass should only apply to deliberate acts.
3. The defendant must have intended to deal with the chattel. [160]
   a. **Note**: A purely *accidental* interference with chattels is not actionable in trespass, because it lacks intent and negligence.
   b. **Example**: Fred was standing watching a horse race. He did not know that Audrey had removed her new hat to straighten her hair. Audrey set the hat on the seat behind Fred. When Fred suddenly sat on the hat, he did not intend to deal with the chattel (hat) in any manner. If Fred performed his act (sitting) negligently, he could still be liable.

C. Injury or interference

1. **Interference** includes: [161]
   a. Removing chattel from possession of another;
   b. Or simply moving the chattel from one place to another.

    (1) Example: *Whelan v Madigan* [1978] 1 IR 136. The land-
        lord moved the tenant's chairs.

2. **Injury** includes: **[162]**
    a. Damaging the chattel.
    b. Destroying the chattel.

3. **Actionable per se?**   **[163]**
    a. Commentators generally write that trespass to chattels is
       actionable per se.
       (1) McMahon has noted that the judiciary do not appear to
            think it is.
       (2) McMahon states that it probably is actionable per se.
    b. English approach
       (1) Street states that trespass to chattels is actionable per se.
            (a) Otherwise people could touch museum objects with
                impunity.
            (b) It also provides a remedy for instances such as when
                a person rightfully refuses to use his own toothbrush
                after another person has used it.
    c. American approach
       (1) According to Prosser, trespass to chattels is not actionable
            per se.
            (a) Trespass remains a remedy for minor interference
                resulting in some damage, but not serious or impor-
                tant enough to amount to conversion (forced judi-
                cial sale of chattel).

D. *Plaintiff in possession or entitled to immediate possession*   **[164]**

    1. **Possession of chattel,** not ownership, is the key. See [124] re:
       land.
    a. **Possession includes**:
       (1) **By borrowing. Example**: If I borrow my sister's book, I
            am in possession of the book.
       (2) **By hiring. Example**: If I hire a car, I am in possession of
            it.
       (3) **By creating a bailment.**   **[165]**
            (a) A bailment is generally a contractual relationship
                where a chattel is delivered to another to hold in
                trust. In other words, the chattel will be returned to
                the person delivering it.
            (b) Example of a bailment: When clothes are left at a
                dry cleaner, the cleaner is in possession of the

clothes and is expected to return them to the owner
of the clothing.

    (c) **Note**: Money deposited into an account does not
create a bailment. **Rationale**: The depositor does
not expect the same coins and notes returned.

2. **Owner v person in possession**   **[166]**
   a. **The owner of the chattels** *cannot* bring an action for trespass
against any person in lawful possession of the chattel.
    (1) **Example**: *Keenan Bros. v CIE* (1962) 97 ILTR 54. The
plaintiff's goods were delayed in transit during a labour
dispute. The High Court refused to compel the defendant
carrier (in lawful possession) to deliver the goods or to
allow the plaintiff to remove the goods from the defendant's railroad cars. The fact that the goods were the plaintiff's did not change the fact that at common law it would
be a trespass to chattels for any person to open the defendant's cars to remove goods without the defendant's consent or some legal right to do so, such as under a contract.
   b. **A superior title holder** may defeat the plaintiff's claim if the
plaintiff's claim to the chattel is based solely on possession.
Webb v Ireland, see [119].

E. Causation   [167]

1. The interference or injury to the plaintiff's chattel must have
been caused by the act(s) of the defendant.
   a. **For liability, interference must be direct.** See [29].
    (1) **Direct interference. Example**: Moving jewellery from
one room to another. *Kirk v Gregory* (1876) 1 Ex D 55.
When the defendant's brother-in-law died, she moved
his jewellery from one room to another, thinking that it
would be safer. The jewellery was subsequently stolen,
and the deceased's executor successfully sued the defendant for trespass.
    (2) **Indirect interference. Example**: *McDonagh v West of
Ireland Fisheries*, unrep. HC 1986. The defendant tem-
porarily removed plaintiff's boat from its moorings. The
boat was damaged, probably due to settling on some
unknown obstruction on the seabed. Such an injury was
held not to be direct and hence not a trespass.

Conversion

A. Historical background   **[168]**

1. Trover developed in the late fifteenth century to fill the void
   between:
   a. Trespass: the wrongful taking of chattels, and
   b. Detinue: the wrongful retention of chattels.
2. Trespass applied if the plaintiff remained the owner of the chattel and his possession was only interrupted or interfered with.
3. Trover applied if the defendant had appropriated (taken possession of) the chattel.
4. Tort of conversion is said to have come about when the basic differences between trespass and trover were highlighted in *Fouldes
   v Willoughby* (1841) 151 ER 1153.   **[169]**
   a. *Fouldes v Willoughby* facts: The plaintiff boarded the defen-
      dant's ferry. The ferry sailed between Birkenhead to Liverpool.
      The defendant wrongfully refused to carry the plaintiff's two
      horses. The defendant told the plaintiff to take the horses
      ashore, but the plaintiff refused. The defendant then took the
      horses from the plaintiff and put them ashore. The plaintiff
      remained on the ferry and was taken across the river. As a
      result, the plaintiff lost his horses. **Holding**: The mere act of
      removing the horses from the ferry was wrongful and action-
      able as a trespass. However, it did not amount to a conversion.
5. Conversion expanded greatly and encroached upon detinue, trespass and replevin. It has expanded to include: **[170]**
   a. **Appropriation of another's chattels** to one's own use;
   b. **Dispossession** of the chattel to another person;
   c. **Dealing** with the chattel in a manner *adverse* to the plaintiff
      and *inconsistent* with the plaintiff's right of possession.

(Modern) conversion definition: Any act to the chattels of
another that constitutes an unjustified denial of his title. (This is
sometimes expressed as the wrongful assertion of dominion over
the chattels of another.)   **[171]**

Definition by McMahon: Wrongfully and directly interfering
with the possession of chattels. Cited in *Farrell v Minister for
Agriculture and Food* (1995) (HC).

> **Required elements of conversion:** **[172]**
>
> A. Voluntary act by the defendant
> B. Intent or negligence by defendant
> C. Plaintiff in possession or entitled to possession of the chattel
> D. Causation

A. *Voluntary act by the defendant* [173]

1. There must be some voluntary act by the defendant. See [14].
   a. **By taking possession**
      (1) Dealing with chattels in a manner *inconsistent* with rights of true owner.
         (a) **Example**: Stealing.
         (b) Intention to *permanently* deprive is not necessary. **Example**: Taking a car for a joy ride. [174]
      (2) **Mistaken assumption of ownership**: An innocent purchaser of stolen goods will commit conversion because the mistaken assumption of ownership *is* a denial of the true owner's title. [175]
         (a) **Rule of commercial convenience**: A bailee who merely takes possession of a chattel for storage, safekeeping or transportation but has no knowledge that the chattel is lost or stolen does not become liable to the true owner for conversion.
         (b) **Exception to rule of commercial convenience**: Misdelivery (giving it or taking it to the wrong person or place) by a carrier or warehouseman will render the bailee liable in conversion. *Lancashire and Yorkshire Ry. v MacNicoll* (1919) 88 LJKB 601.
2. **By detention** [176]
   a. **Required demand and refusal**: Where the defendant has *lawfully gained possession* of a chattel, there *must* be a demand (by the plaintiff) and a refusal to surrender (by the defendant) before conversion arises.
   b. **Conclusive evidence of conversion** is the defendant's refusal to return chattels after demand by person entitled to possession.
   c. However, a refusal may be reasonable to authenticate claims of ownership. *Poole v Burns* [1944] Ir Jur Rep 20.

3. **By wrongful delivery**   [177]
   a. To deprive a person of his chattels by delivering them to someone else.
   b. **Example**: Where chattels have been obtained by fraud, and the original owner has rescinded the contract, a subsequent purchaser converts the chattels. *Hollins v Fowler* (1875) LR 7 (HL). The defendant cotton broker bought and resold cotton that was fraudulently acquired by the seller from the plaintiff. The defendant was not aware of the fraud, and only received a broker's commission. He was held liable for conversion and paid damages equal to the value of the cotton.

4. **By wrongful disposition**   [178]
   a. Where possession has been lawfully acquired, it is a conversion to unlawfully give a third party title to the chattels. **Examples**:
      (1) By pawning the chattels. *Parker v Godin* (1728) 93 ER 866.
      (2) By selling the chattels. *Hollins v Fowler* (1875) LR 7 HL 757.

5. **By wrongful destruction**   [179]
   a. To unlawfully *consume* or otherwise destroy a chattel of another is a conversion.
      (1) Mere damage is *not* enough for conversion, but it may be a trespass.   [180]
      (2) **Test for destruction** is whether the identity or character of the chattel has changed. **Examples**:
         (a) Taking another person's milk and making cheese.
         (b) Taking another person's grapes and making wine.
         (c) Taking another person's corn and grinding it into flour.
   b. **Note: Ownership of chattel** is not changed because of alteration.   [181]
      (1) **Example**: If clay is wrongfully taken and made into bricks, the bricks belong to the true owner of the clay.

6. **By wrongful use**   [182]
   a. Conversion by forfeiture of chattel
      (1) *Moorgate Mercantile Credit Co. Ltd v Finch* [1962] 1 QN 701. The use of another person's car for the unlawful act of smuggling, which resulted in the car being forfeited, was a conversion.
      (2) Infringement of a copyright may be a conversion. *Caxton Publishing Ltd v Sutherland Publishing Co.* [1939] AC 178.

7. **Multiple acts of conversion**   **[183]**
   a. **Note**: A person may act in such a way as to commit several conversions with the same chattel.
   b. **Example**: The defendant stole the plaintiff's painting and sold it to an unsuspecting third party. Later, the defendant bought back the painting, and when discovered by the plaintiff, demand was made for its return. The defendant refused plaintiff's demand to return the chattel.
8. **Not act of conversion**   **[184]**
   a. **Mere receipt of chattels** such as *possession of chattels without title* to them is not a conversion. See finders [194].
      (1) Only adverse detention from the person entitled to possession of chattel is wrongful.
      (2) **However**, buying or receiving a chattel from a person who did not have the lawful authority to dispose of chattel is a conversion.
   b. **Redelivery**   **[185]**
      (1) Any person who innocently receives a chattel and returns it to the person who gave it to him before he has notice of plaintiff's claim to the chattel is not liable for a conversion.
      (2) **Example**: Mr T brings a ring to a jeweller for repairs. The jeweller repairs the ring and gives it back to Mr T before receiving notice from the police that the ring has been stolen from Mrs Gottarock. The jeweller has not committed a conversion.

B. *Intent or negligence by defendant*   **[186]**

1. The plaintiff is not required to prove that the defendant planned to harm or deprive the plaintiff of the chattel.
   a. **Conscious wrongdoer**: It is *not* required that the defendant be a conscious wrongdoer.
2. Plaintiff must show that the defendant *intended* to deal with the chattel in the manner in which he actually dealt with it.   **[187]**
   a. **Mistaken but honest belief** of the defendant that he had the right to deal with chattels is generally *not* a valid defence. *Hollins v Fowler* [177]. See non-valid defences [226].
   b. **Conversion by negligence**: A defendant may breach a duty of care owed to the plaintiff, and if the breach causes the plaintiff to suffer a direct interference with her possession of the chattel, a conversion occurs.   **[188]**

(1) **Example**: *Shield Life Ins. Co. v Ulster Bank Ltd* [1995] 3 IR 225 (HC). The defendant bank accepted for collection, from their own customer, an insurance broker, a £30,000 cheque on which the plaintiffs were the payees. The broker asked the bank to transfer £5,000 to his office account. Court held that the defendant bank should have made inquiries before accepting the cheque. The defendant bank had been negligent in its duty to the plaintiffs.

3. Physical possession not required, as there is no requirement that defendant actually takes physical possession of the chattels. **[189]**
   a. As long as he has dealt with them in such a way as to amount to an absolute denial and repudiation of the plaintiff's rights. *Douglas Valley Finance Co. Ltd v Hughes* [1969] 1 QB 738.
   b. **Example**: An unjustified levy or attachment under legal process held to be conversion although chattel was not taken from the possession of plaintiff. *Tinkler v Poole* (1770) 98 ER 396.
4. Chattels capable of conversion include: **[190]**
   a. Any corporeal (tangible) personal property. **Examples**: Furniture, vehicles, jewellery, clothing, pets, etc.
   b. Realty when severed. **Example**: A growing tree is land; to cut it down, the felled tree is a chattel, and the act of severance (cutting) is a conversion.
   c. Domestic animal and birds.
   d. Non-domestic animals and birds if they have been reduced into possession. **Example**: Game that has been shot or captured may be converted.
   e. Money, papers, title deeds and negotiable instruments.

C. Plaintiff in possession or entitled to possession of the chattel   **[191]**

1. Same requirement as in:
   a. Trespass to land. See [124].
   b. Trespass to chattels. See [164].
2. **Conversion between co-owners**   **[192]**
   a. **General rule**: Each co-owner is entitled to the use and possession of the chattel.
      (1) Neither commits a wrong by taking, restraining or using the chattel.
         (a) This is true even if the other co-owner is deprived from using the chattel.

(2)   One co-owner cannot sue another in conversion unless:
                                                              [193]
    (a)   The acts of the defendant *destroy* the chattel; or
    (b)   The acts of the defendant permanently destroy the
                plaintiff's right to possession. **Example**: Selling the
                chattel to a third person.

3. **Entitlement to possession: The battle of titles**   **[194]**
  a. **General rule**: The **true owner** of the chattel *has a better title*
        to it then either its finder or the occupier of the land where it
        is found. *Webb v Ireland* [1988] IR 353. See [119].
    (1)   **Duties of a finder**   **[195]**
      (a)   To take reasonable care of the chattel, and
      (b)   To return it to the rightful owner.
    (2)   **Unknown true owner**: If the true owner cannot be
            found, the finder has a title as against all others *except* the
            occupier of land where it was found.
      (a)   **Example**: *Quinn v Coleman* (1898). A young girl
                found a purse containing some money. Later,
                through fraud she lost possession of the purse. The
                police recovered it, and it was ultimately returned to
                the girl when the true owner could not be located
                within one year and one day.

  b. **Rules from *Webb***   **[196]**
    (1)   **True owner of chattel** has the *best* title and claim.
      (a)   It is superior to any claim by the owner of land on
                which the chattel is found.
      (b)   It is superior to any claim made by the finder of the
                chattel.
    (2)   **Attached chattels**: If the chattel is attached to or under
            the land, then the owner of the land has a better claim to
            the chattel than the finder.
      (a)   **Exception**: Unless the owner has *never* been in pos-
                session of the land.
    (3)   **Not attached chattels**: If the chattel is on the land but not
            attached to it, the owner of the land will have a better
            claim to the chattel than the finder if the owner has *man-
            ifested an intention to exert control over* the chattel.
      (a)   **Example**: Control may be shown by looking for the
                lost chattel. In deciding this point, the court in
                Webb cited *Parker v British Airways Board* [1982] 1
                All ER 834.   **[197]**

(4) **Antiquities of importance**: The state has the right of ownership over antiquities of importance that have no known owner. See [119].
   (a) Similar to royal prerogative of treasure trove. See [105].
   (b) But in Ireland, based on constitutional grounds (Article 10).

c. **Statutory or contractual finders** [198]
   (1) **General rule**: Are not usually entitled to claim title to found chattels.
   (2) **Statutory finders** are generally public servants, like the police. **Example**: *Crinion v Minister for Justice* [1959] Ir Jur Rep 15. A police officer found money on the footpath. He gave the money to his sergeant, and after a year and one day he sought the money. When the return of the money was refused, he brought an action for conversion. Court held that because he found the money while on duty, he was not entitled to it.
   (3) **Contractual finders** may be employees. [199]
      (a) **Example**: *Grafstein v Holme* (1958) 12 DLR (2d) 727. An employer was found to be entitled to money found in a box in his basement by one of his employees.

D. Causation [200]

1. The defendant's act(s) must have resulted in the unjustified denial of the plaintiff's title to the chattel. In other words, the defendant's act(s) must have resulted in the defendant exercising authority or control over the chattels.
2. Onus shift: Once the plaintiff shows that the act(s) of the defendant resulted in the defendant exercising authority or control over the plaintiff's chattels, then the onus shifts onto the defendant to show that he or she did not act intentionally or negligently.

Remedies for conversion [201]

> 1. **Damages** for lost chattel (treated like forced sale); or
> 2. The trial court has *discretion* to allow return of chattel,
>   a. If the chattel is not injured, and
>   b. There are no special damages as a result of the detention.
> 3. **Note**: Recovery of the chattel does not bar action for conversion, but it may reduce the damages that may be awarded. *Tucker v Wright* (1826) 130 ER 645.

Detinue

A. Historical background [202]

1. Common law definition: The wrongful detention of another person's chattels.
2. Detinue dates back to the twelfth century.
3. At common law, the defendant had the option of
   a. Returning the chattel, or
   b. Paying for damages.
4. Detinue was not helpful if the chattel was returned but damaged.
5. Detinue was almost completely replaced by trover (the forerunner of conversion).

B. Other approaches [203]

1. Detinue has been abolished in England and replaced by statutory provisions.
2. In the US, detinue is regarded generally as one of the many remedies available under the tort of conversion.

> **Definition of detinue**: The wrongful failure of a person in possession of a chattel to deliver it to the person entitled to immediate possession. [204]
>
> **Required elements**
> A. Defendant is in possession of the chattel
> B. The plaintiff demands return of the chattel
> C. The defendant fails or refuses to return the chattel

A. Defendant is in possession of the chattel

1. Detinue protects entitlement to possession of chattel.   **[205]**
   a. Ownership of the chattel is not essential.
2. Detinue usually arises in bailments. See [165].
3. **The finder of chattels:**   **[206]**
   a. Will not be liable in *detinue* if the finder loses possession of the chattel;
   b. However, the finder will be liable (in *conversion*) if he wrongfully disposes of chattel.

B. The plaintiff demands return of the chattel   **[207]**

1. The defendant must adversely possess the plaintiff's chattel.
2. **Establishing adverse possession**
   a. **General rule**: The plaintiff *must* make a *demand* for the return of the chattel.
      (1) **Example**: *Cullen, Allen and Co. v Barclay* (1881) 10 LR Ir. A potato salesman was held not liable in detinue because the owners of the chattels (potato sacks) failed to demand their return. This was true, even though the salesman was contractually required to return chattels.
   b. **Exception to general rule**: The plaintiff is *not* required to demand the return of the chattel if it would be futile to do so.
                                                      [208]
      (1) **Examples**:
         (a) If the chattels were destroyed while in the defendant's possession; or
         (b) The defendant has given or allowed possession of the chattel to go to another person.

C. The defendant fails or refuses to return the chattel   **[209]**

1. Detinue arises if after the plaintiff's demand for possession the defendant *refuses* or *fails* to give the chattel to the plaintiff.
2. **Loss of possession during bailment**: If the defendant wrongfully loses possession of a chattel bailed to him, he will still be liable when he cannot return the chattel at the end of the bailment.
   a. **Example**: Leaving a suit at a dry cleaners, and it is either misplaced or given to the wrong customer.
   b. **Exception**: The defendant's refusal or failure to return may be excused if the refusal or failure *is reasonable*.
      (1) **Reasonable failure or refusal** occurs where: **[210]**

    (a)   There is a fair dispute as to the plaintiff's entitlement to possession. *Poole v Burns* [1944] Ir Jur Rep 20.

    (b)   The chattel was destroyed through *no fault* of the defendant, such as an act of God.

3. Onus is on the defendant to prove the absence of fault. *Sheehy v Faughnan* [1991] 1 IR 424. **[211]**

Remedies for detinue

> 1. **Damages** is the usual remedy for detinue. **[212]**
>   a. For the value of the chattel, and
>   b. Damages for its detention.
> 2. With the discretion of the court, **[213]**
>   a. The return of the chattel may be ordered, and
>   b. For unique items of special value or interest to the plaintiff, damages for the detention of the chattel may be awarded.

Defences to intentional torts to chattels   **[214]**

> A. Consent
> B. Lawful authority
> C. Self-help
> D. Necessity
> E. Contributory negligence
> F. Limitations

A. Consent. See generally [72] et seq.   **[215]**

1. The plaintiff's consent to the defendant's use or interference with his chattels is a valid defence.
   a. The plaintiff's consent may be expressed or implied. **Examples**:
   (1) Expressly: 'Yes, you may read my book.'
   (2) Implied (by conduct): Without speaking, offering your opera glasses to the person seated next to you.
2. For consent to be effective, scope cannot be exceeded. **[216]**
   a. **Example**: Allowing your brother to drive your car does not give him your consent to his painting the car.
3. To be valid, consent cannot be obtained by:
   a. Fraud; or
   b. Duress.

4. ***Volenti non fit injuria*: Voluntary assumption of the risk [217]**
   a. The plaintiff agrees, i.e. consents, to assume the risk of injury to his interests or damage to his chattel.
   b. **Example**: *Arthur v Anker* [1996] 2 WLR 602. The defendant, a company, clamped a car parked on private land and was found to have a defence of consent. Notices displayed prominently on the land had warned that anyone parking without authorisation would be clamped. When the plaintiff parked there, he was deemed to have accepted that risk.
   c. **Note**: *Volenti non fit injuria* is generally associated with negligence rather than trespass.

B. Lawful authority   **[218]**

1. **Judicial authority**: Courts are empowered to grant warrants for the search and seizure of chattels.
2. **Statutory authority**: Police do not commit a trespass to chattels when they exercise their lawful powers of search and seizure.
   a. Examples of statutory powers of seizure:
      (1) Section 15, Proceeds of Crime Act 1996.
      (2) Section 37, Control of Horses Act 1996.
   b. **Power of seizure of the police**   **[219]**
      (1) **Does not extend** to a general right to interfere with possession in the event of a civil dispute.
      (2) **Limited to cases** involving lawful arrest of the person in possession of the chattels.
3. **Leading case of seizure** of chattels *without* a warrant is *Jennings v Quinn* [1968] IR 305.
   a. **Public interest** requires police, under a lawful arrest, to seize property without a warrant which is in the possession or custody of the arrested person when the police believe it is necessary because the property is:
      (1) Evidence in support of the criminal charge;
      (2) Evidence in support of any other criminal charge; or
      (3) Reasonably believed to be stolen property not in the lawful possession of that person.

C. Self-help   **[220]**

1. **Common law**: Under the common law, a person could use *reasonable force* to defend one's property or the property of another.

a. **Example**: Under the common law, a person could chase after and use reasonable force to take back stolen chattels from a pickpocket.
2. **Statutory reform** [221]
   a. **Non-Fatal Offences Against the Person Act 1997, sections 18–20**, basically restates the common law. See [95] *et seq.*
      (1) A person may use reasonable force in the defence of his property or the property of another person.

D. *Necessity* [222]

1. **Definition**: Necessity is the commission of a tortious act to prevent some greater evil where there is no reasonable alternative. See [85] and [140].
   a. The degree of interference or damage to plaintiff's chattel must be balanced against the threatened harm to defendant's interests.
   b. **Example**: *Cresswell v Sirl* [1948] 1 KB 241. The defendant shot the plaintiff's dog, which had been worrying the defendant's sheep. The shooting was held justified by the threatened harm.
      (1) **Statutory reform**: The Control of Dogs Act 1986, section 23 provides that a person who kills a dog he reasonably believes is worrying livestock, or is about to worry livestock, has a defence for any charge for shooting the dog.

E. *Contributory negligence* [223]

1. Civil Liability Act 1961, section 34(2)(d) provides:
   a. That the plaintiff's failure to exercise reasonable care of his own property will be deemed to be contributory negligence.
   b. Except to the extent the defendant is unjustly enriched.

F. *Limitations* [224]

1. **The Statute of Limitations 1957, section 12(11)**
   a. For detinue and conversion
      (1) The limitation period begins to run from the time of the wrongdoing.
      (2) Subsequent acts of detinue and conversion do not give rise to separate periods of limitation.

2. Note **importance of limitations** [225]
    a. The running of the limitation period will bar a civil case, and
    b. Result in extinction of plaintiff's title to the chattel (section 12(2)).

Non-valid defences

A. Mistake [226]

1. **General rule**: A mistake of law or fact is no defence to anyone who intentionally interferes with a chattel in a manner inconsistent with the right of another.
    a. 'Persons deal with the property in chattels or exercise acts of ownership over them at their peril.' *Hollins v Fowler* [1874-80] All ER 118. See [177] for facts.
    b. **Remoteness of damage**: It is no defence that the loss suffered was not intended, or even that it was not the natural or probable result of the act. *Hiort v Bott* (1974) LR 9 Ex 86.

B. Jus Tertii [227]

1. It is not a valid defence to argue that the chattels belonged to someone other than the plaintiff.
2. **Example**: Polly was given her brother's bicycle to go to the shop. While Polly was in the shop, Nellie took the bicycle so she would not have to walk home. Nellie cannot claim as a defence that Polly was not the rightful owner of the bicycle. Polly was in possession.

Chapter 2 Questions

1. Henry was having a problem with his garden flooding. He knew that his neighbour, Nicola, had a drain in her garden, so he moved his chutes to allow the water off of his roof to run down into her garden. Name the tort.
2. Tim was driving fast on a narrow road. On a bend he hit Michael and sent him over the ditch into Fred's field.
    (a) Did Michael commit a trespass onto Fred's land?
    (b) Did Tim commit a trespass to Fred's land?
3. Pauline is eight months pregnant. In the busy bus station there are no empty seats, except one next to Naomi. Naomi is reading a novel and her bag is on the seat next to her. If Pauline moves the bag to the floor:

    (a) Has she committed a tort?

    (b) Does she have a valid defense?

4. Cyril fell asleep during a boring film. When he awoke the cinema was empty and people were entering for another film. Cyril decided to stay and watch the new film.

    (a) What made Cyril's initial entry into the cinema legal?

    (b) Has Cyril committed a trespass to land?

5. Mai Dai was protesting the opening of a DIY superstore in Waterford. During the protest she threw a stone which broke two windows that were on special offer near the entrance of the store.

    (a) Has Mai Dai committed a trespass to the DIY's land?

    (b) Has Mai Dai committed a conversion?

6. I took my pedigree cat, Toulouse, to the vet for an ear operation. The vet mistakenly neutered Toulouse. Name the tort.

7. Miss Marbles found an elderly gentleman sitting in her garden enjoying the sun. Before he left the garden he picked a small rose and stuck it in his buttonhole.

    (a) Has the elderly gentleman committed trespass to Miss Marbles's land?

    (b) When the gentleman picked the flower, what tort did he commit?

8. By mistake, Chris grabbed and used her flatmate Fiona's toothbrush. Name the tort.

9. Melanie found John's thermos and drank all of his tea.

    (a) What act is a conversion?

    (b) What act is a trespass to chattels?

10. Sean threw a firecracker into his friend Shane's open sitting room window. Unfortunately, it caused a fire. When Sean realised that the sitting room curtains were burning, he reached into the window and ripped down the burning curtains.

    (a) Identify the acts that are a trespass to land.

    (b) Is necessity a good defence for Sean to the trespass to land?

    (c) Identify Sean's act of conversion.

11. Susan is angry that her husband, Michael, has been having an affair. When Michael came home from work, he found Susan burning their wedding photos in the fire. Name the tort.

12. Nicholas is hired by Finbar to plough a field. While ploughing, Nicholas unearthed an unusual stone. On closer examination the stone is found to be an important dolmen or standing stone. Who has the best title to the stone?

13. Bob Crachett is very poor. He went to the local shop to buy a Christmas tree and was dismayed to find that he could not afford to buy one. Thinking that if one of the trees was slightly damaged he might be able to purchase it at a reduced rate, he quickly snapped off a couple of limbs. Unfortunately, the shop owner refused to reduce the price, so Bob left the slightly damaged tree and went to the Scrooge farm. Quietly, to avoid detection, Bob chopped down one of Scrooge's ornamental pine trees to use as a Christmas tree. He then dragged the tree to his home. Identify all the intentional torts to land and chattels in the problem.

14. Ziggy was hired as a rat catcher by Limerick Corporation. Under statute he may enter any dwelling in search of rats. Mary saw a rat in her flat and called for Ziggy. Ziggy arrived and entered the flat. Quickly he began moving furniture away from the walls, looking for rats. Mary left the flat in terror. After Mary left, Ziggy opened the drawers in Mary's dresser, looking for her knickers. He selected a bright red pair with black lace to add to his knicker collection.

    (a) Has Ziggy committed trespass *ab initio*?
    (b) When Ziggy moved the furniture, was he committing a trespass to chattels?
    (c) When Ziggy opened the drawer in Mary's dresser, was he committing a conversion?

15. Sean bought a very old desk from an old family friend. He called ABC Antique Restorers to come to his home and give him an estimate on refinishing the desk. Sean agreed to the price quoted for refinishing the desk and helped the men load the desk into their van. After several months, Sean contacts ABC and learns that they cannot locate his desk. It is believed that the desk may have been destroyed in an accidental fire in one of their workshops.

    (a) Can Sean maintain an action for detinue against ABC?
    (b) Does ABC have a valid defence because Sean did not make a formal written demand for the return of his desk?

16. 'An allegedly injured party took Supermac's to court seeking up to €38,000 compensation in November 2001. However, the claim was withdrawn when the plaintiff learned the alleged accident was captured by hidden cameras. The plaintiff did not fall, but pretended to slip after purposely splashing water on the floor of the toilets…' (*Irish Independent*, 7 March 2002, Initiative Supplement) Assume the alleged injured party is named Patrick. Has Patrick committed a trespass to Supermac's land?

17. The Three Bears came home and found Goldilocks sleeping in their house. When they asked her to leave, she told them that she wasn't going to vacate the premises because she knows that Yogi Bear owns the house.
    (a) Can the three bears use force to eject Goldilocks?
    (b) Can the three bears maintain a cause of action for trespass against Goldilocks?

SECTION II:
STRICT LIABILITY

3

COMMON LAW AND
STATUTORY STRICT LIABILITY

Chapter synopsis

I.   Common law strict liability
     Fire
     Animals
     Vicarious liability
     Rule in *Rylands v Fletcher*
II. Statutory-based strict liability
     Liability for Defective Products Act 1991

Strict liability chart   [228]

Common law strict liability	Fire	See Fire chart [243].
	Animals	See Animal chart [261].
	Vicarious liability	Where one person is held strictly liable for the acts of another. Usually arises in the employer/employee relationship. See [262] *et seq.*
	Rule in *Rylands v Fletcher*	An occupier who brings onto his land anything likely to do damage if it escapes, and keeps it on his land, will be held strictly liable for the damage caused if it escapes. See [273] *et seq.*
Statutory strict liability	Liability for Defective Products Act 1991	This statute imposes strict liability on a producer for damage caused wholly or partly by a defect in his or her product. See [296] *et seq.* and chart [325].
	Control of Dogs Acts 1986 and 1994	See Animal chart [261].

I. Common law strict liability   [229]

A. Historical background of strict liability

1. **Definition**: Liability imposed without intent or fault by the defendant.
2. Early law of torts *not* concerned with moral responsibility.
   a. **Example**: Affirmative duties.
   b. It was argued that early torts provided a remedy that would be accepted instead of private vengeance. For more on Holmes, see [337].
3. Originally, strict liability was imposed in the sense that any person who injured another, even if by pure accident or self-defence, was responsible for damages.
   a. Until the end of the nineteenth century, tort liability slowly began to lean toward recognition of *fault* or moral responsibility as its primary concern:
      (1) Due to growing moral consciousness in the community.
      (2) Led to legal liability based on achieving conduct expected of a good member of the community, i.e. negligence.
   b. **Near death of strict liability**   [230]
      (1) Eventually, arguments emerged that there should never be liability without fault.
      (2) McMahon refers to this period in tort history as the 'no liability without fault' era.
   c. Twentieth century: Since the beginning of the twentieth century, it has been generally accepted that in some cases a defendant may be liable although he has:
      (1) No moral wrongdoing; nor
      (2) Departed from a reasonable standard of care.

B. Reasons for imposing strict liability   [231]

1. **Social justice**: Who best can bear the loss?
   a. Often referred to as *loss shifting* by creating liability where there was no fault.
   b. **Deep pockets**: The person or entity with the 'deepest pockets' (resources) is made responsible for the loss.
      (1) **Example**: Workers' compensation statutes.
2. **Social policy**: What is best for the public or society at large?   [232]
   a. Strict liability imposed on the keepers of animals, and
   b. Abnormally dangerous activities or conditions.

Fire

<table><tr><td>A. Historical background   **[233]**
B. Present fire liability: The Accidental Fires Act 1943
C. Survival of common law strict liability
D. Other actions for fires</td></tr></table>

Fire

A. Historical background   **[234]**

1. **Early common law** imposed strict liability on land owners for fire.
   a. Allegation was for 'negligently' keeping fire, but commentators think that this was not the negligence of today. (Wigmore)
   b. Defences included:
   (1) Act of God;
   (2) Act of stranger.
   c. Strict liability rule was considered unduly harsh.
2. **Early fire statutes**   **[235]**
   a. England passed statutes in the early eighteenth century.
   (1) The Prevention of Fires (Metropolis) Act (1707) 6 Anne.6. c 31, made permanent by (1774) 10 Anne.1.c. 14.
   (a) No tort action allowed for a fire accidentally occurring in a person's 'building or estate'.
   (2) An Act for Preventing Mischief That May Happen by Fire (1715) 2 Geo.1.c 5.
   (a) No tort action allowed against a person 'in whose house, chamber, or out-house' a fire was accidentally caused.
   b. English courts held that a landholder would not be liable:
   (1) Unless the fire started or spread through landholder's negligence, *Vaughan v Menlove* [335] or
   (2) The fire was intentionally started. *Filliter v Phippard* [1847] ER 490.
   c. **Note**: Strict liability applied to *arson* or intentional fires.
3. **Industrialisation**   **[236]**
   a. **Caused a reversion to common law strict liability** for fires started because of *abnormally dangerous activities*. *Musgrove v Pandelis* [1919] 2 K B 43. *Musgrove* facts: A fire accidentally started in the carburettor of the defendant's automobile. The

defendant's employee negligently failed to turn off the petrol tap and the fire spread. The defendant was held liable for the spreading of the fire, but not for the original fire.
   b. Led to the Railway Fires Act 1905 and 1923, which provided statutory compensation for damages to land caused by sparks from railway engines.
4. **Irish approach** [237]
   a. *Richardson v Athlone Woollen Mills* [1942] IR 581. A fire accidentally started in a factory. The court held that it was not protected by the 1715 statute, and the owners were liable for damages to adjoining premises. The reasoning was that factories were not covered by the Act.
   b. In response to this case, the Accidental Fires Act 1943 was enacted.

B. *Present fire liability: The Accidental Fires Act 1943* [238]

1. **No legal action** can be initiated by any person who has suffered damage because of a fire accidentally occurring on or in the buildings or lands of another person.
   a. Definitions:
      (1) Building: Any structure made of any material.
      (2) Any person: Appears to extend to any occupier.
      (3) Accidental: Means without negligence. *Rutledge v Land* [1930] I R 537.
   b. **Purpose**: The Act grants immunity for non-negligent fires.
      (1) A similar statute in Northern Ireland (Accidental Fires Act 1944) suggests that accidental includes all *non-intentional* fires.
2. **Occupiers** [239]
   a. May be vicariously liable for negligent act of anyone but a stranger. *Balfour v Barty-King* [1957] 1 Q B 496.
      (1) A stranger is not a(n):
         (a) Member of the occupier's family;
         (b) Guests of the occupier;
         (c) Employees acting within the course of employment; or
         (d) Licensee of the occupier.
      (2) Negligent act may include:
         (a) Creation of the fire; or
         (b) Failure to control a fire caused by:
            i. The defendant or the defendant's employee;

        ii. The act of stranger, such as a trespasser;

        iii. Natural sources, such as lightening; or

        iv. Fires of unknown origin.

    (c) *McKenzie v O'Neil and Rose Ltd* (1977) unrep. (HC). The defendant's employee burned papers on the defendant's land. The day was windy. Although the employee thought that the fire was out, it spread to another's land. Liability was imposed for negligent failure to control the fire.

  b. **Immunity** under Act includes: [240]

    (1) Injuries to land,

    (2) Injuries to chattels, and

    (3) Personal injuries.

  c. Onus: The burden of proof is on the plaintiff to show that fire was caused by a non-accident. *Woods v O'Connor* [1958] Ir Jur Rep 71.

C. Survival of common law strict liability [241]

  1. **Intentional fires**

    a. **Accidental Fires Act 1943** provides *no immunity* for intentional fires such as arson.

    b. The person starting the fire will be held strictly liable.

  2. *Rylands v Fletcher* may apply against an occupier of land for fires negligently started by independent contractors, provided the fire arises from a non-natural use of the land and escapes. See [273] *et seq.*

D. Other actions for fires [242]

  1. Negligence actions

    a. Liability may be imposed on the manufacturer of a dangerous product that goes on fire when used by the consumer. *Robinson v Technico Ltd* (1954) (SC). See [450].

    b. The Accidental Fires Act 1943 provides no immunity for fires negligently started or negligently allowed to spread. *Kelly v McElligott* (1949) 85 ILTR (1) See [239] *et seq.*

  2. Under the Liability for Defective Products Act 1991, imposes strict liability on a producer of a product for damage caused wholly or partly by a defect in his or her product. See [296] *et seq.*

Fire chart [243]

Early common law	Imposed strict liability on landowners for damages caused by fire. See [234].
Early fire statutes	Granted immunity to occupiers and landowners for damages caused by accidental fires or caused by accidental fires occurring in a person's buildings or estate. Strict liability still applied to arson or intentional fires. See [235].
Industrialisation	Caused a reversion to common law strict liability for fires started by abnormally dangerous activities, *Richardson v Athlone Woollen Mills* [1942]. See [236].
Accidental Fires Act 1943	No legal action can be initiated by any person who has suffered damage because of a fire accidentally occurring on or in the buildings or lands of another person. Strict liability still applies to arson or intentional fires. See [241].

Animals

A. Historical background [244]
B. Present strict liability for animals
C. Cattle trespass

A. Historical background [245]

1. Earliest common law held the owner of chattel strictly liable for any harm caused by the chattel.
   a. Owner held strictly liable for damage to an animal, slave or other chattel inflicted on others.
   b. Owner could escape liability by surrendering the chattel to:
      (1) The injured party; or
      (2) The king.
      (3) This was referred to as *noxal surrender*.
2. Today, ancient notions of strict liability have survived because of modern social policy. [246]
   a. **Rationale:** Certain animals create an obvious danger to others, even if they are carefully kept.
      (1) Strict liability for dangerous animals is of ancient origin.
      (2) First modern case dealing with dangerous animals was *May v Bundett* [1846] 115 ER 1213.

b. Those who keep animals are required to protect the community from damage caused by the animals.

B. *Present strict liability for animals*   [247]

1. In general, liability for injuries caused by animals can be:
   a. Strict; and/or
   b. Based on fault, i.e. negligence. See Chapter 4 for negligence principles.
2. The law has divided animals into classes.   [248]
   a. *Ferae naturae*, or wild animals. **Examples**: Elephants, bears, seals, alligators, tigers.
   b. *Mansuetae naturae*, or domestic animals. **Examples**: Dogs, cats, bees, horses, cattle, pheasants.
   c. **Distinction** between domestic and wild animals is: [249]
      (1) Based on the traits of the species *rather* than an individual animal, and
      (2) Determined by the likelihood of finding such an animal in jurisdiction.
         (a) **Example**: An elephant is a common domesticated animal in Asia, but is not native to Ireland. Hence, the elephant is considered wild even if the particular animal is domesticated.

3. **Liability**   [250]
   a. **Domestic animals**: Under common law, the keepers of domestic or tame animals with vicious, fierce or 'mischievous propensity' to do the damage suffered were held strictly liable for the damage suffered.
      (1) Liability based on *possession or control* rather than ownership. *Breen v Slotkin* [1948] 4 DLR 46.
      (2) Onus: Plaintiff has the burden of establishing the defendant's knowledge of the dangerous nature of the animal.
      (3) *Scienter* doctrine: Once the defendant had knowledge of the dangerous nature of an animal in his possession, strict liability would attach.
         (a) *Scienter* simply means knowledge of the dangerous propensity.
      (4) **Knowledge**:   [251]
         (a) *Must* be proved for domestic animals.
         (b) May be imputed to the owner.
            i. **Example**: *Bennet v Walsh* [1936] 70 ILTR 252. The defendant's nine-year-old daughter knew of

the animal's mischievous propensity. The defendant was held to have imputed knowledge.

(c) Knowledge *must* be of the *damage suffered*. **Examples**:

   i. *Quinn v Quinn* 39 ILTR. The defendant's sow had previously killed fowl, then killed the plaintiff's cow. Defendant held to have knowledge of dangerous propensity of sow.

   ii. *Glansville v Sutton and Co. Ltd* [1928] 1 KB 571. The defendant's horse had a bad habit of biting other horses, but this was not proof that the horse had a vicious tendency to bite humans.

(d) Awareness does not require injury. An animal can display dangerous or mischievous propensity without inflicting injury.

   i. **Example**: *Duggan v Armstrong* [1992] 2 IR 161 (SC). A dog showed aggressive behaviour toward children although he did not bite. Owner held to have knowledge of mischievous propensity.

(e) **Mere friskiness** is not dangerous or mischievous propensity.

   i. **Example**: Excited dogs may jump on people and bark. A horse may run about wildly kicking up its heels.

b. **Wild animals**: Under common law, the keeper of a wild animal keeps the animal at his peril.   **[252]**

   (1) The keeper of a wild animal is *strictly liable* for all damages caused by such an animal.

      (a) Liability is based on *possession or control* rather than ownership.

   (2) **Doctrine of *Scienter***   **[253]**

      (a) **Knowledge is presumed** of the dangerous nature of a wild animal.

      (b) **This presumption cannot be rebutted**. *Behrens v Bertram Mills Circus Ltd* [1957] 1 All ER 583.

4. **Dogs**: Statutory liability.   **[254]**

   a. **Control of Dogs Acts 1986 and 1992** impose strict liability on dog owners for:

   (1) Damage caused by the dog attacking a person; or

   (2) Damage done to livestock by the dog (section 21 of the 1986 Act).

    b. Old common law rule of 'one free bite' abolished.
- (1) **One free bite** was allowed because the owner needed knowledge of the dog's dangerous propensity to bite for liability to attach, thus it was said that the dog was allowed one free bite.
- (2) **Note**: Today the owner *does not* need knowledge of the dog's dangerous propensity for liability to attach.

    c. **Owner**: Includes occupiers of land where dog: **[255]**
- (1) Is kept; or
- (2) Allowed to stay.
  - (a) This requires knowledge and consent. *Leahy v Leader and Cork Diocesan Trustees* (1999) (HC). The plaintiff was bitten on the defendant's church property. The dog belonged to another and the parish priest had no knowledge that the dog was present. No liability.
  - (b) **Exception**: If the occupier of land where the dog is kept or allowed to stay can prove he is not the owner of the dog.

    d. **Statutory exceptions to strict liability**   **[256]**
- (1) If a dog injures a trespasser, strict liability will not apply. The trespasser must prove negligence to bring action.
- (2) If a dog injures trespassing livestock, strict liability will not apply, unless the defendant caused the dog to attack the livestock.

C. *Cattle trespass*   **[257]**

1. **Definition**: The person keeping livestock that strays onto the land or chattels of another is held strictly liable for the trespass itself and any resulting harm.
2. **Does not apply** if cattle are being lawfully driven on road and break into property adjoining the road.
3. Cattle trespass applies to all farm animals.
   a. Exception: Cats, dogs and wild animals.
4. **Resulting harm** includes:
   a. Damage to land;
   b. Damage to chattels (crops and other animals); and
   c. Personal injuries. *Wormald v Cole* [1954] 1 All ER 683.
5. Under common law, livestock *straying* onto the public road did not commit cattle trespass.
   a. **Animals Act 1985, section 2** provides that any person placing

animals on land is required to take reasonable care to avoid damage being caused by the animals straying onto a public road.

6. **Defences to cattle trespass**   **[258]**
   a. **Act of God**
      (1) **Definition**: A result of natural forces.
          (a) **Example**: In tornado country, it is common for livestock to be picked up in a tornado and put down several miles away unharmed.
   b. **Contributory negligence**   **[259]**
      (1) Where the acts of the plaintiff caused the defendant's cattle to trespass.
      (2) **Example**: The plaintiff left the defendant's gate open and the defendant's horses trampled the plaintiff's garden.
   c. **Act of stranger**   **[260]**
      (1) Where the acts of a third party cause the defendant's cattle to trespass.
      (2) **Example**: *Moloney v Stephens* [1945] Ir Jur Rep 37. A third person left the defendant's gates open so that his cattle strayed onto the plaintiff's land. Act of stranger was a valid defence.

Strict liability for animals chart   [261]

Common law	*Ferae naturae*	Strict liability: Under the common law, the keeper of a wild animal keeps the animal at his peril. See **[252]**
	Mansuetae naturae	Strict liability: Only attached to the keepers of domestic or tame animals with vicious, fierce or mischievous propensity to do the damage suffered. See **[250]**
	Cattle trespass	Strict liability: The person keeping livestock that strays onto the land or chattels of another is strictly liable for the trespass itself and any resulting harm. (Note: It does not apply to cattle lawfully driven on the road.) See **[257]**
Statutory	Control of Dogs Act 1986	Section 21: Imposes strict liability on the owner or keeper of a dog for damage caused in an attack on any person and for injury done to livestock. See **[254]**

Vicarious liability

A. General background   **[262]**
B. The doctrine of *respondeat superior*
C. Duty to control others

A. General background   **[263]**

1. **Definition**: Where one person is held liable for the acts of another person.
2. The modern form of vicarious liability dates from the end of the seventeenth century.
3. Vicarious liability arises in:
   a. **Formal legal relationships,** such as:
      (1) Employer/employee; see [432] *et seq.*
      (2) Principal/agent;
      (3) Firm/partner, which is imposed by liability of partners under the Partnership Act 1961.
   b. **Informal relationships** where one person has *control* over another.
      (1) Driver/passenger. *Curly v Mannion*, see [269].
      (2) Social host/guest. *Moynihan v Moynihan*, see [272].
      (3) Owner of vehicle/driver. **Section 118, Road Traffic Act.**

B. The doctrine of respondeat superior, *see [420] et seq.*   **[264]**

1. **Definition**: An employer is vicariously liable for any tortious acts committed by his employees within the scope of the employ-ment.
2. **General rule**: An employer may be liable for the tortious acts committed by employees within the scope of employment. See [420] for crucial requirements.
   a. An employee may be: **[265]**
      (1) An ordinary worker;
      (2) A casual or part-time worker; or
      (3) An unpaid volunteer.   **[266]**
   b. **Factors for determining** if employment relationship exists.
      (1) **Dominant factor**: The right to *control* the worker.
      (2) Method of payment (salary or fee).
      (3) Right to hire and fire worker.
      (4) Degree of skill of worker.

(5)   Whether the worker provides his own employment.
(6)   Contract for services or of services?
(7)   Worker integrated into the business?
  c. **Medical staff** in the full-time service of hospitals are employees for vicarious liability purposes.
3. **Independent contractors**   **[267]**
  a. **General rule**: There is no vicarious liability to employers for the tortious acts of independent contractors.
    (1)   Legal commentators generally agree that:
        (a)   There is no precise rule for determining the difference between an employee and independent contractor.
        (b)   Some courts have gone to extraordinary lengths to find that contractors are employees.
  b. **Exception**: An employer may be vicariously liable for torts committed by independent contractors if the employer's degree of control was *comparable* to that of an employee.   **[268]**
    (1)   *Phelan v Coillte Teo* [1993] 1 IR 18. The plaintiff was injured due to negligence of an independent contractor, a welder/fitter with whom the plaintiff was working.
    (2)   Test of control is not settled.
    (3)   English approach regarding issue of control:
        (a)   Was the wrongful act authorised by the employer? Or
        (b)   Was the act authorised by the employer, but the method of performance was not authorised?

C. Duty to control others, see [418] et seq.   **[269]**

1. **Parent/child relationship**
  a. **General rule**: Parents are not vicariously liable for the torts committed by their child. See [426].
2. **Owners of vehicles**
  a. **General rule**: A driver has a duty to control her passengers so that third parties using the public road are not injured.
  b. **Example**: *Curly v Manion* [1965] IR 543 (SC). The driver of a car was held vicariously liable for the negligent acts of her passenger. The passenger, a child, negligently opened the car door, causing injury to the plaintiff, a cyclist.
  c. **Road Traffic Act 1961, section 118** imposes liability on the owner of a vehicle for the conduct of any person using the vehicle with the owner's consent.   **[270]**

(1) To hold the owner vicariously liable, the plaintiff must show that the driver had the owner's consent to use the vehicle, *and*

(2) The conduct causing the injury was within the scope of the consent.

   (a) **Example**: *Guerin v Guerin and McGrath* [1992] 2 IR 287 (HC). The owner of a car left the country. He gave the keys to his father, but before leaving he asked a neighbour to drive his family. However, the father asked another person to drive the family, and the plaintiff was injured. Held: The consent granted by the owner extended to any person driving on behalf of his family, and was not confined to the neighbour.

(3) **Fraud**: Consent obtained by fraud bars vicarious liability. *Kelly v Lombard Motor Co. Ltd* [1974] IR 142.

(4) Onus is on the owner to show that conduct is outside the scope of the consent. *Buckley v Musgrave Brook Bond Ltd* [1969] IR 440.

3. **Partners** [271]

   a. **Common law**: Persons who engaged in a partnership or joint venture were vicariously liable for the conduct of the other members within the scope of the enterprise.

      (1) **Rationale**: Persons engaged in a partnership or joint venture had an equal right to control the operation of the enterprise.

   b. **Partnership Act 1890**

      (1) Each partner is vicariously liable for the tortious acts of the other partners committed in the course of the partnership's business.

         (a) Extends to all activities that the partner has authority to do.

         (b) This may include fraud. *Allied Pharmaceutical Distributors Ltd and All-Phar Services Ltd v Walsh* (1990) unrep. (HC).

4. **Gratuitous services** [272]

   a. Hostess/social guest. *Moynihan v Moynihan* [1975] IR 192. A two-year-old was burned by a pot of tea that the child pulled off of her granny's table. The tea was left on the table by her aunt, who went to answer the phone. The mother and granny were in the kitchen doing the dishes. **Held**: The gran was vicariously liable for the negligence of her daughter, the mother. As the hostess, the grandmother was in control of her daughter, the serving of the tea and/or if the tea was to be served.

Rule in Rylands v Fletcher

A. *Historical background* [273]

1. **Landmark case – *Rylands* facts:** The defendant, a mill owner, hired an independent contractor to make a reservoir on his land to supply water to a mill. During construction of the reservoir, the independent contractor found a shaft of an old coal mine on the site. The contractor could have blocked the mineshaft, but he did not. He was not aware that it joined shafts of mines on neighbouring land. When the reservoir was filled with water, it flooded the shaft, thus flooding the plaintiff's mine – (1868) LR 3 HL 330.

2. The ***Rylands* Rule** was developed because under existing law the plaintiff was without a cause of action. [274]
   a. **Negligence:** The defendant was not negligent because he did not know about the shafts.
   b. **Vicarious liability:** The defendant could not be vicariously liable because the contractor was an independent contractor.
   c. **Trespass:** The plaintiff could not bring an action in trespass because the damages he suffered were not direct and immediate.
   d. **Nuisance:** The plaintiff could not bring an action for nuisance because it did not apply to a single event.

3. **The rule:** An occupier who brings onto his land anything likely to do damage if it escapes, and keeps it on his land, will be held strictly liable for the damage caused if it escapes. [275]

4. **Note:** There are very few Irish cases.

B. Rylands *requirements* [276]

1. Accumulation
2. Non-natural use of land
3. Dangerous or hazardous thing
4. An escape
5. Damage and causation

1. **Accumulation**   **[277]**
   a. Thing must be brought onto land by the defendant.
      (1) Does not include things naturally occurring or already
          on the land.
      (2) *Healy v Bray Urban District Council* [1963-4] Ir Jur Rep
          9. Stones forming part of a hillside injured the plaintiff.
          The stones had not been brought to the land by the
          defendant.
   b. Accumulation must be for the benefit of the defendant.
   c. Early cases required that the parties be owners or occupiers of
      land.
      (1) Requirement has been eased.   **[278]**
          (a) In *Crown River Cruises Ltd v Kimbolton Fireworks
              Ltd* [1996] 2 Lloyd's Rep 533, it was held that a
              barge moored to a riverbank could qualify as land.
              (Defendant not held liable under rule in *Rylands*.)
          (b) Liability can be incurred for bringing a dangerous
              thing onto the highway. *Rigby v Chief Constable of
              Northampton* [1985] 2 All ER 985 (QB). While
              attempting to capture a man, police fired tear gas
              into a shop where he was hiding. The tear gas set the
              shop on fire. **Held**: The rule would apply to a thing
              escaping from the highway.
2. **Non-natural use of land**   **[279]**
   a. The principle is applied *only* to the non-natural use of the
      land.
   b. Non-natural use of land is a vague concept.
      (1) Without a meaningful test. *Burnie Port Authority v
          General Jones Pty Ltd* (1994) 68 ALJR 331 (HC)
          (Australian).
      (2) Natural does not mean primitive. *Read v Lyons* [1947]
          AC 156 (HL).
   c. English decisions have placed an emphasis on the use being:
      (1) Abnormal,
      (2) Inappropriate,
      (3) Extraordinary, or
      (4) Exceptional, etc.
   d. **Special use** is required that must bring with it an increased
      danger to others, not merely ordinary use or use of land for
      the benefit of the community. *Rickards v Lothian*, see [286].

3. **Dangerous or hazardous thing** [280]
   a. **Definition**: Anything likely to do mischief if it escapes.
      (1) **Examples**: Fireworks, water, poisonous gases and chemicals.
      (2) **Not relevant** that thing could be safe if not allowed to escape.
         (a) Dangerous chemical substances: *Hanrahan v Merck Sharp and Dohme*, see [723]. Decided on non-*Rylands* grounds. See generally [523].
         (b) However, see *obiter* Goff, J. in *Cambridge Water*, the storage of chemicals was a classic case of non-natural use. Liability denied, see [283].
   b. **Standard of foreseeability**: The defendant will not be liable for damages caused by something that could not be foreseen as causing damage if it escaped.
      (1) **Strict liability**: The fact that the possibility of escape is not foreseeable is not a defence.

4. **An escape** [281]
   a. Required from the defendant's occupation or control.
   b. *Read v Lyons* [1947] AC 156. While inspecting the defendant's munitions factory, the plaintiff, an inspector, was injured when a shell exploded. The defendant had not been negligent, so the plaintiff sued under *Rylands*. The court held that the dangerous thing was required to escape. **Held**: The plaintiff was injured on the defendant's premises, liability was denied as there had not been an escape.

5. **Damage and causation** [282]
   a. Occupier of neighbouring land can recover for:
      (1) Damage to chattels and land.
      (2) Economic loss suffered because of damage to land.
      (3) Personal injuries.
   b. A person with no right of occupation of land, such as a guest, may not be able to recover under *Rylands*.
      (1) Quill argues that person with no right of occupation:
         (a) Should have the right to recover under *Rylands*. Otherwise two persons with similar damage in the same incident would be treated differently.
         (b) Should be treated the same as in nuisance. Once the damage falls within the risk generated by the activity, the injured party should be allowed to recover independently of any interest in the property on which the injuries occurred. [283]

c. **Foreseeability requirement**: The damage suffered must be foreseeable. *Cambridge Water Co. v Eastern Counties Leather* [1994] 2 AC 264 (HL).
  (1) If damage is foreseeable: The manner in which the damage occurs need not be foreseeable.
     (a) Having escaped, was the damage the type or the kind that was a reasonable consequence of the escape?
     (b) Was the damage the type that was foreseeable at the time of the escape?
  (2) *Cambridge Water*: Notwithstanding the fact that the storage of chemicals is a classic case of non-natural use (*obiter* Goff, J.), it was held that it was not foreseeable that a solvent used in industry that seeped into the ground would be found in a bore hole over a mile away. Liability under *Rylands* denied.
     (a) Per Lord Goff: The historical basis of *Rylands* was the tort of nuisance, with a particular application to isolated escapes.
  (3) Applied in *Superquinn Ltd v Bray UDC* (1998) (HC). See [288].
d. **Causation**, see [530] *et seq* regarding causation. **[284]**
  (1) Plaintiff must prove:
     (a) That the escape of the dangerous accumulation caused the loss and
     (b) The loss was not too remote a consequence of the accumulation and escape.

C. Defences **[285]**

---

1. Act of stranger
2. Act of God
3. Consent
4. Contributory negligence

---

1. **Act of stranger** **[286]**
  a. **General rule**: Where a stranger causes the release of the dangerous accumulation, the defendant will not be liable in the absence of negligence.
  b. **Example**: *Rickards v Lothian* [1913] AC 263 (HL). An unknown person blocked a sink and left a tap turned on in

the defendant's premises, thereby causing damage in the plaintiff's premises on a lower floor.

    (1) **Stranger**: Any person without authority to interfere with the dangerous accumulation.

2. **Act of God** [287]

  a. **General rule**: Without negligence, a defendant will not be liable if a natural force caused the escape. *Greenock Corporation v Caledonian Railway Co.* [1917] AC 556 (HL). The corporation built a concrete paddling pool for children, and changed the flow of a stream. After an exceptionally heavy rain the stream flooded, and water poured down a public street into the plaintiff's premises. **Held**: The rainfall was not an act of God that the defendants could not have predicted.

  b. **Exception**: There is no liability if the escape is caused by a natural force in circumstances which the defendant could not have been expected to foresee or guard against. [288]

    (1) *Nichols v Marsland* [1874-80] All ER Rep 40. The defendant damned a natural stream on his land in order to create three artificial lakes. The lakes were well built, and precautions against flooding were adequate. However, an exceptionally heavy rain caused the banks of the lakes to burst. The flooding water swept away four bridges on the plaintiff's land. **Held**: No liability because the storm could not have been reasonably predicted. Witnesses had described it as the heaviest rain in living memory.

    (2) *Superquinn Ltd v Bray Urban District Council* (1998) unrep. (HC). The defense was successful for flooding caused by Hurricane Charlie.

3. **Consent** [289]

  a. **Complete defence**: If the plaintiff consented to the risk associated with the dangerous accumulation.

  b. **Partial defence**: If the plaintiff consented to the accumulation, but the defendant would remain responsible for any negligence.

  c. *Victor Weston (Eire) Ltd v Kenny* [1954] IR 191 (HC). The flat occupied by the plaintiff was flooded by water from the defendant landlord's flat. The water was part of the ordinary supply to the building. **Held**: No liability. The plaintiff implicitly consented to the accumulation of the water for supply to the building as a whole, and there was no negligence

committed by the defendant.
(1) In other jurisdictions, this defence is called *common benefit*. The presence of the thing brings a benefit to the plaintiff.
4. **Contributory negligence**: If the plaintiff causes the dangerous thing to escape, she may be held contributorily negligent. See [586] *et seq.*   **[290]**

D. *Other approaches*   **[291]**

1. **English approach**
   a. The principle in *Rylands v Fletcher* is a sub-species of the tort of nuisance.
   b. Therefore, it protects land and it is questionable whether personal injuries are recoverable. *Transco v Stockport Metropolitan Borough Council* [2003] UK HL.
2. **Australian approach**   **[292]**
   a. The principle in *Rylands* has been subsumed within the general law of negligence. *Burnie Port Authority v General Jones Pty* (1994) 68 ALJR 331 (HC).
   b. This means that it is fault based and not based on strict liability principles.
   c. **Note**: Before *Burnie Port*, the tort in Australia covered personal injuries.
3. **American approach**   **[293]**
   a. **General rule: Section 519, 2nd restatement**. A person who maintains an abnormally dangerous condition or activity on his land or engages in an activity that presents an unavoidable risk of harm to others may be liable for the harm caused even though reasonable care has been exercised.
      (1) Untra-hazardous activities: This term was used in the 1st Restatement.
         (a) **Examples**: Blasting, manufacturing explosives, etc.
         (b) Examples of merely dangerous activities: Use of vehicles, fire, boilers, etc.
      (2) Abnormally dangerous activities: Used in the 2nd Restatement.
         (a) Terminology changed to give more weight to the context in which the activity was performed.
   b. **Factors for determining** if an activity is abnormally dangerous:
      (1) Involves a high degree of risk?
      (2) The gravity of the risk.

(3) Can the risk be eliminated by the exercise of reasonable care?
(4) Is the activity a matter of common usage?
(5) Is it appropriate to where it is being conducted?
(6) The value of the activity to the community.

II. Statutory-based strict liability

A. Statutes may impose [294]

1. **Strict liability**: Liability imposed where the defendant may not be at fault.
   a. **Exercise of reasonable care**: The defendant's exercise of reasonable care will *not* relieve the defendant of liability.
   b. **Example**: Section 21 of the Control of Dogs Act 1986 imposes strict liability on the owner or keeper of a dog for damage caused in an attack on any person and for injury done to any livestock. See [254].

B. Common features of strict liability statutes include: [295]

1. The language of statute phrased in the *imperative* form.
   a. **Example**: Language such as 'shall' or 'must' instead of 'may' or 'should.'
2. A strict liability statute does *not* provide restrictions, defences or conditions for meeting the duty imposed.
   a. **Example**: The Control of Dogs Act 1986. See [254].
3. However, a strict liability statute may provide limitations on amounts recoverable under the statute and types of damages covered.
   a. **Example**: The Warsaw Convention on International Aeroplane Crashes is designed to meet the problems of international legal conflicts, and it provides the victims of any international air mishap with a strict liability recovery of a limited amount of damages. There is no recovery for emotional distress without some physical injury.

Liability for Defective Products Act 1991 (LFDPA 1991)

A. General background [296]

1. **Focus**: The law of products' liability focuses on the liability of a manufacturer, or other supplier of a product, for harm to the person or property of the plaintiff caused by a defect in the product.

a. Harm to the person can be physical or psychological.
b. **Strict liability**: **Section 2** imposes strict liability on a producer for damage caused wholly or partly by a defect in his product.
c. **Rationale** for strict liability: It is imposed on the party best able to stop similar future harm.

2. **Sales problems** are *not* covered under products' liability. **[297]**
   a. Sales problems include issues regarding:
      (1) **Performance.** Where a product simply does not perform as well as expected, causing a purely economic loss to the buyer.
      (2) **Damage.** Where the product is damaged and it is worth less than the price paid for the product.
   b. Sales problems may be covered under:
      (1) Contract law; or
      (2) The Sale of Goods Act 1893 and the Sales of Goods and Supply of Services Act 1980 (SGSSA 1980).
   c. The Act differs from the SGSSA 1980.
      (1) Act is based on safety.
      (2) SGSSA 1980: Places two implied conditions in every contract for sale:
         (a) That the product or goods are of merchantable quality, and
         (b) That they are reasonably fit for the purpose for which they are intended.
   d. **Note**: The Sale of Goods legislation provides remedies not available in the LFDPA for flaws in products that have *not* caused any personal injuries or damage to other property.

3. **EEC Directive 85/374/EEC of 30 July 1985**   **[298]**
   a. **LFDPA 1991** gives effect to the Directive.
   b. **Note: LFDPA supplements existing law**
      (1) **Section 10** provides that the Act *supplements*, rather than replaces, the existing remedies in tort and contract.
      (2) See [450] *et seq* for common law products liability.
   c. **Not retrospective**
      (1) **Article 17**: The LFDPA is *not* retrospective in its operation.
      (2) It does not apply to products put into circulation *before* the date the Act went into force.
         (a) The Act went into force on 16 December 1991.
   d. **Failed to comply**: Member States were to give effect to the Directive within three years.

(1) Ireland did not comply.
(2) **Grey area**: There is the question of the 'direct effects' of the Directive during the period after 30 July 1988 and before implementation on 16 December 1991.
4. *Prima facie* case under the LFDPA   **[299]**

> To succeed, an injured party is required to prove:
> a. A covered **injury**; and
> b. **Causation.** The injury must have been caused by a defect in the product which was produced or manufactured by the defendant.

B. *Definitions: The Act provides definitions of the requisite elements.*
    [300]

1. **Producer**: Under section 2 a producer is:
   a. The manufacturer or producer of a finished product,
   b. Producer of a component,
   c. Manufacturer or producer of any raw material,
   d. Person who holds himself out as being a producer, which may be done by:
      (1) Applying a trademark; or
      (2) Own brand on the product.
   e. Importer of products from outside the EU,
   f. The person who carried out the processing in the case of products of soil, or stock farming, and of fisheries and game, which have undergone initial processing.
      (1) Initial processing: Any processing of an industrial nature of these products which could cause a defect.
   g. **Extended definition: Section 2(3)**   **[301]**
      (1) **The supplier,** e.g. the retailer, may be liable to the plaintiff if the producer cannot be identified by taking reasonable steps.
         (a) **Reasonable steps**: If the plaintiff requests, the supplier must identify any person who is the producer of the product within a reasonable time.
      (2) The importer of a product brought into the EU for supply in the course of business may be considered the producer of the product.
      (3) A person holding themselves out as the producer by placing a trademark on the product or using some

distinguishable feature of his or her business in connection with the product.

h. **A producer is not**:   [302]
   (1) A repairer. (Common law still applies, see [455].)
   (2) Or installer of a product. (Common law still applies, see [456].)

2. **Product**: Is defined under section 1 as including all **movables**, except primary agricultural produce.   [303]

   a. **Directive 99/34/EC** (effective 4 December 2000) provides that primary agricultural produce is no longer exempt from the definition of products.

   b. **Includes incorporated movables,** whether as a component part, raw material or otherwise into:
      (1) Another product, or
      (2) An immovable.
         (a) **Example**: A house (immovable) collapses because of faulty bricks (movables). The producer of the bricks may be liable under the LFDPA.

   c. **Electricity is a product.**   [304]
      (1) Where damage is caused as a result of a *failure* in the process of generation.
         (a) **Examples**: Damage resulting from a surge in electricity, or conversely, damages resulting from inadequate voltage being produced.
      (2) Does *not* cover defects that are due to external agents intervening after the electricity has been put into the network.
         (a) **Example**: Damage resulting to a television from a surge in electricity caused by lightning.
      (3) Does *not* cover *damage from failure* to supply.
         (a) **Example**: LFDPA would not cover food in a freezer that thaws and is ruined because of a power failure lasting several days.

3. **Defective product**: Under section 5 a defective product is one that fails to provide the safety that a reasonable person is entitled to expect, taking all circumstances into account.   [305]

   a. **Circumstances** include:
      (1) Presentation of the product,
         (a) Presentation includes advertising, labelling and instructions for use.
      (2) The use to which it could *reasonably* be expected that the product would be put.

(a) The more unusual or extreme the use, the less likely it could be said to be reasonably expected.

(b) **Example**: The producers of a haemorrhoid cream would not reasonably expect that the product would be used to reduce 'bags' under the eyes or that it would be placed over fresh tattoos to reduce swelling.

(3) The time when the product was put into circulation.

b. **Exception**: A product is not considered under the LFDPA to be defective because a better product is later put into circulation.

4. **Damage**: **Section 1** provides that damage means death or personal injury, or loss of, damage to or destruction of any item of property other than the defective product itself. **[306]**

a. **Personal injury** includes:

(1) Mental impairment,

(2) However, there is some doubt as to whether pain and suffering is included. (McMahon)

b. **Requirements for damaged property** **[307]**

(1) **Type**: The property must be of a type *ordinarily* intended for private use or consumption, and

(a) **Private use**: The property must have been used by the injured person mainly for his own *private* use or consumption.

(2) **Damage to defective product itself** is not covered. **[308]**

(a) **Example**: An electric kettle is defective and starts a fire. Under the LFDPA, no damage occurs unless it causes injuries to a person or damage to other property.

C. Liability **[309]**

1. **The producer under section 2** is strictly liable for damage caused *wholly or partly* by a defect in his product.

2. **A retailer may be liable under section 2(3)** if:

a. He or she does not; or

b. Cannot identify someone above him or her in the chain of distribution, i.e. manufacturer, producer, importer, etc. See [301].

(1) Within a reasonable time of being requested to do so.

3. **Joint and several liability**: **Section 8** is where two or more persons are liable under the Act for the same damage. **[310]**

a. They are held jointly and severally liable as *concurrent wrongdoers*. See [534] *et seq*.

  b. Persons may be concurrent wrongdoers where:
   (1) One has *vicarious liability* for another,
   (2) There is a *breach* of a joint duty,
   (3) Where there is a *conspiracy* or a concerted action to a common end.
  c. **Concurrent wrongdoers** are each liable for the whole of the damages.
   (1) **Note**: Important to an injured party, particularly if one or more of the responsible parties is unable to pay their share of the damages.

4. **Reduction of liability: Section 9**   **[311]**
  a. The liability of a producer *cannot be reduced* when damage is caused both by a defect in his product and by an act or omission of a third party.
  b. **Note**: The doctrine of contributory negligence applies where the plaintiff's act or omission contributed or caused the plaintiff's damages. See [586].

5. **Prohibition on exclusion from liability: Section 10** **[312]**
  a. A producer is *prohibited* from limiting or excluding his liability:
   (1) Contractually,
   (2) By notice, or
   (3) By any other provision.

D. Damages   **[313]**

1. **Section 4** provides that the *onus* is on the injured person to prove:
  a. *Damages*;
  b. The *defect*; and
  c. The *causal relationship* between the defect and damage.
2. **Section 3** provides limitation on damages: **[314]**
  a. **No award** if property damage is *less* than £350.
  b. For damage to property greater than £350, *only* the amount in excess of £350 shall be awarded.

E. Defences: Pursuant to section 6, a producer shall not be liable if he proves: **[315]**

1. **Circulation**: That he did not put the product into circulation.
  a. **Put into circulation** means when:
   (1) The product is delivered to another in the course of business; or
   (2) It is incorporated into another immovable product.

2. **No defect at circulation.** [316]
   a. Having regard to the circumstances, it is *probable* that the defect did not exist at the time:
      (1) When the product was put into circulation; or
      (2) That the defect came into being afterwards.
   b. *Difficulty*: Determining when precisely a defect came into being.
3. **Private non-commercial transactions.** The product was neither: [317]
   a. Manufactured by him for sale or any form of distribution for an *economic purpose*, nor
   b. Manufactured or distributed by him in the *course of his business*.
4. **Compliance with law** [318]
   a. The defect is *due* to compliance by the product with any requirement imposed by or under any enactment or any requirement of the law of the European Communities.
   b. In other words, any producer who abides by the law, and in doing so causes a defect in his product, will have a good defence to the strict liability in observing the law.
5. **State of the art** [319]
   a. The *state* of scientific and technical knowledge at the time when the product was *put into circulation* did not enable the existence of the defect to be discovered.
   b. Also known as the 'development risks' defence.
   c. To avail, a producer will have to show that *no* producer of a similar product *could have* been expected to have discovered the defect which caused the injury.
   d. The Act does not specify whether EU or international 'state of the art' standards should apply.
   e. This defence was optional in the Directive.
      (1) Complete exclusion: Found in legislation of Luxembourg and Finland.
      (2) Partial exclusion: Spain excluded it for medicines and human foods, but included it for everything else. [320]
   f. **Scope of the defence** was considered in *EC Commission v UK* [1997] 3 CMLR 923. Commission alleged that the UK had failed to properly implement the Directive. Although the wording of the defence written into UK legislation was different from the wording of the EU Directive, the Court of Justice concluded that there was no substantial difference in

the effect. Important factor was that the English courts had not interpreted the language of the UK legislation.
- g. **Defence is controversial.** Commentators see it as undermining strict liability sought to be imposed by Act.
  - (1) **American approach**: In the US, strict liability for defective products developed within the common law.
  - (2) **Statutory intervention for vaccines.**
    - (a) In 1986, the US Congress enacted legislation (42 USC, sections 300aa-10 *et seq*) to insulate the producers of vaccines from liability with a modified no fault compensation scheme for injuries resulting from certain childhood vaccines.
    - (b) **Rationale**: Vaccines are important, but there is a great liability risk for any company producing them.
6. **Component and raw material producers** have a defence if the defect is attributable entirely to: **[321]**
   - a. The *design* of the product in which the component has been fitted or the raw material has been incorporated.
   - b. The *instructions given* by the manufacturer of the product.
   - c. This defence protects subcontractors where:
     - (1) Their products are clearly not responsible for the defect, or
     - (2) They produced specifically to order and the defect is the result of the design of the product or as a result of the instructions given by the manufacturer.
7. **Contributory negligence**: **Section 9**   **[322]**
   - a. Will apply where any damage is caused:
     - (1) *Partly* by a defect in the product; and
     - (2) *Partly* by the fault of the injured person or of any person for whom the injured person is responsible.
   - b. **Proportion**: The plaintiff will have her damages reduced in proportion to his or her fault. See generally the defence of contributory negligence [586].

F. *Limitations of actions: Section 7*   **[323]**

1. All actions under the Act must be brought within *three years*:
   - a. After the date on which the cause of action accrued, or
   - b. The date on which the plaintiff *became aware*, or *should reasonably have become aware*, of the damage, the defect and the identity of the producer.
2. **Action barred**: A right of action shall be *barred ten years* from the

date on which the producer put into circulation the actual product which caused the injury, regardless of whether or not the
right of action accrued during the ten years.
   a. **Exception**: If the injured person has instituted proceedings
      against the producer within the ten years, the action is not
      barred.

G. Criticism of LFDPA [324]

1. Quill argues that the Irish (and European) approach to product
   liability is not truly strict liability given the range of defences
   available.
2. Quill notes that a preferable approach for injured consumers
   would be similar to the American approach, where strict liability
   for defective products developed within the common law for personal and property damage caused by dangerous products.
3. The American law is not encumbered by the variety of defences
   present under the Act.

Liability for Defective Products Act 1991 Chart [325]

S. 2	Strict liability	The producer of a product is strictly liable for damage caused wholly or partly by a defect in his or her product. **See [296]**.
S. 1	Product	Includes all movables. (Before December 2000, primary agricultural produce was excluded.) **See [302]**.
S. 2	Producer	• The manufacturer or producer of a finished product. • Producer of a component. • Manufacturer or producer of raw material. • Person who holds himself out as being a producer, which may be done by applying a trademark or own brand on the product. • Importer of product from outside the EU. • Extended to include a supplier if the producer cannot be identified by taking reasonable steps. **See [300]**.

S. 5	Defective product	One that fails to provide the safety that a reasonable person is entitled to expect taking all circumstances into account. **See [305]**.
S. 1	Damage	Means death or personal injury, or loss of, damage to or destruction of any item of property other than the defective product itself. **See [306]**.
S. 4	Onus	The onus is on the injured person to prove damage, the defect and the causal relationship between the defect and the damage. **See [313]**.
S. 3	Limitation of damages	• No award of damages if the property damage is less than £350. • For damage to property greater than £350, only the amount in excess shall be awarded. **See [314]**.
S. 7	Limitation of action	• All actions under the Act must be brought within three years after the date on which the cause of action accrued, or the date on which the plaintiff became aware, or should have reasonably have become aware, of the damage, the defect and the identity of the producer. • A right of action shall be barred ten years from the date on which the producer put the actual product into circulation. **See [323]**.
S. 8	Joint and several liability	Where two or more persons are liable under the Act for the same damage, they shall be held jointly and severally liable as concurrent wrongdoers. **See [310]**.
S. 9	Reduction of liability	• Liability is not reduced where damage is caused by a defect in the product and the act or omission of a third person. **See [311]**. • Contributory negligence does apply. **See [322]**.

S. 6	Defences	• The producer did not put the product into circulation. • At the time of circulation there was no defect. • Private non-commercial transaction – the produce was not manufactured for sale or for an economic purpose, or manufactured or disturbed in the course of the defendant's business. • The defect is due to compliance with the law. • State of the art – at the time the product was put into circulation, the state of the scientific and technical knowledge did not enable the existence of the defect to be discovered. • A component and raw material producer will have a defence if the defect is entirely due to the design of the product, or to the instructions given by the manufacturer. **See [315]** *et seq.*

Chapter 3 Questions

1. Conor started a tourist dude ranch near Ennis. After building a replica Wild West town, Conor imported rattlesnakes to keep in a glass enclosure in the gift shop. One of the snakes escaped and bit Rose in the bunkhouse. Can Rose bring an action based on the rule in *Rylands* against Conor?

2. Fred has a bull named Jean Luke. Jean Luke is a huge inquisitive animal that enjoys exploring. Hillary, a hillwalker, lost her way and opened the gate to enter Jean Luke's field when the bull rushed out past her.
   (a) If the bull injures Hillary, will Fred be held strictly liable?
   (b) If Jean Luke injures Michael, the milkman, will Fred have a valid defence?

3. The day after Irene's big party, she was not feeling well. While ironing her blouse for work she had to make a rush to the loo. Unfortunately, the blouse caught fire. Upon returning to her ironing, Irene grabbed a glass and threw the contents on the fire. The glass contained vodka and it caused the fire to spread rapidly. If the neighbours' chattels are destroyed by the fire, will Irene be held strictly liable?

4. Cyril the sheep dog saw ten heifers enter his master's field. Knowing the heifers did not belong to his master, Cyril chased the heifers over the ditch into the road. One of the heifers was injured going over the ditch. Under the Control of Dogs Acts 1986 and 1992, is Cyril's master strictly liable for the injured heifer?

5. Bobby, a bouncer at the Dew Drop Inn Disco, was irritated by an obnoxious patron named Patrick. Bobby broke Patrick's arm throwing Patrick out of the disco. Is Bobby's employer strictly liable for Patrick's injuries?

6. The Zipper Circus visited Cork. Someone let Larry the lion out of his cage. As Larry lazily wandered the streets of Cork, everyone ran from him. Conor saw the lion and tried to capture him by enticing him into a horse box. When Larry would not climb into the horse box, Conor hit the lion with a long whip to drive him into the trailer. Larry knocked Conor to the ground and continued his walk about until he was tired, and then he returned to his cage.

    (a) Will Larry's owner be able to escape some liability by alleging that Conor was contributorily negligent?

    (b) Assume that Aine climbed onto a chair to look out her kitchen window to watch Larry as he strolled by. While leaning forward to get a better view, Aine fell off of the chair and broke her leg. Will Larry's owner be held strictly liable for the injuries suffered by Aine?

7. Johnny asked his neighbour, Michael, if he objected to Johnny building a large goldfish pond in his back garden. Johnny intended to put in several fountains in the pond and wanted to make certain that the sound of running water would not disturb Michael. Michael's house is located very close to the proposed site of the pond and slightly downhill. Michael assured Johnny that the sound of the water would not disturb him, but he stressed to Johnny that the pool must be well made and maintained because he did not want several hundred gallons of water and fish to flow into his kitchen. If the pond water escapes and floods Michael's kitchen, will Johnny escape all liability because Michael consented to the accumulation?

8. Maurice, a mechanic, fixed the brakes on Stephanie's car. Later the same day, the brakes failed and Stephanie crashed into Walter. Both Stephanie and Walter were injured in the crash.

    (a) Can Stephanie sue Maurice under the Liability for Defective Products Act 1991?

    (b) Can Walter sue Maurice under the Liability for Defective Products Act 1991?

9. Jane bought a Curl Up and Dye brand hair dryer at Schultze's Department Store for £25. The next morning she washed her hair. When Jane turned on the dryer it worked fine for a few minutes then burst into flames, setting her hair on fire. Jane quickly threw down the dryer and smothered the flames in her hair with a towel. The dryer landed on the floor and ruined her new carpeting. While recovering from her burns, Jane has found out that a North Korean manufacturer makes the Curl Up and Dye brand hair dryer.

   (a) Pursuant to the Liability for Defective Products Act 1991, can Jane bring a cause of action against the North Korean manufacturer?

   (b) Pursuant to the Liability for Defective Products Act 1991, can Jane bring a cause of action against Schultze's Department Store, even though she knows the name of the manufacturer?

   (c) Pursuant to the liability for Defective Products Act 1991, will Jane have her damages reduced due to contributory negligence?

   (d) Pursuant to the Liability for Defective Products Act 1991, will Jane recover for the cost of the hair dryer?

   (e) Pursuant to the Liability for Defective Products Act 1991, will Jane recover for the entire cost of her carpeting?

   (f) Pursuant to the Liability for Defective Products Act 1991, will Jane recover for her personal injuries if her medical bills are less than £350?

10. Iggy the inventor designed a rat trap in 1990 for his mother. His mother liked the trap so much that Iggy decided to manufacture his rat trap. Iggy sold thousands of traps from 1990 to 1999, when he retired. In 2001 Ziggy, a Dublin rat catcher, was injured by one of Iggy's 1990 rat traps.

   (a) Can Ziggy bring a cause of action under the Liability for Defective Products Act 1991 against Iggy?

   (b) Assume that Ziggy was injured when he attempted to use the rat trap as a paper weight on his desk. Is the rat trap defective?

11. 'Defibrillator Spark Sets Clothing Aflame', New London, Conn (Associated Press, 28 January 2004) 'A spark from a defibrillator set a woman's clothing on fire when a paramedic tried to restart her heart in an ambulance. Brenda Jewett, 47, was pronounced dead at a hospital Monday. An autopsy was scheduled to determine the cause of her death…Mary Newman of the National Center for Early Defibrillation in Pittsburgh said the Center had never heard of such a case before. She said she doubted the fire or the defibrillator caused

Jewett's death. "When you defibrillate a person, they are already dead," she said.' Assume that these event occurred in Ireland.

(a) Will the Accidental Fires Act 1943 protect the paramedic from being sued for causing the fire that damaged Brenda Jewett's clothing?

(b) Assume that Ms Jewett survived. She claims that the fire destroyed clothing worth €150 and she suffered severe burns to her chest from the fire. The manufacturer of the machine in question is Shock-R-Us. Will Ms Jewett be able to bring an action against Shock-R-Us under the Liability for Defective Products Act 1991 for her ruined clothing and her personal injuries?

12. 'Child Savaged to Death by Dogs' (*Irish Independent*, 27 June 2000) – 'Two dogs savaged a 6 year old boy to death as he made his way to swimming class in a Hamburg schoolyard yesterday…The animals were accompanied by their owner, a 23 year old man, and a woman when a witness said the dogs – a pit bull and Stafordshire terrier – broke away and jumped over a school fence. The pit bull immediately went for the boy's throat and the other dog snapped at him. The two adults and a couple of passers-by attempted to get them off of the boy before police arrived, shooting both dogs…' Assume these events took place in Dublin. Under the Control of Dogs Acts, will the (a) owner (b) woman walking with him and (c) the school be liable?

13. 'Camel that Got the Hump with Circus Life' (*Irish Independent*, 9 March 2002) 'A lone camel got the hump and escaped from its circus home yesterday causing alarm to motorists who spotted it on a busy road in Co. Offaly. AA Roadwatch issued a warning after the animal, named Saraha, was spotted just outside Tullamore…at 7.40 a.m.…and spent most of the morning grazing at the road side.'

(a) Excluding the rule in *Rylands v Fletcher*, discuss the potential liability of the circus regarding Saraha's escape.

(b) Assume that Michael did not know of the escape and was out walking his dog Shep, and they found Saraha grazing on the side of the road. Discuss Michael's liability if Shep escapes from his lead and attacks and injures Saraha.

14. 'Half-ton Bullock Attacked Motor Car' (*Munster Express*, 17 March 2000) 'A half-ton bullock attacked a car, smashed the windscreen and jumped onto the roof…causing a teenage passenger in the car to sustain a serious hand injury. The mother of the teenager was

driving when she was confronted by the animal. She stopped the car, but the animal turned around and ran at the car, smashing the windscreen, and climbed onto the roof. Glass and bullock hair was found in the teenager's wound.' Finbar is the owner of the bullock.
(a) Will Finbar be held strictly liable for cattle trespass?
(b) Will Finbar be held strictly liable under the Animals Act 1985?
(c) Will Finbar be held strictly liable under the common law?

15. 'Families Evacuated After Gas Leak at Landfill Site' (*Irish Times*, 8 June 2001) 'Four families living within 250 metres of the Baskertstown landfill…have been evacuated from their homes by the county council after an electronic carbon dioxide monitor was activated.' It is believed that the gas is generated and accumulated at the landfill. Ignoring the issue of the defendant being a public authority, could the rule in *Rylands v Fletcher* be applied successfully?

16. 'Couple Forced to Abandon Home over Burst Tank' (*Irish Independent*, 9 March 2000) A house was swamped by mud and slime after a 10,000 gallon industrial water storage tank ruptured and collapsed. Shocked householders…are now living in a hotel after their Cork bungalow was swamped with mud and debris from the brief flood. The tank, which holds up to 10,000 gallons, was shattered by the rupture, with one entire concrete wall being flattened by the force of the flood. The tank was located uphill from the home. It is understood the flood resulted from a crack in one of the tank walls which widened and then, under the immense water pressure, finally collapsed the entire concrete support wall.' Could the rule in *Rylands v Fletcher* be applied successfully?

17. 'Warm Air Boiler Exploded in Housewife's Face' (*Evening Herald*, 25 October 2001) 'A 60-year-old housewife was injured when the warm air boiler in her home exploded in her face…The boiler had been serviced only ten weeks prior to the accident by the defendant. The plaintiff stated that her hair, eyebrows, and eyelashes had been badly singed and her face had been blackened with soot. While her face was not badly burned she suffered severe post traumatic stress following the explosion. The system sends warm air to rooms in the house and had been installed 30 years ago when the house was built.' The plaintiff denied that the system was obsolete. Will the Liability for Defective Products Act 1991 apply to (a) the manufacturer of the boiler and (b) Mr Warren Cosy, who serviced the boiler ten weeks ago?

SECTION III:
FAULT-BASED LIABILITY

4

GENERAL PRINCIPLES OF COMMON LAW NEGLIGENCE

Chapter synopsis

I. Historical background
II. Basic present requirements for negligence
III. Influencing policies

I. Historical background   [326]

A. Common law liability based on fault

1. Prior to the development of the tort of negligence, a plaintiff had to establish provisions of the appropriate writ. The two writs used were:
   a. Trespass, and
   b. Trespass on the case. See [3].
2. **Direct and immediate harms**: The writ of trespass was used with liability being strict. See [2].
3. **Indirect harms**: Required a plaintiff to use trespass on the case.
   a. Because trespass on the case was the proper writ for fault-based liability, it was the forerunner to negligence.
   b. Therefore, negligence is *not* actionable per se.

B. Before duty   [326a]

1. While negligence liability existed for centuries, there was no concept of duty until the nineteenth century.
2. Generally, the word 'negligence' was used to describe 'inadventure or indifference' by a person while entering into the commission of other torts.
3. Liability existed within *defined contractual relationships* of those who held themselves out to the public as being competent.
   a. **Examples**: Doctors, innkeepers, blacksmiths.

4. If the case fell outside the recognised relationships, there was no liability.

C. *The Industrial Revolution*   [327]

1. The Industrial Revolution is credited with bringing about social, industrial and technological changes, including the need for a **test** to determine whether liability existed *outside* the recognised relationships.
2. The economic view was that a duty should not be imposed unless:
   a. The person *agreed* to it; and
   b. That by requiring persons injured by industry to prove fault (as opposed to direct harm under the trespass writ), defendants were much more likely to avoid liability.
3. '[P]erhaps one of the chief agencies in the growth [of the tort of negligence]…is industrial machinery. Early railway trains, in particular…killed any object from a Minister of State to a wandering cow, and this naturally reacted on the law.' (Winfield)
4. **Denial of negligence**: Many legal commentators in the early part of the twentieth century, such as Salmond (*Law of Torts*, 6th ed., 1924), continued to argue that negligence was not a separate tort, but merely one way of committing other torts.
   a. Negligence was seen as having no legal significance.
   b. These assertions were laid to rest in England with the famous case of *Donoghue v Stevenson* [1932] AC 562 (HL). See [371] for facts of case.

D. *Importance of* Donoghue v Stevenson   [328]

1. **Destroyed** the privity of contract requirement. See [370] and [372] *et seq.*
2. **Created a new category of duty** where manufacturers of dangerous products owe a duty to the ultimate consumer of their products.
3. **Birth of neighbour principle**
   a. Lord Atkin stated his famous neighbour principle as a *general test* for determining whether a duty of care existed.
4. *Donoghue v Stevenson* was accepted into Irish law by *Kirby v Burke* [1944] IR 207 (HC).
   a. Quill has noted that Gavin Duffy J. indicated that *Donoghue* alone would not be sufficiently convincing authority.

b. However, he accepted the neighbour principle, as it conformed to the views expressed by the American jurist Oliver Wendell Holmes. See [337].

II. Basic present requirements for negligence   [329]

> A. Duty of care
> B. Breach of the duty of care
> C. Causation
> D. Injury, loss or damage

A. Duty of care   [330]

1. The defendant *owed* the plaintiff a *legal duty of care*.
   a. **Duty**: A legally recognised relationship between the parties.
2. There are two types of duties generally owed.
   a. **General duty to act as a reasonable person.** See Chapter 5.
   b. **Special duties that are imposed by statute or case law.**
      (1) **Special duties** may be in addition to, or in place of, the general duty to act as a reasonable person.
      (2) Duties imposed by statute are covered in Chapter 9.
3. Different tests have been advanced since *Donoghue* for determining whether a duty of care existed between the parties.
   a. **Two stage test**: *Anns v Merton London Borough Council* [1978] AC 728 (HL). (Lord Wilberforce)
      (1) The Irish decision *Ward v McMaster* [1989] ILRM 400 (see [479]) was influenced by *Anns*, but as McMahon has opined, *Ward* was more liberal, as less emphasis was placed on policy factors inhibiting recognition of a duty of care.
   b. **Three stage test**: *Caparo Industries v Dickman* [1990] 2 AC 605 (HL). See [399] and [407].
      (1) Endorsed by the Supreme Court in *Glencar Explorations v Mayo Co. Council* [2002] 1 IR 84. See [399].

B. Breach of the duty of care   [331]

1. By failing to achieve the standard of care required.
   a. Standard of care: The required level of conduct expected.
   b. Most common standard is the 'reasonable person'.
2. By performing an act or omission (failure to perform a required act).
3. See Chapter 6.

C. Causation   [332]

1. The defendant breached the duty of care that he owed to the plaintiff and caused the plaintiff's injury, loss or damage.
2. **Actual cause** (cause in fact): The plaintiff's harm *must* have the required nexus to the defendant's breach of duty.
3. **Proximate cause** (legal cause): There are *no* policy reasons to relieve the defendant of liability.
4. See Chapter 7 [530], *et seq.*

D. Injury, loss or damage   [333]

1. The plaintiff suffered an *injury, loss* or *damage* as a result of the defendant's act or omission.
2. **Note**: Negligence is not actionable per se.
3. See Chapter 8, [586] *et seq.*

E. *Note: Negligence is the most important area of tort law.*   [334]

1. To successfully approach a negligence problem, you should always systematically start with duty of care.
2. Only after concluding that the defendant owed the plaintiff a duty of care should you analyse breach, etc.
3. *Never assume* that the defendant owed a duty of care to the plaintiff.
4. For more helpful hints regarding answering exam questions, see Chapter 13.

III. Influencing policies   [334a]

A. Whether a duty exists is largely a policy-based determination rather than the application of legal rules or principles.

B. Some of the various policies that influence duty include:

1. Foreseeability of the harm to the plaintiff.
2. The degree of certainty that the plaintiff would suffer harm.
3. The closeness of the connection between the defendant's conduct and the injury suffered by the plaintiff.
4. The moral blame attached to the defendant's conduct.
5. The policy of preventing future harm.
6. The burden to the defendant.
7. The consequences to society for imposing a duty.

COMMON LAW DUTY OF CARE

Chapter synopsis

I. Common law general duty of care   [335]

A. Reasonable person standard

   1. This model or standard:
      a. Applies to *all* persons.
      b. Is used to *test* the defendant's act or conduct for conformity with what is required at any given time and place to avoid unnecessary danger.
         (1) The reasonable person standard is based on a fictitious person 'who never existed on land or sea'. (Quote from Prosser)
         (2) Was first articulated as the 'man of ordinary prudence' in *Vaughan v Menlove* (1837) 132 ER 490, and continued to

be known as the reasonable man standard until recently.

    (3) 'Instead, therefore, of saying that the liability for negligence should be co-extensive with the judgment of each individual, which would be as variable as the length of the foot of each individual, we ought rather to adhere to the rule which requires in all cases a regard to caution such as a man of ordinary prudence would observe.'

  c. Most commentators generally agree that the standard should now be known as the reasonable person.

2. Objective standard   **[336]**

  a. The reasonable person standard is an objective standard.

  b. The defendant's good faith belief is *not* material.

  c. **Reasonable person standard** serves as a *goal* to be worked toward.

  d. It is not based on how any specific person would have acted, but rather it is based on how the reasonable person would have acted.

  e. **Flexible**: Although situations and circumstances change, the standard remains the same, 'the reasonable person' under the same or similar circumstances.

3. **Rationale** for objective standard   **[337]**

  a. Subjective standard would be difficult to use.

  b. Oliver Wendell Holmes, Jr., *The Common Law* (1881), reasoned:

    (1) '[T]he impossibility of nicely measuring a man's powers and limitations is far clearer than that of ascertaining his knowledge of law.'

    (2) Further, society members should be able to expect a certain level of behaviour from others.

    (3) 'If a man is born hasty and awkward, and is always hurting himself or his neighbours…his slips are no less troublesome than if they sprang from guilty neglect. His neighbours accordingly require him, at his peril, to come up to their standard, and the courts which they establish decline to take his *personal equation* into account.'

  c. **Criticism**: A person can be negligent for failing to meet some standard that he cannot meet.

    (1) McMahon alleges that to 'eliminate the *personal equation*' completely and apply objective standard would result in considerable injustice and hardship.

4. **Characteristics of the reasonable person** [338]
   a. **Knowledge**: The reasonable person is expected to know:
      (1) Facts of common experience.
         (a) **Example**: Laws of nature, normal incidents of weather, characteristics of common animals.
      (2) His or her own *personal limitations* and act accordingly.
         (a) **Example**: A reasonable person coming into contact with an unfamiliar breed of snake will not handle the snake.
   b. **Physically** [339]
      (1) The reasonable person is physically the same as the defendant.
      (2) Standard becomes reasonable person afflicted with same physical limitation.
         (a) **Example**: A blind person is not required to see.
      (3) However, a physically challenged person must be reasonable in light of her impairment.
         (a) **Example**: A blind person would be negligent in driving a car.
   c. **Voluntary intoxication** [340]
      (1) If physical impairment results from voluntary intoxication, impairment is not taken into account.
      (2) Intoxicated persons are held to the *same standard of care* as a sober, reasonable person.

5. **Standard for children**: Very few Irish cases. [341]
   a. Appears to be *subjective* standard, taking into account the child's:
      (1) Age,
      (2) Intelligence, and
      (3) Experiences.
   b. Adult activity exception: In the US, Canada, New Zealand and Australia, a child engaging in adult activities, such as driving cars, motorcycles, motorboats or aeroplanes, is held to the adult standard.

6. **Mentally disabled persons** [342]
   a. **General rule**: The objective reasonable person standard applies.
      (1) In other words, a mentally disabled person is held to the same standard (reasonable person standard) as persons who are not mentally disabled.
   b. **Rationale** for disparity of treatment between physical and mental disabilities includes:

(1) Difficulty in determining what types of mental disabilities will reduce the duty of care owed; and

(2) Fear of complicating tort law in much the same way that the insanity defence has complicated criminal trials in some jurisdictions.

c. **Law Reform Commission** (LRC 18-1985) recommended single rule for negligence and contributory negligence, i.e. the ordinary standard of care (reasonable person) would apply to a person unless:

(1) At the time of the act the person was suffering from a serious mental disability which affected that person in the performance of the act; and

(2) The disability rendered the person unable to behave according to the standard of care appropriate to the reasonable person.

d. US approach: 2nd Restatement – the ordinary standard of care should be applied to mentally disabled persons unless they are children.

7. **Standard of care for learners** [343]

a. **General rule**: A person who engages in an activity with known risks is held to the same standard of care as an experienced, reasonable person.

(1) **Classic example**: Driving a car on a public road.

b. **Rationale**: Learners who engage in such activities should bear the risk of harm rather than the person injured.

B. *Standard of care for professionals* [344]

1. **General rule**: A person holding themselves out to the public as being *skilled* must have the standard of care customarily exercised by the members of that profession. *O'Donovan v Cork Co. Council* [1967] IR 173 (SC).

a. **Profession**: There is much debate about what is a profession.

b. Nursing was held *not* to be a profession for professional negligence purposes. *Kelly v St Laurence's Hospital* [1989] ILRM 437.

c. Mechanics were held to be professionals because they exercise and profess special skills.

2. The professional standard of care *only* applies if the defendant is acting in her professional capacity. [345]

a. **Example**: A solicitor driving a vehicle is held to the same standard as all other drivers.

b. **Duty of care**: A professional owes a general duty of care to his (clients, patients or customers) to exercise the skills of a reasonable (mechanic, doctor, solicitor, accountant, etc.). *Roche v Peilow* [1985] IR 232 (SC) and *Dunne v National Maternity Hospital* [1989] IR 91 (SC). **[346]**

c. **Concurrent liability**: Because most clients have entered into a contractual relationship with the professional, liability may be based in contract or tort.

    (1) **Note**: Relationship between professional and client is *not* required to be contractual.

    (2) **Example**: Relationship could arise in a gratuitous situation, such as free legal aid, and the professional still owes a general duty of care to that client or patient.

3. **Advocate immunity** **[347]**

a. **Established** in *Rondel v Worsley* [1969] 1 AC 191, where it was generally held that barristers cannot be sued for negligently conducting a client's case in court or for work closely connected with the conduct of the case in court.

b. **Rationale for immunity**: While barristers owe a duty to their clients, they owe a broader duty to assist in the administration of justice. To achieve the broader duty, activities in court need to be protected. **[348]**

c. **Application in Ireland**: To actions of the attorney general.

    (1) *HMW v Ireland* [1997] 2 IR 141 (HC). The plaintiff was the victim of a convicted paedophile. She sued the attorney general in negligence for the injuries she sustained as a result of the delay in extraditing the paedophile. The court held that the attorney general did not owe the plaintiff a duty of care. It also rejected arguments that the plaintiff's constitutional right to bodily integrity had been infringed. Constitutional rights are not absolute.

d. **Advocate immunity abolished** by the House of Lords in *Hall (Arthur JJ) and Co. v Simons* [2000] 3 All ER 673. **[349]**

    (1) McMahon noted that it was abolished 'under the shadow of the European Convention on Human Rights'.

    (2) McMahon recommends that Ireland also abolish advocate immunity.

C. Standard of care for solicitors [350]

1. **Traditionally**: No negligence actions were allowed because the relationship between a solicitor and his client was based on contract.
2. **Modern view**: The tort of negligence applies if the negligence arises due to a breach of a general professional duty of care. *Finaly v Murtagh* [1979] IR 249 (SC).
   a. The tort of negligence does not apply if the breach *is* due to a special term in a contract.
   b. **The test**: Would a solicitor be liable if the contract had not contained the term?
3. General duties of solicitors [351]
   a. Barron J. in *McMullen v Farrell* [1993] 1 IR 123 (HC), affirmed in part by the Supreme Court (February 1994), found as follows:
      (1) A solicitor is a professional person and cannot fulfil his or her obligations to the client merely by carrying out what he or she is instructed to do.
      (2) The solicitor is required to exercise professional skill and judgment in the interests of the client.
      (3) When consulted, a solicitor has an obligation to consider not only what the client wishes done, but also the legal implications of the facts that the client brings to the solicitor's attention.
      (4) If necessary, the solicitor must follow the facts (investigate) to ensure that the real problem is appreciated.
      (5) The solicitor must advise the client of his or her views and all reasonable approaches to the problem.
      (6) The solicitor must then act on the basis of the instructions that are received in light of advice.
   b. **Legal advice**: A solicitor's primary duty is to his or her client. [352]
      (1) With regard to possible negligence for giving incorrect legal advice to the client, the leading case is *Roche v Peilow* [1985] IR 232 (SC). The defendant was found to be negligent in following the universal practice of solicitors in failing to execute a search against a building company until after the completion of the building and the payment of some instalments of the purchase price.
      (2) If the law being advised upon is clear, there will be negligence, but if the law is not clear or is difficult, the advice may be reasonable.

   c. **Failure to advise**: See [408] *et seq*, solicitors' duties to third parties.

   d. **Conflicts of interest**   **[353]**

     (1) Leading case is *Phelan Holdings (Kilkenny) Ltd v Hogan* (1996) (HC).

     (2) **Facts**: The defendant solicitor represented his client in a transaction involving the solicitor himself as a party to the transaction. The defendant was in breach of his duty as a solicitor toward his client and deprived the client of an opportunity to obtain proper independent advice in relation to all of his legal problems.

4. **Litigation**   **[354]**

   a. A solicitor may commit negligence with regard to litigation by:

     (1) Choosing the wrong court. *Lopes v Walker* (1997) (SC).

     (2) The manner in which a solicitor liaises with counsel on behalf of the client.

     (3) Improper performance of advocacy duties, and

     (4) Unreasonable delays in initiating or processing litigation.

   b. **Liaising with counsel**   **[355]**

     (1) **General rule**: It is well settled that where a solicitor lays his client's claim fully before competent counsel and acts on counsel's advice, he is not liable for negligence. *Millard v McMahon* (1968) (HC).

     (2) The duties of a solicitor regarding litigation include:

       (a) Briefing appropriate and competent counsel.

       (b) Instructing the counsel properly with regard to the facts of the case which he has obtained from his client.

       (c) Making provision for the attendance of appropriate witnesses and other proofs.

     (3) **Note**: A solicitor is not vicariously responsible for the individual conduct of counsel. Per Finlay CJ (for the court) in *Fallon v Gannon* [1988] ILRM 193 (SC).

5. Buying and selling property   **[356]**

   a. Buying and selling property for clients are dangerous activities in terms of potential negligence litigation.

     (1) *Hanafin v Gaynor* (HC 1990). The defendant solicitor was not negligent, as he had acted with the ordinary care that a solicitor of equal status and skill would have acted.

     (2) *Doran v Delancey* [1998] 2 ILRM 1 (SC). The vendors'

solicitors were not negligent toward the plaintiff buyers for transmitting their client's instructions where it was clear that the solicitors were not assuming responsibility for the information transmitted.

b. Liquor licenses requisitions on title and requests for full particulars of exemptions and other privileges often require a duty to investigate.

(1) *Taylor v Ryan* [1985] IR 212. Liability in negligence was imposed on the defendant solicitor for his failure to pursue his requisition when the vendors' solicitors simply replied ordinary license and that a copy of the license had been furnished. However, only the face of the license was copied.

(2) *Kelly v Crowley* [1985] IR 212 (HC). Liability in negligence was imposed on the defendant solicitor who failed to pursue his requisition as to the exact type of license. The vendor's solicitor merely referred the defendant to the license which was attached but made no statement as to the nature of the license or the privileges attached to it.

(3) *Pierse v Allen* (1993) (HC). The defendant solicitor acted for the plaintiff, who bought premises on the representation of the vendor that it was a hotel. The premises had lost its status as a hotel some time earlier. The court held that the defendant solicitor had not been negligent for his failure to make pre-contract enquiries or requisitions.

6. Criticism   [357]

a. McMahon notes that the Irish courts appear to focus more on the facts of the case in discussing solicitors' negligence.

b. However, where the courts discuss medical negligence, more judicial discussion takes place at a higher level of abstraction where principles and policy are more openly acknowledged.

D. Standard of care for doctors (medical malpractice)   [358]

1. **General rule**: A doctor must exercise the skills of a reasonable doctor.

a. **Specialist**: Must exercise the skills of a reasonable specialist in that particular area of medicine.

b. **General practitioner**: Must exercise skills of a reasonable general practitioner.

(1) Knowledge of limitations: A reasonable GP realises and refers patients to specialists when special care is needed.

2. Malpractice allegations usually arise in: **[359]**
   a. Diagnosis, and/or
   b. Treatment.
3. The actions of a doctor will be judged according to the standards accepted at the time of the acts. *Roe v Minister of Health* [1954] 2 QB 66.
   a. However, once a risk becomes known, a doctor may be under a duty to investigate the suspected risk.
   b. *N. v UK Medical Research Council* [1996] 7 Med LR 309 (QB). In 1959, the defendant began a medical trial of human growth hormone for children with growth problems. In 1976, the defendants were warned that the hormone could cause Creutzfeld Jakob Disease, the deadly human form of mad cow disease. In 1977, the defendants were told that two of the four methods of giving the hormone carried the risk of transmitting CJD. Several children in the trial died of CJD. The court held that the failure to investigate the risks in 1976 was negligent.
4. The onus or burden is on the plaintiff to establish that: **[360]**
   a. The doctor did not meet the applicable standard of care, and
   b. This failure resulted in an injury or harm to the plaintiff.
5. **Note**: Perfection is not the duty owed by a doctor to her patient. In other words, a bad result does not mean that a doctor has been negligent.
6. Standard of care owed by doctors **[361]**
   a. English approach
      (1) ***Bolam* rule**: The *Bolam* rule applied, which simply meant that the standard of care owed by a doctor was one of the 'custom of the profession'.
         (a) *Bolam v Frien Barnet Hospital Management Committee* [1957] 1 WLR 582. The plaintiff suffered broken bones as the result of drugs given to him before electric shock treatments. Doctors were split over the use of such drugs in the procedure. It was found that the doctor was *not* negligent because *he acted in accordance with the accepted practice.*
         (b) **Important effect of *Bolam***: So long as the defendant doctor could find a medical expert to state that his or her actions were within the bounds of a responsible body of medical opinion, there would *never* be a finding of negligence.

(2) **Bolitho**: More recently in England, there has been an erosion of the *Bolam* rule with the *Bolitho v Hackney Health Authority* [1998] AC 232 case.

  (a) **Bolitho facts**: A two-year-old was taken to the hospital with breathing problems. The child was not seen by a doctor, suffered a heart attack and died. The mother sued, alleging that the doctor was negligent in not seeing the child and failing to intubate (place a tube down the throat to aid breathing). The doctor countered that even if she had seen the child she would not have intubated because it was not the proper procedure, therefore her alleged negligence was not the cause of the child's death. Under *Bolem* the doctor would have won, but the House of Lords set forth a new test.

  (b) **Bolitho test**: The plaintiff could prove causation if:
    i.   The plaintiff proved that the defendant would have intubated if she had attended; or
    ii. That she should have intubated if she had attended because she had a duty to do so.

  (c) **Note**: The *Bolitho* decision did not reject *Bolam* outright.

  (d) The *Bolitho* court held that it was not required to find a doctor not liable in negligence *merely* because a medical expert had testified that the doctor had acted within accepted practices.

  (e) **Note**: There was no recovery for the plaintiff in *Bolitho*.

(3) **Bolitho test**: [362]

  (a) **Reasonable**: Was the medical expert's opinion reasonable?

  (b) **Properly balanced**: Had the medical expert weighed up the associated risks and benefits?

  (c) **Logical basis**: Was there a logical basis for the expert's conclusion?

(4) **Bolitho test applied**: *Wisniewski v Central Manchester Health Authority* [1998] PIQR P 324. A trace during labour revealed that the baby was under stress. The midwife negligently failed to bring the trace to the attention of the doctor. The baby was born with cerebral palsy. The plaintiff claimed that had any reasonable doctor been

shown the trace, the baby would have been delivered by a C-section and thereby avoided injury. Experts for the defendant said that a reasonable doctor may have delayed and the harm would have occurred anyway. When the doctor on duty at the birth declined to testify, the judge applied adverse inferences to this fact, upholding the plaintiff's expert that no reasonable doctor would have delayed. Court of appeals held that this is *not* the type of case outlined in *Bolitho* for special treatment. The appeal was dismissed on other grounds, upholding the defendant's liability.

b. **Irish approach** [363]
   (1) The Supreme Court has *not* followed *Bolam*.
   (2) The Supreme Court in *Dunne v National Maternity Hospital* [1989] IR 91 set forth the standard of care owed by a doctor to his or her patient.
      (a) **Diagnosis and treatment**: A doctor will be negligent if no practitioner of *equal status* (specialist or GP) and *skill*, acting with *ordinary care*, would have done the same.
      (b) **Deviations from general and approved practice**: Will not be negligent unless *no* doctor of *equal status* and *skill*, acting with *ordinary care*, would have done the same.
      (c) **Alternative treatments**: If there are two or more accepted medical treatments, it is *well settled* that the doctor is protected from liability if he or she follows one of the accepted medical treatments. Follows holding in *Daniels v Heskin* [1954] IR 73, see [524].
      (d) **Inherent defects**: It is not a defence for a doctor to allege that he followed an established practice of conduct if the practice has *inherent defects* that should be obvious to any person giving due consideration to the matter. [364]
         i. **Example**: *Collins v Mid-Western Board* [1991] (SC). A system that vested all hospital admissions to one senior house officer was found inherently defective.
   (3) Onus: The plaintiff *must establish* that the doctor did not meet the applicable standard of care and this resulted in injury to the plaintiff.

7. **Duty to disclose medical information (informed consent)** [365]
   a. **Debate**: A debate has endured over whether battery or negligence is the correct tort for medical personnel treating a patient without the patient's consent. See [78]–[81].
   b. **Negligence** is the proper tort if the plaintiff was not fully advised concerning the risks and/or side effects of any proposed procedures. *Walsh v Family Planning Services Ltd* [1992] 1 IR 496 (SC).
      (1) *Walsh* facts: The plaintiff suffered a serious but rare injury following a vasectomy.
      (2) The Supreme Court held that there was a duty to warn of the risks, but the doctors had given sufficient warnings to the plaintiff in the case.
   c. **Battery**: Is the proper tort if there was no consent for contact (treatment) of the patient.
      (1) **Example**: *Wells v Surrey Area Health Authority* (1978) *The Times*, 20 July. The plaintiff, while in distress during a long labour, was seen by a consultant who recommended a caesarean section and sterilisation. The plaintiff signed the consent form agreeing to both procedures. Later, she alleged that she had she not been in distress she would never have agreed to sterilisation on religious grounds. Her claim for trespass failed because she had consented to the procedure. Her claim for negligence succeeded because she was not properly counseled before the operation.
   d. **Informed consent approaches** [366]
      (1) **English approach**: Under *Bolam*, the decision of what to tell a patient is a medical decision determined by the doctor.
      (2) **US approach**: In the US, the disclosure of all material risks is required.
         (a) The doctor has a duty to give all information concerning risks.
         (b) Providing information on all material risks allows the patient to make an informed choice concerning treatment.
      (3) **Australian approach**: In Australia, *Bolam* traditionally applied. [367]
         (a) However, *Bolam* has been limited to treatment and diagnosis.

   (b) *Bolam* does not apply to the decision to inform a
        patient of the inherent risks of a procedure. *Rogers v
        Witiker* (1992) ATR 81.
   (c) A middle-of-the-road approach has been used
        wherein *Bolam* applies except where a particular risk
        must be disclosed for the patient to make an
        informed choice such that no reasonably prudent
        medical person would fail to disclose the risk.
        Sidaway v Gov of the Bethlem Royal Hospital [1985]
        AC 871.   **[368]**
(4) **Irish approach**: A patient must be informed of any
    material risk, whether the patient inquires or not, regard-
    less of the infrequency of the risk arising. *Geoghegan v
    Harris* [2000] 3 IR 536 (HC).
   (a) McMahon views the *Geoghegan* decision as the most
        sophisticated and closely reasoned discussion of the
        subject of the duty of disclosure by an Irish court.
   (b) Kearns J. in *Geoghegan* critically analysed the deci-
        sion in *Walsh v Family Planning Services*.

E. Foreseeable plaintiffs   [369]

1. To whom is a common law duty of care owed?
   a. Historically, the earliest duties were found in contractual rela-
      tionships between a professional and his or her client or patient.
   b. However, the law has expanded to impose a duty to persons
      reasonably foreseen to be injured, i.e. foreseeable plaintiffs.
   c. **Note**: Not everyone who is careless will be liable in negligence.
   d. **Liability** is *limited* to:
      (1) Circumstances where the *law imposes a duty of care*; and
      (2) **The duty of care owed**: Is owed to any person *reasonably
           foreseen* to be injured by defendant's acts or omissions.
2. **Foreseeable plaintiffs**   [370]
   a. First articulated in England in *Donoghue v Stevenson* (1932).
      (1) This famous case introduced the 'neighbour principle'.
           See [328].
      (2) **Neighbour principle**: 'The rule that you are to love your
           neighbour becomes in law you must not injure your
           neighbour…[or] persons who are so closely and directly
           affected by [your] act that [you] ought *reasonably to have
           them in contemplation as being so affected…*' (Lord Atkin)
                                                          [371]

(3) ***Donoghue v Stevenson* facts**: The plaintiff's friend purchased a bottle of ginger beer from a retailer and gave it to the plaintiff to drink. The bottle was opaque (not clear glass). The plaintiff drank a part of the ginger beer, and when she poured the rest of the bottle into a glass, the remains of a small snail allegedly came out of the bottle. The plaintiff became seriously ill and sued the defendant manufacturer in negligence. The defendant argued that he did not owe a duty of care to the plaintiff as she had not purchased the bottle of ginger beer (no privity of contract).

(4) **Reasoning**: The defendant had prepared the product in such a way as to show that he intended it to reach the ultimate consumer in the form in which it left his control. He could reasonably foresee that someone other than the original purchaser might consume the product. Thus, he was held liable to the plaintiff. See [451] *et seq*.

[372]

b. The neighbour principle as espoused in *Donoghue v Stevenson* was accepted into Irish law in *Kirby v Burke* [1944] IR 207.

(1) Quill has highlighted the fact that according to Gavan Duffy J., *Donoghue v Stevenson* alone would not have been a sufficiently convincing authority, but the neighbour principle was accepted because it also conformed to the views expressed by Holmes in *The Common Law* (1881). See generally [337] and [328].

3. **Foreseeability** [373]

a. Legal commentators often use the famous US case of *Palsgraf v Long Island Railway* (1928) 248 NY 339 to illustrate issues concerning foreseeability that are still debated today.

(1) In *Palsgraf*, a passenger was running to catch one of the defendant's trains. The train was beginning to pull away from the platform when one of the defendant's employees helped the passenger onto the train. In helping the passenger, the employee knocked an innocent-looking parcel from the passenger. It contained fireworks and when it hit the ground an explosion occurred. It shook the platform, causing a heavy scale at the end to fall on Helen Palsgraf, injuring her.

b. **Majority opinion written by Justice Cardozo.** [374]

(1) The defendant owes a duty of care only to those persons that the *reasonable person* would have foreseen as at risk

of harm under the circumstances.
   (2) The plaintiff must be *a foreseeable plaintiff* and injured in a *foreseeable zone of danger*.
   (3) Helen Palsgraf was not owed a duty of care by the defendant railroad because she was neither a *foreseeable plaintiff* nor in a *foreseeable zone of danger*.
   c. **Dissenting opinion written by Justice Andrews** is much broader. **[375]**
   (1) The defendant railroad did owe Helen Palsgraf a duty of care.
   (2) Andrews reasoned that if a duty was owed to passengers on the train, then it was owed to everyone who suffered injuries as a proximate result of the defendant's breach of that duty, regardless if the injured were 'foreseeable plaintiffs'.
4. **Special foreseeability issues** **[376]**
   a. **Rescuers**: Traditionally, rescuers injured during or in the course of rescuing had no cause of action.
   b. The courts used a number of theories to disallow the claims of rescuers.
   (1) The rescuer had voluntarily assumed the risks. See [595].
   (2) The rescuer was not a foreseeable plaintiff.
   (3) The rescuer was contributorily negligent. See [586].
   c. **Present status**: **[377]**
   (1) Today, a defendant's duty to act as a reasonable person is owed to any rescuer who comes to the aid of the defendant or another who was placed in peril because of the defendant's conduct.
   (2) **Example**: *Phillips v Durgan* [1991] ILRM 321 (SC). The defendant hired his sister to paint his house. The kitchen was a greasy mess. The sister tripped or slipped and started a fire. It spread quickly. Her husband rescued her. They both sustained personal injuries. **Held**: The defendant failed to warn his sister of the risks and the rescue efforts of her husband were foreseeable and provoked by the defendant's negligence.
   (3) **Rationale**: For imposing liability on a defendant for injuries to a rescuer:
      (a) 'Danger invites rescue.' Cardozo J. in *Wagner v Intern'l Railroad Co.* (1921) 232 NYS 176. **[378]**

(b) If the defendant unreasonably acts so as to put himself or another in peril, it is foreseeable that a rescue attempt could take place.

(4) **Reasonable care required**: To recover, the rescuer must exercise reasonable care.

    (a) If a rescuer is contributory negligent, his damages will be reduced.

    (b) If a rescuer is foolhardy under the circumstances, no damages will be awarded.

(5) **Note**: The law does not distinguish between professional and non-professional rescuers. **[379]**

    (a) Thus, a lifeguard does not assume the risk when rescuing a swimmer although it is part of her job. See defences to negligence [586] *et seq.*

    (b) The rescuer must be *provoked* into action by the defendant's negligence that created the peril.

II. Special duty issues

A. Affirmative duties
B. Duties owed to third parties
C. Duty to control third parties
D. Common law duties owed by an employer to employees
E. Common law duties regarding dangerous products
F. Common law duties owed to children by schools.
Note: Duties imposed by statute are covered in Chapter 9.

A. Affirmative duties [380]

1. The law *distinguishes* between misfeasance and nonfeasance.

  a. **Misfeasance**: Doing a lawful act in a wrongful manner.

    (1) Due care is required.

    (2) Do not confuse misfeasance with *malfeasance*, i.e. doing an unlawful act.

  b. **Nonfeasance**: Is not acting.

    (1) Generally with nonfeasance there is no duty owed.

  c. 'There is no distinction more deeply rooted in the common law and more fundamental than that between *misfeasance* and *nonfeasance*, between active conduct working positive injury to others and passive inaction, a failure to take positive steps to benefit others, or to protect them from harm not created by any wrongful act of the defendant...In the case of active misfeasance the victim is positively worse off as a result of the wrongful act. In cases of passive inaction plaintiff is in reality no worse off at all. His situation is unchanged; he is merely deprived of a protection which, had it been afforded to him, would have benefited him.' Franicis H. Bohlen, 'The Moral Duty to Aid Others as a Basis of Tort Liability', 56, *U.Pa.L.Rev* 217, 219–220 (1908).

2. **Misfeasance**   **[381]**
   a. **General rule**: Tort liability is normally based on the defendant doing a lawful act in a wrongful manner.
     (1) Generally, a person is liable for positive acts that create an unreasonable risk of harm, but not for nonfeasance.
     (2) **Example of affirmative misfeasance**: Operating a motor boat at a high rate of speed through a group of swimmers.
     (3) **Note**: Generally, a person is always liable for malfeasance.   **[382]**
       (a) Example: *Kennedy et al. v Ireland and the AG* [1988] ILRM 472 (HC). The plaintiff's constitutional rights were infringed deliberately where the plaintiff's phone was tapped without justification.
   b. **Exception to general rule**: Misfeasance can also be by a negligent omission.
     (1) **Negligent omission**: Failing to do something that a reasonable person would do while engaged in other activity.   **[383]**
       (a) **Example**: Not paying attention while driving a car.
     (2) A negligent omission is a type of nonfeasance, but because it is a risk creating failure to act, liability may be imposed.

3. **Nonfeasance**   **[384]**
   a. **General rule**: A person does not owe a duty for *not* acting.
     (1) Usually arises when the plaintiff asserts that the defendant should have acted or intervened in order to prevent harm to the plaintiff.
     (2) **Examples**: The defendant:
       (a) Failed to prevent harm to the plaintiff by controlling a third party.
       (b) Failed to take steps to protect the plaintiff from injury.
       (c) Failed to rescue the plaintiff.   **[385]**

b. **Note:** Unlike omissions [511] and acts constituting misfeasance [381], the defendant in nonfeasance took no action and therefore did not create the risks that injured the plaintiff.

    (1) **Example:** P fell while rollerblading. D saw the accident, but walked past P. P suffered extensive brain injuries because he was not found, and therefore did not receive medical treatment for several hours. P alleges that if D had summoned help at the time of the accident, P would not have suffered his brain injury. D does not owe P a duty of care.

c. **Exception to general rule: Negligent omission** is a failure to do something that a reasonable person would do while engaged in other activity. **[386]**

    (1) Negligent omissions are a type of nonfeasance for which liability may be imposed.

    (2) **Example:** Not paying attention while driving a car. See [383].

4. **Affirmative duties** are another type of nonfeasance where liability may be imposed. **[387]**

a. **Special relationship** between the parties may give rise to a legal duty for the defendant to act. **Examples:**

    (1) Occupier to entrant. See [649] *et seq.*

    (2) Parent and child.

    (3) Employer/employee.

b. **Assumption of duty by acting:** If the defendant gratuitously acts for the benefit of the plaintiff, he must act like a reasonable person. **[388]**

    (1) **Gratuitous act:** Where the defendant was not required to act, but elected or chose to act.

    (2) **Example:** A road authority does not have a duty to keep roads in repair, but if it elects to repair the road, it must meet the duty, i.e. not be negligent by leaving the road in a dangerous condition. *Phelan v Kilkenny Co. Council* [1943] IR Jur 1 (SC).

    (3) **Example:** Coastguard responding to an emergency at sea. *OLL Ltd v Sec. of State for Transport* [1997] 2 All ER 897 (QB).

c. **Assumption of duty by promise:** If the defendant gratuitously undertakes to perform an act and causes the plaintiff to rely on it to her detriment, liability may be imposed. **[389]**

    (1) **Example:** The defendant promised to send an ambulance, but did not. Liability was imposed. *Kent v Griffiths*

[2000] 2 WLR 1158 (CA).

5. **Examples of affirmative duties**   **[390]**

   a. **Duty to warn**

      (1) *McKenna v Best Travel* (1997) (SC). Travel companies generally found to owe a duty to warn customers of known dangers at destination. Plaintiff lost, as dangers were not known to the defendant.

      (a) Regarding defective products. See [460].

      (b) Regarding risks. See *Phillips v Durgan* [377].

   b. **Duty to protect**

      (1) General rule: See [429].

      (2) Exception to general rule: See *Osman v UK* [431].

   c. **Duty to control**: See [417] *et seq.*

   d. **Duty to investigate**: See *N. v UK* [359].

   e. **Duty to disclose**: See *Doolan v Murray* [403] *et seq.*

   f. **Duty to advise third party**: See [408].

6. **No duty to rescue**   **[391]**

   a. **General rule**: In common law jurisdictions there is no general duty to rescue or go to the aid of others in danger.

      (1) **Example**: A person may witness a neighbour's toddler drowning in a small fountain in the park, and he has no duty to go to the aid of the toddler even if he is in no risk of injury.

   b. **Rationale**: Tort law is not concerned with purely moral obligations.   **[392]**

   c. **Exceptions** to general rule regarding no duty to rescue. **[393]**

      (1) **Special relationship**: The defendant will owe a duty to go to the aid of another where some *special relationship* exists between defendant and victim. **Examples**:

      (a) Parent/child;

      (b) Jailer/prisoner; *McKevitt v Ireland* [1987] ILRM 541 (SC): The police owed a duty of care to an intoxicated person in custody to take all reasonable steps to keep person from injuring himself.

      (c) Employer/employee.

      (2) **Responsible for peril**: If defendant is responsible for the injury or peril, the defendant is under a duty to aid the plaintiff and in doing so the defendant *must* exercise reasonable care in aiding.

      (a) **Example**: *Adderly v Great Northern Railway Co.* [1905] 2 IR 378 (CA). The plaintiff was injured by the acts of an intoxicated passenger. The defendant railway was held liable, as it chose to accept the intoxicated passenger. It owed a duty to take reasonable care to prevent injuries to other passengers.

7. **US statutory exceptions to affirmative duties**   **[394]**
   a. **Motor vehicle codes**: In some common law jurisdictions in the US, it is a criminal offence to fail to go to the aid of another motorist involved in a car accident even though the defendant was not at fault for the accident. (Civil liability may be imposed.)
   b. **Limitation of liability for doctors**: Every state in the US has adopted legislation shielding doctors from negligence liability when they render aid in an emergency. **Rationale**: To encourage doctors to go to the aid of injured persons without fear of malpractice claims.
   c. **Duty to rescue statutes**: A few states (Vermont and Minnesota) have passed statutes requiring all persons to render reasonable aid to anyone exposed to grave physical injury.
      (1) **Exception**: If acting to aid another would endanger the actor, or interfere with important duties that person owes to others.
      (2) **Examples**: Parent responsible for small child is not required to abandon the child to effect a rescue, nor is a teacher on a school trip responsible for young students required to abandon the students to effect a rescue.

B. *Duties owed to third parties*   **[395]**

1. Negligent infliction of emotional distress
2. Negligent misstatements
3. Solicitors' duties to third parties
4. Doctors' duties to third parties

1. **Negligent infliction of emotional distress**   **[396]**
   a. See nervous shock [482] *et seq.*
2. **Negligent misstatements**   **[397]**
   a. **Traditional common law rule**: A duty of care was *only* imposed for negligent statements *causing* economic loss where:
      (1) There was a fiduciary relationship between the parties; or
         (a) **Fiduciary relationship** generally arises where one person holds property in trust for the use and benefit of another.

(2)   Where the statement was prepared pursuant to a contract between the parties.

b. **Expansion**: **Duty to third parties under the *Hedley Byrne* principle.** *Hedley Byrne v Heller* [1964] AC 465 (HL). The plaintiff was asked by a firm to buy advertising for them. To check the firm's credit, the plaintiff asked its own bank to check on the firm. The plaintiff's bank contacted the defendant (the firm's bank) twice to make credit inquiries. Both times the defendant gave favourable references, with a disclaimer of liability for the statement. Relying on the advice, the plaintiff entered into a contract, but the firm went into liquidation, leaving the plaintiff with £17,000 in unpaid advertising fees. The defendant escaped liability because of the express disclaimers. **Holding**: A duty exists where there is a *special relationship* between the parties and the person making the statement can *foresee* the person receiving the statement *relying* on it to his detriment. **Important elements**:

(1)   Special relationship between the parties.   **[398]**

(2)   The defendant can foresee the plaintiff relying on the statement.

(3)   The plaintiff relied on the statement to his detriment.

c. **Irish approach**: *Hedley* principle interpreted broadly. **[399]**

(1)   Approved in Ireland in *Securities Trust Ltd v Hugh Moore and Alexander Ltd* [1964] IR 417 (HC). See [402].

(a)   *Hedley* principle has merged with the broader concept of the *Donoghue* duty of care. See [328] and [370].

(2)   **Duty of care**: Requirements from *Ward v McMaster* [1988] IR 337 (SC). See [479].

(a)   Proximity of the parties.

(b)   Foreseeability of the damage.

(c)   Absence of any compelling public policy.

(3)   The Supreme Court in *Glencar Exploration plc v Mayo County Council* [2002] 1 ILRM 481 has reinterpreted *Ward v McMaster* (see [479]) in line with the House of Lords decision in *Caparo Industries v Dickman* [1990] 2 AC 605. See [330] and [407].

(a)   Proximity of the parties.

(b)   Foreseeability of the damage.

(c)   Imposition of a duty must be fair, just and reasonable in the circumstances.   **[400]**

(4) Quill notes that the *Caparo* [407] approach (three stage test) is virtually identical to the *Anns v Merton London Borough Council* approach [330] (two stage test), except the *Caparo* approach employs less plaintiff-friendly language. See [330].

(5) Auditors and accountants in Ireland are exposed to a broader obligation and hence more potential liability than English auditors and accountants.

d. Proximity of the parties (special relationship) [401]

(1) Generally, the defendant owes a duty of care only to the persons he *made* the negligent statement to, *or* to those persons he could *foresee* would rely on it.

(2) There is *no duty* owed to the world at large. **[402]**

  (a) *Securities Trust*, see [399]. Because of a printing error in the Articles of Association, the plaintiff invested to its detriment in the defendant company. The action failed because the defendant did not owe a duty to the world at large to avoid mistakes and printing errors. However, the court found that the relationship between a limited company and its shareholders is close enough to be considered special.

  (b) *Bank of Ireland v Smith* [1966] IL 646 (HC). The defendant auctioneer published an ad incorrectly stating that land was in pasture. The plaintiff bought it relying on the statement. No special relationship found.

(3) The duty of care is owed by the party preparing a reference to the subject as well as the recipient of the reference. *Spring v Guardian Assuarance* [1995] AC 296 (HL).

  (a) **Example**: Homer is a lousy employee. He falls asleep at work, is habitually late in arriving to work and is often absent. Homer's employer, Mr Smithers, is very happy when he learns that Homer has applied for a job at a rival company. When the human resource manager of the rival company asks for a work reference for Homer, Mr Smithers falsely states that Homer is a highly qualified and motivated employee who is punctual, dedicated and has good attendance at work. Mr Smithers owes a duty of care to both the rival company as well as Homer.

(4) **Note:** There is no requirement that the misrepresentation be limited to auditors, accountants or commercial
matters.   **[403]**
  (a) The defendant in *Treston v Mayo Co. Council* (1998)
      (HC) was found liable for negligently misrepresent-
      ing to the plaintiff that it intended to upgrade
      houses in an estate. In reliance, the plaintiff bought
      a house, then the defendant gave neighbouring
      houses to known troublemakers.
  (b) Likewise in *Doolan v Murray* (1993) (HC). The
      owner of land negotiated and executed deeds repre-
      senting an intended right of way as being for pedes-
      trians. In fact, under planning permission vehicular
      access was necessary, so the owner was found liable
      for negligent misstatement.
  (c) *T v Surrey County Council* [1990] 4 All ER 577. The
      local authority was held liable for negligent mis-
      statement regarding the suitability of a childminder.
e. Defendant made statement to   **[404]**
  (1) *Treston v Mayo Co. Council* (1998) (HC). The defendant
      was found liable for negligently misrepresenting to the
      plaintiff that it intended to upgrade houses in an estate.
      In reliance, the plaintiff bought a house, then the defen-
      dant gave neighbouring houses to known troublemakers.
  (2) *Doolan v Murray* (1993) (HC). The owner of land nego-
      tiated and executed deeds representing an intended right
      of way as being for pedestrians. In fact, under planning
      permission vehicular access was necessary. Owner found
      liable.
f. Defendant should have foreseen reliance on statement **[405]**
  (1) *Potterton Ltd v Northern Bank* [1993] ILRM (HC). The
      defendant deliberately put a false statement on cheque
      where the plaintiff was payee.
  (2) *McCullogh v PB Gunne* (1997) (HC). A couple relied
      heavily on the defendant's employee, an auctioneer.
      Court found that auctioneer had taken a pro-active role
      with the couple and knew they relied on his statements.
  (3) *Grayson v AIB* (2000) (HC). The plaintiff, a customer of
      the defendant, had a bogus foreign account. The plain-
      tiff alleged that the defendant's employee, during a brief
      exchange, told the plaintiff not to avail of the 1988 tax

amnesty. Case dismissed, as remarks by employee did not show assumption of responsibility.

g. **Foreseeability of damage**   **[406]**

    (1) The damage *must* be caused by the plaintiff's reliance on the statement.

        (a) *Kelly v Haughey Boland and Co.* [1989]. The defendants were negligent in the performance of yearly audits of a company. The plaintiff relied upon the audits in a takeover, and then sustained heavy losses. While a duty was recognised, the plaintiff failed because the accounts did not give a misleading account of the company's financial status.

    (2) **Causation**: The incorrectness of the statement must lead to the plaintiff's damage. *Potterton Ltd v Northern Bank Ltd* (SC) (1997).   **[407]**

    (3) **Purpose of statement**: In weighing foreseeability, a court may look to the purpose of the statement.

        (a) *Caparo Industries v Dickman* [1990]. The plaintiff took over a company, relying on statements prepared by the defendant auditors pursuant to the Companies Act. No liability was imposed for the negligent statements, as they were not designed to guide potential investors. See [330] and [400].

        (b) *Reeman v Department of Transport* [1997]. The defendant department issued an annual certificate of seaworthiness for a fishing boat later bought by the plaintiff. Plaintiff relied on the certificate when he bought it, and sued when it was found that the inspector had been negligent. No liability. The object of the certificate was to promote safety, not to establish commercial value. When the certificate was issued it was not foreseeable that plaintiff would rely on the statement.

3. **Solicitors' duties to third parties**, see [350], professional duty of care.   **[408]**

    a. **Advice or information**: While a solicitor's primary duty is to his client, he may also have a duty to advise others in certain circumstances.

        (1) *Doran v Delaney* [1998] 2 ILRM 1 (SC). Duty found to exist between the defendant solicitor (for vendor) and the plaintiff buyer where defendant was aware of a

boundary dispute but answered inquiry concerning whether litigation was pending or threatened with 'Vendor says none'.

(2) The Supreme Court drew up *general terms* regarding the solicitors' duty for advice or information supplied to third parties in *Doran v Delaney*.

(3) **Solicitor** must have *expressly* or by *implication* led the third party to believe that he had the required skill or knowledge to advise or give information.

    (a) **Detrimental reliance**: The third party must have relied on the advice or information to his detriment.

    (b) **Solicitor must be aware** that the third party was likely to rely on the advice or information.

b. **Negligent acts or work** (not statements)　　　　　**[409]**

(1) **Wills**: A solicitor drawing up a will has a duty of care to the *intended beneficiaries*, but his **primary duty is to his client**. *Wall v Hegarty* [1980] ILRM 124.

    (a) *Ross v Caunters* [1979] 3 All ER 580. A solicitor negligently drafted a will breaking the probate law. The intended beneficiary successfully sued for the value of her lost inheritance.

    (b) *White v Jones* [1995] 1 All ER 691. A father disowned two of his daughters, and later instructed his solicitor to reinstate his original legacies to the two. After a long period of time the father died, and the solicitor had failed to make the necessary changes. The daughters successfully sued the solicitor for his negligent work.

(2) **No extension** of the duty to other transactions affecting the value of assets the beneficiary is to receive.

    (a) *Clarke v Bruce Lance and Co.* [1998] 1 All ER 364. The plaintiff was not entitled to have the value of a potential benefit preserved during the lifetime of the testator by solicitor.

c. **Voluntary assumption of responsibility**　　　　　**[410]**

(1) **General rule**: A solicitor does not owe a duty to the opposing party in contested litigation.

(2) **Exception**: When the solicitor voluntarily assumes responsibility toward the opposing party.

    (a) *al-Kandari v J.R. Browne and Co.* [1988] QB 655. The defendant solicitors represented the plaintiff's husband in a divorce. The defendant solicitors agreed to hold the husband's passport to prevent him from taking the children out of the jurisdiction. The defendants sent the passport to the Kuwaiti embassy and it was returned to the husband, who took the children and fled. The defendant solicitors were found to owe a duty to plaintiff because they had voluntarily assumed a responsibility toward her.

4. **Doctors' duties to third parties** [411]
   a. In general, arises in cases involving:
      (1) Injury to unborn;
      (2) Contraceptive failures; and
      (3) Patient's condition is a danger to third parties.
   b. **Injury to unborn** [412]
      (1) A duty is owed by a doctor treating a pregnant woman to her unborn child. *Dunne v National Maternity Hospital* [1989] IR 91.
      (2) English approach: The right to refuse medical treatment is paramount even if the refusal results in the death of the patient's unborn child. See [81].
   c. **Failed contraceptives: There are no Irish cases**. [413]
      (1) A duty may be owed by a doctor performing a failed sterilisation procedure resulting in an unwanted pregnancy for the cost of raising the child. *Emeh v Kensington and Chelsea and Westminister Area Health Authority* [1985] QB 1012.
         (a) The decision not to abort did not break the chain of causation. *Emeh*.
      (2) **Limited duty**: No duty owed to unknown partners. [414]
         (a) *Goodwill v British Pregnancy Advisory Service* [1996] 1 WLR 1392. A man had a vasectomy and was assured that he was sterile. Several years later, the plaintiff became pregnant. No duty owed to the plaintiff. However, *obiter* if a partner was known to the doctor the procedure would have benefited both and doctor would have owed her a duty.
         (b) *McFarlane v Tayside Health Board* (1998) BMLR (Scottish). Where it was assumed that a duty was owed to the wife of a man who had a vasectomy and was negligently advised that he was sterile.

(3) **Public policy**: Debates have raged over: [415]
   (a) Whether a healthy child conceived after a failed contraceptive surgery should be regarded as a blessing or damages.
   (b) Whether a woman having the child suffers damages as a result of the 'natural process', etc.
   (c) Public policy arguments were rejected by the House of Lords in *McFarlane* [414]. Question involved law, not social policy.

d. **Patient's condition a danger to third parties** [416]
   (1) In the US, where a doctor has reason to know that a patient is likely to harm a specific third party, the doctor owes a duty of care to that person to warn the intended victim or the police. *Tarsoff v Regents of the University of California*, 17 Cal.3d 425 (1976).
      (a) *Hammon v County of Maricipa*, 775 P.2d 1122 (Arizona 1989). A psychiatrist who knew, or should have known, of the risk of violence to others, owed a duty to the violent child's parents even though no specific threat of violence was made against them by the child.
   (2) *Urbanski v Patel* (1978) 84 DLR 3d 650. A doctor who negligently removed a patient's only kidney, leaving her in a very dangerous position, was found to have owed a duty of care to the patient's father, who donated one of his kidneys to her.

C. Duty to control third parties [417]

1. General principles
2. Vicarious liability
3. Doctrine of *respondeat superior*
4. Liability of parents for torts of child
5. Publican liability
6. Police liability

1. General principles [418]
   a. A defendant may be held liable for nonfeasance in the failure to control the conduct of third persons where the defendant had the power of control. Nonfeasance, see [384].
   b. **Direct liability**: Where the defendant is *present* at the time of the third person's wrongful conduct, his failure to exercise

control to stop such conduct may be an act of negligence.

(1) **Examples**:

    (a) A driver may have a duty to control passengers so they do not injure other road users. *Curley v Manion*, see [269].

    (b) A publican may have a duty to protect a patron against a battery by another patron. *Hall and Kennedy v Routledge* (1993). See [428].

c. **Indirect liability**: Where the defendant is *not present*, he may be liable for the acts of third persons in limited situations such as vicarious liability.

2. **Vicarious liability,** see Chapter 3, [262].   **[419]**

a. **Definition**: Where one person is held strictly liable for the acts of another person.

b. Vicarious liability may be imposed by common law or by statute.

c. Vicarious liability arises in:

(1) **Formal legal relationships** such as:

    (a) Employer/employee, see [420];

    (b) Principal/agent;

    (c) Firm/partner; imposed by liability of partners under the Partnership Act 1961.

(2) **Informal relationships** where one person has control over another person.

    (a) Driver/passenger. See *Curley v Manion* [269].

    (b) Social host/guest. See *Moynihan v Moynihan* [272].

    (c) Owner of vehicle/driver(s). 118, Road Traffic Act.

    [420]

3. **Doctrine of *respondeat superior*:** Employer vicarious liability.

a. **General rule**: An employer may be liable for the tortious acts committed by employees within the scope of employment.

b. **Crucial requirement**: The act must be within the *scope of employment*.   **[421]**

c. **Scope of employment**: Vicarious liability will not apply if tort is committed outside scope of employment.

(1) Scope does *not* include travel to and from primary place of employment.   **[422]**

    (a) **Examples**: After reaching primary place of employment (shop, office, farm, etc.), travelling to see clients or being sent to run errands for employer would be within scope of employment.

(2) **Detour and frolic:** Leaving the place of employment on *private or personal* business is usually outside scope of employment.
- (a) **Example:** *O'Connell v Bateman* [1932] LJ IR 160. A man borrowed his employer's lorry to visit his family. **Held:** The employer was not liable for the damage caused when the lorry crashed.
- (b) **Example: Detour** – *Jameston v Byrne and MaGuire* (1926) 60 ILTR 11. An employee made a detour on his route for personal reasons and crashed. **Held:** There was no evidence that might infer that the employee was acting within the scope of his employment.

d. Intentional torts committed by employees   [423]
(1) **General rule:** An employer may be vicariously liable for the intentional torts (such as batteries) committed by his employees within the scope of their employment.
- (a) Where the employee's duties involve the use of physical force on others, such as bodyguards and bouncers.
- (b) Or where force is used to further the employer's interests.
- (c) **Example:** *Farry v Great Northern Railway Co.* [1898] 2 IR 352. A stationmaster detained the plaintiff to force the plaintiff to surrender his ticket after a dispute arose over his trip. The employer railway was held vicariously liable for false imprisonment of the plaintiff. **Rationale:** The stationmaster had been acting to protect the interests of his employer.

(2) **Criminal conduct by an employee   [424]**
- (a) **Irish approach:** *Johnson and Johnson (Ireland) Ltd v c.P. Security Ltd* [1985] IR 362. A security guard employed by the defendant to protect the plaintiff's premises assisted others in stealing plaintiff's goods. The employer was held vicariously liable because it was specifically engaged to safeguard plaintiff's property.
- (b) **English approach:** *Trotman v North Yorkshire Co. Council* (1998) *The Times*, 10 September. A mentally handicapped teenager suffering from epilepsy

required attendance during the night because of his seizures. During a school trip, the deputy headmaster sexually assaulted the teenager in the room they shared and was convicted of sexual assault. Where an employee performs an act that actually negates the employer's duty (to take care of the teenager), the employer cannot be held vicariously liable.   **[425]**

 e. **Independent contractors**: An employer may be vicariously liable for torts committed by independent contractors if the employer's degree of control was comparable to that of an employee.

  (1) **Example**: *Phelan v Coillte Teo* [1993] 1 IR 18. The plaintiff was injured due to the negligence of an independent contractor, a welder/fitter with whom the plaintiff was working.

  (2) **Test of control** is not settled.

  (3) English approach regarding issue of control:

   (a) Was the wrongful act authorised by the employer? Or

   (b) Was the act authorised by the employer, but the method of performance was not authorised?

4. **Liability of parents for torts of child**   **[426]**

 a. **Common law rule**: No vicarious liability.

  (1) Generally, a parent is *not* vicariously liable for torts committed by his child.

  (2) **Rationale**: Parents do not have sufficient control to justify imputing liability where parent was not otherwise negligent.

 b. **Liability based on parent's own negligence**: A parent, or anyone else having care or custody of a child, may be liable for injuries caused by a child where the parent was negligent by: **[427]**

  (1) Failing to control the acts of a child committed in the presence of parent.

   (a) **Example**: *Curley v Manion*, see [269].

  (2) Failing to exercise reasonable care to protect against the child's known dangerous tendencies.

   (a) **Example**: Allowing a child previously caught setting fires to have access to matches.

  (3) Failing to warn others who are likely to come into contact with child of the child's dangerous tendencies.

      (a) **Example**: *Ellis v D'Angelo*, 116 Cal.App.2d 310 (1953). A childminder was injured by a four-year-old child subject to violent behaviour.

   (4) Failing to prevent the child's foreseeable use of inherently dangerous things.

      (a) **Examples**: Leaving loaded shotgun within reach of child, or leaving child in vehicle with keys.

5. **Publican liability**   **[428]**

  a. **General rule**: Under the common law, a publican is not liable for injuries to third parties resulting from a patron's intoxication.

  b. **Exception to general rule**: A publican has a duty to protect a patron on his premises from a battery by another patron. *Hall and Kennedy v Routledge* (1993) unrep. (HC).

  c. **Note**: A publican may owe other duties, such as in his capacity as an occupier. See occupiers' liability [649] *et seq.*

   (1) **Example**: *Meagher v Shamrock Houses Ltd* [2005] IEHC 35. The plaintiff suffered a fractured jaw when assaulted outside the defendant's nightclub. **Held**: The owner of a licensed premise owes a duty to patrons to take all reasonable care for his safety while on the premises, which included ensuring that another patron on the premises did not assault the plaintiff. The defendant had not provided sufficient protection to patrons by ensuring that at least four security men remained on duty until all patrons had left the premises.

6. **Police liability**   **[429]**

  a. **General rule**: The police are typically not liable for failing to protect individual persons.

   (1) **Public policy rationale**:   **[430]**

      (a) To impose such a duty would determine how the limited police resources should be allocated.

      (b) Floodgate concerns.

      (c) **Example**: *Hill v Chief Constable of West Yorkshire Police* [1993] 4 All ER 344. The plaintiff's daughter was the last victim of the Yorkshire Ripper. He sued the police for negligently conducting the investigation of the previous murders. The plaintiff contended that had a proper investigation taken place, the killer would have been caught sooner. Case dismissed on public policy grounds.

b. **Exception to general rule**: An individual may be owed a duty of protection from the police where there is a specific, increased risk of harm. **[431]**

   (1) **Example**: *Osman v UK* [1999] 1 FLR 193 (ECHR) 1998. A teacher harassed the plaintiff's family for over ten months. Armed with a shotgun, the teacher shot two members of the family. The plaintiffs sued the police for negligently failing to protect. After being dismissed in the English courts, the case was appealed to European Court of Human Rights.

      (a) ECHR found relationship of proximity to police and harm caused was foreseeable. Blanket immunity for police violated article 6 regarding right to a court.

      (b) Distinguished from *Hill*: *Osman* family members were identified. The Ripper's next victim was not.

   (2) Blanket immunities for police questioned. See also *Hall (Arthur JJ) and Co. v Simons* [349].

   (3) See *A v UK* [88] for another example of state omissions resulting in liability.

D. Common law duties owed by an employer to employees   **[432]**

1. Historical background

  a. During the nineteenth century, with increased industrialisation, injured employees sought redress for their injuries through the courts.

   (1) The response of most courts in most jurisdictions was hostile.

   (2) Liability generally rested on the terms of employment, and the terms of employment tended to be dictated by the employer. **[433]**

  b. The judicial response to workers seeking redress included:

   (1) The doctrine of common employment;

   (2) *Volenti non fit injuria*; and

   (3) Contributory negligence.

  c. **The doctrine of common employment**   **[435]**

   (1) Excluded claims for injuries caused by co-workers.

      (a) This was true even if the co-worker was performing an activity on the employer's behalf.

   (2) Doctrine was abolished by section 1, Law Reform (Personal Injuries) Act 1958. **[436]**

  d. ***Volenti non fit injuria*** (voluntary assumption of the risk)

(1)   Excluded claims for injuries caused by the place, system, method or lack of safety equipment on the job.

(2)   In agreeing to work, the injured employee agreed to assume the risk of injury. Application of this doctrine has been greatly curtailed by:

    (a)   Various work safety acts (see [433]) and the

    (b)   Civil Liabilities Act 1961.

e.   **Contributory negligence**   **[437]**

(1)   **Total bar**: Before the Civil Liabilities Act 1961, contributory negligence was a total bar to any recovery by an injured employee.

2.   **Employers also owe common law duties to third parties. [438]**

a.   As occupiers, see occupiers' liability [649] *et seq.*

b.   If manufacturing, see products' liability [296] *et seq.*

c.   If a professional, see professional negligence [344] *et seq.*

d.   Under the doctrine of vicarious liability, see [262] and [419].

3.   **Present status of law: Employers' common law duty of reasonable care to employees**   **[439]**

a.   Four primary duties owed, to provide:

(1)   **Safe place of work,**

(2)   **Safe system of work,**

(3)   **Safe work equipment, and**

(4)   **Competent co-workers.**

Note: In most cases, the various duties owed overlap.

b.   **Safe place of work**   **[440]**

(1)   **General rule**: An employer must take reasonable steps to ensure that employees have a safe place to work.

(2)   Physical environment must be safe. **Examples**:

    (a)   *Kielthy v Ascon* [1970] IR 122. One of the methods of access to employer's premises was not safe.

    (b)   *Gallagher v Mogul of Ireland Ltd* [1975] IR 204 (SC). The roof of the employer's mine collapsed due to insufficient support.

(3)   **Extended**: To a place where the employee is *sent* by the employer to work.

    (a)   **Example**: *Dunne v Honeywell Control Systems Ltd and Virginia Milk Products Ltd* [1991] ILRM 595 (HC). The plaintiff was injured when he fell off of a ladder after repairing equipment at Virginia Milk Product's premises. His employer could not control the premise where the employee was sent, but he could inspect and warn the employee of dangers.

(4) **However, no duty to inspect place where employee sent to work.** [441]

    (a) **Example**: *Mulcare v Southern Health Board* [1988] ILRM 689. The plaintiff was employed to provide home care to elderly patients. She injured an ankle on an uneven floor in one of the homes she visited, and alleged that her employer was negligent for failing to inspect the premises and warn her. Recovery denied because the house was not sufficiently unsafe, and the plaintiff had been in the house numerous times over seven years.

c. **Safe system of work** [442]

(1) **General rule**: The employer has a duty to provide a safe system of work.

    (a) Proper training and supervision and

    (b) Suitable methods of operation, including:

        i.   Design, and

        ii.   Operation of work practices.

(2) **Proper training and supervision. Examples**: [443]

    (a) *Heeney v Dublin Corp.* (1991) unrep. (SC). The plaintiff's decedent died while employed as a firefighter as a result of injuries suffered while fighting a fire without a suitable breathing apparatus. Besides the obvious failure to provide equipment, the defendants were held liable for failing to implement a Labour Court recommendation to assign tasks pursuant to medical exams and the failure to supervise by failing to give instructions for firefighters not to enter burning buildings without proper breathing apparatus.

    (b) *General Cleaning Contractors v Christmas* [1953] AC 180 (HL). The plaintiff window cleaner was told by his employer to hold onto the window sash while cleaning. A window fell on the plaintiff's fingers and the plaintiff fell to the ground. The employer was held liable for failing to have a safe system of work because he failed to tell the plaintiff to test the sashes and wedge all loose sashes.

    (c) *Dunne v Honeywell*, see [440]. The employer was also found negligent for failing to warn the employee concerning the danger of the hand-held tool case on ladders. To improve image, the employer had replaced the employee's shoulder satchel for carrying tools with a case that had to be held in the hand.

(3) **Suitable methods of operation** [444]

    (a) **High-risk activities** require every precaution to be taken. **Example**: *Walsh v Securicor (Ireland)* [1993] 2 IR 507 (HC). The plaintiff was a driver of a security van being escorted by police when he was injured by armed raiders. The employer was held liable for negligently failing to alter the delivery route for over seven years.

    (b) Design of a safe system of work requires more than provision of safety equipment. **Example**: *Barry v Nitrigin Eireann Teo* [1994] 2 ILRM 523 (HC). An unsuitable work system was found to exist due to incompatible equipment. The protective earmuffs had to be removed for the plaintiff to use his communication system.

(4) **Unsafe design of operation** [445]

    (a) **Example**: *McDermid v Nash Dredging and Reclamaiton Co.* [1987] AC 906 (HL). The plaintiff's employer failed to operate a safe system of work. The plaintiff was injured when a tugboat captain failed to wait for the double knock of the plaintiff on the door of the bridge. That was the means of communicating that it was safe to proceed. The plaintiff was seriously injured when he was tangled in ropes and dragged into the sea.

d. **Safe equipment** [446]

  (1) **General rule**: The employer must provide and maintain suitable equipment.

  Note: Duty is *not* limited to safety equipment.

  (2) **Incompatible safety equipment**

    (a) **Example**: *Barry v Nitrigin Eireann Teo*, see [444]). The plaintiff's safety goggles and earmuffs were not compatible. The goggles pushed the earmuffs slightly out of place.

  (3) **Inferior-quality equipment**

    (a) **Example**: *Deegan v Langan* [1966] IR 373. The plaintiff carpenter was injured due to the inferior quality of the nails provided by the employer.

(4) **Failure to maintain equipment** [447]

    (a) **Example**: *Burke v John Paul and Co. Ltd* [1967] IR 277. See causation [531]. The plaintiff was cutting steel rods and complained to his employer that the blades were dull. Liability was imposed on the employer for negligently failing to maintain the blades for the hernia the plaintiff suffered. See [583].

    (b) Duty has been bolstered by statutory protections.

       i.   Factories Act 1955

       ii. Mines and Quarries Act 1965

       iii. Safety, Health, Welfare at Work Act 1989

(5) **Building material may be equipment** [448]

    (a) **Example**: *Knowles v Liverpool City Council* [1993] ICR 21. The plaintiff was injured when a flagstone he was handling broke. The court of appeal held that the flagstone was equipment.

e. **Competent co-workers** [449]

(1) **General rule**: The employer has a duty to exercise reasonable care to provide competent staff.
Note: This provision is less important since the abolition of the doctrine of common employment.

(2) **Qualifications and experience** must be properly considered when hiring someone to work in a position that carries the potential to put others at risk.

    (a) **Example**: *Black v Fife Coal Co. Ltd* [1912] AC 149. The employer was held to have negligently hired a colliery manager who was without experience with carbon monoxide, which was a known hazard at the work site.

(3) **Monitoring staff**: It may be negligent to continue to employ a person who continually engages in practical jokes and/or horseplay resulting in injuries to co-workers. *Hudson v Ridge Manufacturing Co.* [1957] 2 QB 348.

    (a) **Example**: *Hough v Irish Base Metal Ltd* (1967) unrep. (SC). It was held that the employer was not negligent for failure to provide competent staff when the plaintiff was injured by a prank. The prank was not reasonably capable of detection, it was of recent origin and there was no failure to supervise staff.

E. *Common law duties regarding dangerous products*   **[450]**

Remember: The Liability for Defective Products Act 1991 sup-
plements rather than replaces the common law. See [296].
*   Furthermore, the common law principles for defective prod-
    ucts are based on *negligence* rather than strict liability.
*   Thus, if a possible defendant is not a producer, under the Act
    it may be possible to bring a negligence cause of action against
    him.
*   Always determine whether the Liability for Defective
    Products Act 1991 applies *before* attempting to determine if
    the common law applies.   **[451]**

---

1. **Historically**: The manufacturer or supplier of a product could
    only be held liable for injuries sustained through the use of the
    product with which he was in privity of contract. See
    [327]–[328].
    a. This was quite restrictive because it only allowed the parties to
        a contract to sue upon the contract.
        (1) If the plaintiff was not a purchaser of the defective product,
             there was usually no privity of contract and therefore the
             plaintiff did not have the ability to sue the manufacturer.
        (2) **Classic example**: *Winterbottom v Wright* (1842) 152 ER
             402. The plaintiff, a coach driver, was seriously injured
             when his coach broke down due to a latent defect. The
             plaintiff's employer had a contract with the Postmaster
             General to deliver mail. The Postmaster General had a
             contract with the defendant to keep the coaches in good
             repair. The plaintiff could not recover against the defen-
             dant because he had no privity of contract with the
             defendant.
    b. **Inroads on the privity of contract requirement**   **[452]**
        (1) **False representation of safety**: If the defendant knew
             that a product was dangerous, yet he made false repre-
             sentations as to the product's safety, a basis of recovery
             was recognised. *Langridge v Levy* (1837) 150 ER 863.
        (2) **Failure to warn**: Liability was also recognised in cases
             where there was a failure to give a warning when there
             was an awareness of a defect. *Quinn v Tedcastles and Co.*
             (1898) 32 ILTR 137.

(3) **Inherently dangerous things**: Later, liability was also recognised for inherently dangerous things. *O'Gorman v O'Gorman* [1903] 2 IR 573.

c. **Abolition of privity requirement**: Despite early inroads on the privity requirement, the abolition of the requirement came about in the US in the landmark case of *MacPherson v Buick Motor Co.* (1916) 217 NYS 382. **[453]**

(1) **Duty of care owed to all foreseeable users**: Justice Cardozo reasoned that if the reasonable person could foresee that the chattel would create a risk of harm to human life or limb if the chattel were not carefully made or supplied, the manufacturer or supplier of such a chattel is under a duty of care in the manufacture or supply thereof. Cardozo J., see [374], [377]–[378]. **[454]**

(2) **Duty of care owed to the ultimate consumer**: Lord Atkin, in *Donoghue v Stevenson* [1932] AC 562 in addressing the case of a plaintiff who allegedly found a decomposed snail in her ginger beer that had been purchased by a friend, stated that the manufacturer of products which sells the product in such a way as he intends the product to reach the ultimate consumer, with no reasonable possibility of examination, with the absence of reasonable care in the preparation will result in an injury to the consumer's health or property; the manufacturer owes a duty of care to the consumer to take reasonable care.

(3) This principle was accepted into Ireland in the case of *Kirby* v *Burke* [1944] IR 207 (HC). See [372].

2. **Duty owed to consumer expanded**: Eventually the duty owed to the consumer was expanded to include *all persons who may be exposed to the danger by a repaired chattel*, if it was foreseeable that the chattel would be used without inspection.

a. **Repairers**: **[455]**

(1) Owe a duty of care to *all persons* exposed to the danger.

(a) **Example**: *Power v Bedford Motor Co.* [1959] IR 391 (SC). Liability was imposed on the defendant garage for the negligent repair of a car. The repair left the steering mechanism in a dangerous state. The court held that the duty of care extended to all persons exposed to the danger – other drivers, passengers and property owners adjoining the road, etc.

(2) Duty to inspect for defects or warn if product not inspected.   **[456]**

    (a) **Example**: *Andrew v Hopkins* [1957] 1 QB 229. A garage selling a used car was found to have a duty to inspect the car for defects or to warn the buyer that the car had not been inspected for defects.

    (b) **Installers and assemblers**: The duty owed to the consumer was also expanded to include *installers and assemblers* and *extended to all persons injured by the defective work.*

       i. **Example**: *Brown v Cotterill* (1934) 51 TLR 21. Liability was imposed on a monument mason when a tombstone that he had erected fell on a little girl who was placing flowers on her granny's grave. The court held that the mason could not shift responsibility away from himself onto the person who had contracted with him for the erection of the tombstone. Further, it has been held that the supplier of a chattel for reward or hire owes a duty to all persons likely to use or be injured by the chattel.

    (c) **Suppliers of chattels for reward**: Duty is owed to all persons likely to use or be injured by the chattel.   **[457]**

       i. **Example**: *Keegan v Owens* [1953] IR 267 (SC). It was held that there was evidence capable of supporting a verdict for the plaintiff against the supplier of swingboats, hired out to a carnival committee, for injuries sustained by a worker (a volunteer) who assisted the committee by operating the swingboats. The duty owed to the consumer was also expanded to include *installers and assemblers* and *extended to all persons injured by the defective work.*

3. **Dangerous substances**: There was also an expansion to include dangerous substances.   **[458]**

    a. A person in control of a dangerous substance, whether as a *supplier, manufacturer* or *vendor*, has a duty to take reasonable care that any person acquiring the substance from him does not suffer injury or loss. *Bolands v Trouw Ireland Ltd* (1978) unrep. (HC).

(1) In *Bolands* the vendor of an ingredient in a poultry food mixture was found not to owe a duty to explain to the purchaser who compounded the food mixture the manner in which the ingredients could be used safely with other ingredients. It was found that the purchaser (as a compounder) had, or should have had, special knowledge of the product and its correct usage. Finley J. did not find the product to be particularly dangerous.

4. **Non-dangerous substances**: A manufacturer of a product which is not dangerous may be liable for what he knew or should have known when the product was released on the market. *Donoghue v Stevenson*, see [370].   **[459]**

   a. **Example**: *Kearney v Paul and Vincent Ltd* (1985) unrep. (HC). The plaintiff claimed that his calves died as a result of the defendant's product. **Held**: No liability because the plaintiff had failed to produce scientific evidence that the deaths were due to the product.

5. **Duty to warn**: Under the common law, an affirmative duty to warn has also been recognised.   **[460]**

   a. **New products**: Manufacturers placing new products on the market have a duty to inform consumers of the dangers which are known, or should be known, if the product is used in a certain manner.

      (1) **Example**: *O'Byrne v Gloucester* (1988) unrep. (SC). The makers of a brushed cotton skirt were held liable in negligence for failing to attach a warning that the skirt was highly flammable. The teenage plaintiff suffered severe burns after the hem of the skirt touched a butane heater.

   b. **Continuing nature of duty to warn**: The duty to warn is of a *continuing nature*.

      (1) In other words, if the manufacturer discovered a defect after the product was put into circulation, the manufacturer must issue a warning concerning the dangers. *Hobbs (Farms) v Baxenden Chemical Co.* [1992] 1 LR 54.

      (2) Recall of the product may be the proper course of action if the risk is serious enough.

         (a) **Example**: Adulterated baby food.

F. Common law duties owed to children by schools   **[461]**

1. **Schools**
   a. *Loco parentis*: Teachers and school managers owe a duty of care to students.
      (1) Lord Esher in *Williams v Eady* (1893) 10 TLR 41 famously stated that 'the schoolmaster [is] bound to take such care of his boys as a careful father would take of his boys…'
      (2) Cited with approval in *Lennon v McCathy* (1966) (SC).
2. **Negligence in instruction**: Generally cases involve dangerous exercise, inadequate equipment and lack of supervision.
   a. **Supervision in school and yard**   **[462]**
      (1) Duty to supervise begins when children allowed onto premises. *Greene v Mundow* (CC) (2000).
      (2) Normal healthy children in the playground do not need *constant* supervision. O'Dalaigh, CJ in *Lennon v McCarthy* (1966) (SC).
      (3) Teachers have a duty to act as a reasonable parent and therefore cannot be expected, even with young children, to supervise their behaviour constantly. *Mullins v Richards* [1998] 1 All ER 920.
      (4) Sliding down banisters.
         (a) *Ryan v Madden* [1944] IR154 (HC) liability imposed.
         (b) *O'Neill v Tipperary SR VEC* [1996] (CC). No liability on school where plaintiff, aged twelve, was injured by another student sliding down the banister. The offending student had previous sliding incident.
      (5) In measuring the duty of care, the court must take into account all of the relevant factors. *Mapp v Gilhooley* (1989) (HC).   **[463]**
         (a) Ages of the children.
         (b) The activities that children are doing.
         (c) The degree of supervision (if any) required having regard to the circumstances and the opportunity (if any) which those in charge of the child had to prevent.
         (d) It is impossible to keep very young children under complete control when at play.
   b. **Supervision outside school hours**: Duty to supervise does not necessarily end at the school gate.

3. **Injuries off the premises**   **[464]**
   a. Liability may be imposed for a lack of supervision or because of an inadequate safety system.
      (1) **Example**: *Hosty v McDonagh* (1973) (SC). A ten-year-old girl was injured when she came through the school gates at lunch, ran into the road and was injured by a car.
4. **Other acts of negligence**   **[465]**
   a. Extent to which schools owe a duty of care toward students besides physical injury has not been litigated.
   b. Leaving dangerous thing within reach of students. *Williams v Eady* (1893) 10 TLR 41.
   c. Sending a student on a risky task which is beyond the student's abilities. *Smith v Martin* [1911] 2 KB 775.
5. **Structural dangers**: Students are considered visitors under the Occupier's Liability Act 1995, see for duties owed [649].
   a. **Example**: *Hall v Meechan* [2004] IEHC 401. Gilligan J. held that the placing of kerbing with rough, sharp edges was not appropriate on school premises where students would be running. As occupier, the defendant was negligent and breached its duty of care to the plaintiff in failing to take reasonable care to prevent the plaintiff's injuries from an unusual danger.

III. Duty may be limited by type of harm suffered

A. Pure economic loss
B. Nervous shock
C. Death

A. Pure economic loss   **[466]**

1. **Traditional common law approach**
   a. **Exclusionary rule**: Did not allow any recovery for negligently inflicted *pure* economic loss.
   b. **Definition**: Pure economic loss is economic loss without property or protected personal interests being affected, i.e. no property damage or injuries to the person.
      (1) **Example** of a pure economic loss: Captain Marvel negligently sailed his ship into the Waterford Bridge, damaging the bridge to the extent that it had to remain closed to vehicle and ship traffic for one week. Pauline owns a shop on the quay in Waterford that caters to tourists. The ship damaged neither her shop nor her person.

However, due to the bridge closure, Pauline's business suffers heavy losses. Pauline has suffered a pure economic loss.

  c. **Rationale** for traditional common law approach: No duty of care was found because of public policy concerns about potential crushing liability being out of proportion to the defendant's fault.   **[467]**

   (1) **Criticism**: Persons with similar losses are not treated the same.

   (2) **Example**: Herbie ran into an ESB pole late Friday night. The pole hit the corner of the ABC frozen fish factory, and various wires disconnected from the pole. All of the frozen food businesses on the street were without electricity all weekend. All suffered similar economic losses, but only ABC (which also suffered a physical injury) would be able to recover for the economic losses sustained.

2. **Direct or restrictive approach**: Favoured in England.   **[468]**

  a. **Recovery**: Allowed only where the loss is a *direct* result of the defendant's conduct and the plaintiff is the *immediate* victim.

  b. **Damage to property**: Allowed only for persons with a proprietary interest in the property.

  c. **Pure economic loss**: Allowed only when there is a high degree of proximity between defendant's act and the plaintiff's pure economic injury.

  d. **Benefit of restrictive approach**: It limits potentially crushing liability or floodgates.

  e. **Restrictive approach applied**:   **[469]**

   (1) English case: *Leigh and Sillavan Ltd v Aliakmon Shipping Co. Ltd* [1986] AC 785. Goods were damaged in transit by the defendant's negligence. At the time of the injury, the plaintiff had no proprietary interest in the goods, just a financial risk because it covered the risk of damage to the goods. The House of Lords denied a recovery because the plaintiff had no proprietary interest in goods nor the required proximity.

   (2) Irish case: *Irish Paper Sacks Ltd v John Sisk and Son (Dublin) Ltd* unrep. (HC) (1972). While digging, the defendants cut a cable that supplied electricity to the plaintiff's factory. The plaintiff suffered economic loss, but no property loss. No recovery allowed.

3. **Broad approach**: Favoured in Ireland. [479]
   a. Treats economic loss with the same principles as physical damage.
      (1) *Ward v McMaster* [1985] IR 29 (SC). The case involved a house with dangerous and non-dangerous defects. See generally [330].
      (2) Requirements from *Ward v McMaster*:
         (a) **Proximity**: There must be sufficient proximity between the parties.
         (b) **Reasonable foreseeable damage**: The damage must be a reasonable foreseeable consequence of the defendant's conduct.
         (c) **No adverse public policy considerations.**
      (3) Same approach as in negligent misstatements. See [399].
   b. **Applied in** *McShane Wholesale and Vegetable Ltd v Johnston Haulage Co. Ltd* [1997] I ILRM 86 (HC). The defendant's premises suffered a fire and the fire caused the plaintiff's factory to lose electricity.
   c. **Criticism** of approach: There are problems with determining foreseeability. [480]
      (1) **Example**: *Madden v Irish Turf Club* [1997] 2 ILRM 148 (SC). The plaintiff bet on a horse that came in second to a horse that was not eligible to run in the race. The plaintiff sued the defendant for failing to stop the ineligible horse from running. Case dismissed. The defendant's function was to regulate and control racing, not betting.
4. **Vulnerability approach**: Favoured in Australia. [481]
   a. **Vulnerability**: This is the relevant criterion for determining whether a duty of care exists.
   b. Where a person knows or ought to know that his act(s) or omissions may cause the loss or impairment of legal rights possessed, enjoyed or exercised by another, whether as an individual or as a member of a class, *and the latter person is in no position to protect his interest*, there is a relationship such that the law should impose a duty of care on the actor to take reasonable steps to avoid foreseeable risk of economic loss resulting from the loss or impairment of those rights. Gaudron J.: *Perre and Others v Apand Pty Ltd* [1999] 164 ALR 606 (HC).
      (1) *Perre* facts: Potato farmers in a rural locality were prohibited from exporting their crops after the defendant

negligently supplied diseased seed that introduced potato wilt onto neighbouring lands. The potato farmers
were placed by the government in a five-year exclusion
zone that prohibited exporting their crops. **Held**: A duty
of care was owed to all the farmers affected.

(2) Detrimental reliance and assumption of responsibility
are indicators of the plaintiff's vulnerability to harm
from the defendant's conduct.

B. *Nervous shock*   [482]

Exam hint: This is a favorite question area for examiners. If you
are given a problem question involving nervous shock, make certain that if the event took place in Ireland you apply the *Kelly v
Hennessey* [494] principles rather than the *Alcock* [495] test.

---

1. **Definition**: **Nervous shock** or negligent infliction of emotional
   distress is psychiatric harm suffered by the plaintiff due to a sudden or unexpected shock.
2. **Historical development**   [483]
   a. **Traditional general rule**: If a defendant acted negligently,
      causing a mental injury (nervous shock) to the plaintiff, there
      was no liability.
      (1) However, if the defendant acted negligently and thereby
          caused a physical and mental injury (nervous shock) to
          the plaintiff, the plaintiff could generally recover for both
          the physical and mental injury.
      (2) This is generally referred to as dependent nervous shock
          and in most lawsuits is simply called 'pain and suffering'.
   b. There has been much criticism over the years for nervous
      shock.   [484]
      (1) The criticism has primarily centered on the fear of fraud-
          ulent claims, or 'floodgates' fears. (One negligent act
          potentially leading to limitless claims.)
      (2) The erosion of the traditional approach of not allowing
          claims for nervous shock is said to be due to the devel-
          opment of the railway systems of the nineteenth century.
3. **Earliest recognition of nervous shock**: Person in fear of his or
   her own safety.   [485]
   a. With resulting physical injury.

(1) *Byrne v Southern and Western Railway Co.* (1884) unrep. CA. The plaintiff was in a building struck by a train. Plaintiff suffered no physical injuries (at time of the crash), but the resulting shock led to a deterioration of his health.

b. With resulting mental injuries, but no physical injury.
   (1) *Bell v Great Northern Railway Co.* (1890) 26 LR 428. The plaintiff was a passenger in a train carriage which detached from the train and careered backward down a hill. Plaintiff's mental health suffered.

c. With resulting physical harm to unborn child.   **[486]**
   (1) **Dulieu v White and Sons** [1901] 2 KB 669. *Dulieu* is often cited as the first successful nervous shock case. A publican's wife suffered a severe fright when a horse-drawn vehicle crashed through the window of the pub where she was working. Soon after the event, her child was born premature and died. (Court relied upon *Bell* and *Byrne*.)
       (a) **Kennedy limitation**: The shock must be a *reasonable fear* of *immediate personal injury* to oneself.
       (b) Limitation was used for some time to *limit* the scope of liability for nervous shock.

4. **Expansion** to include: **[487]**
   a. **Parent in fear for safety of child**.
      (1) Parents must perceive the injury or near miss with their own unaided senses.
          (a) *Hambrook v Stokes Bros.* [1925] 1 KB 141. The plaintiff saw a lorry out of control heading for her four children. She suffered nervous shock, suffered a miscarriage and died. Although the mother herself was never in harm's way, the court extended liability to include the experience she witnessed with her own *unaided senses*. **Reasoning**: Absurdity to deny remedy where had mother feared for her own safety the claim would have succeeded.
          (b) *Kralj v McGrath* [1986] 1 All ER 907. Recovery allowed for a mother who suffered nervous shock when she saw the condition of her baby, who was the victim of a negligent delivery.
   b. **Person in fear for safety of family member**, but person did not witness the accident or occurrence.

(1) *McLoughlin v O'Brian* [1982] 2 All ER 298. The plaintiff recovered for the severe psychological injuries she suffered (including a personality change) after seeing the injuries of her spouse and children (in hospital) caused by the defendant's negligent driving.

(2) *Mullally v Bus Éireann* [1992] ILRM 722 (HC). The plaintiff recovered for post traumatic stress disorder she suffered as a result of searching for her family members in two different hospitals and viewing her family members and victims immediately after a bus crash caused by the defendant's negligence.

(3) **Shock need not be caused by accident.** [488]

(a) *Broomfield v The Midland Health Board* (1990) (HC). The defendant's hospital gave the plaintiff another person's baby. After nine days, the mistake was ratified. The defendant refused or failed to give the plaintiff documents concerning her child until a year after the event.

c. **Person in fear of safety of friend.**

(1) *Dooley v Cammell Laird and Co. Ltd* [1951] 1 Lloyd's Rep 271. The plaintiff, a crane operator, witnessed a load dropping into the hold of a ship and feared injury to his workmates. A duty was held to be owed to the plaintiff.

5. **No expansion** [489]

a. **Person in fear of injury to property** is generally not recognised.

(1) *Attia v British Gas* [1988] QB 304. The defendant negligently installed central heating in the plaintiff's home, causing a fire. When the plaintiff returned home and found her home on fire, she suffered nervous shock. Claim allowed.

(2) *Campbell v Animal Quarantine Station* 632 P.2d 1066 (Hawaii 1981). The plaintiffs recovered for 'emotional distress' where their nine-year-old pet dog died of heat stroke after being negligently put into a van with no ventilation by the defendants. [490]

b. **Non-sudden shocks**: For liability the shock *must* be sudden.

(1) *Sion v Hampstead Health Authority* (1994) unrep. The plaintiff was denied recovery for his stress-related psychiatric illness caused from watching his son slowly die in intensive care because of negligent medical treatment.

Recovery denied because the illness was not caused by a sudden shock.

c. **Person in fear for safety of a stranger: Generally cannot recover.** [491]

   (1) *Bourhill v Young* [1943] AC 92. A woman exiting a tram heard a serious accident outside her field of vision. She went to the scene of the accident and suffered nervous shock. Her child was stillborn shortly thereafter. Claim for nervous shock failed. Reasoning:

     (a) Plaintiff outside '*area of impact*'.

     (b) Person injured was a total *stranger*.

     (c) Plaintiff outside *foresight of shock*.

   (2) **Rescuers exception**: A rescuer may recover for nervous shock based upon fear for the safety of a stranger if the rescuer comes upon an accident and assists and also exposes himself to potential physical injury. [492]

     (a) *Chadwick v British Railways Board* [1967] 2 All ER 945. The plaintiff helped the official rescue teams at the scene of a train crash. He suffered nervous shock and eventually committed suicide. Recovery allowed. **Note**: The rescuer in *Chadwick* was distinguished in *White* [496] because he was foreseeably exposed to physical injury in entering the damaged railroad cars.

     (b) **Rescuer as a primary victim**: A rescuer that witnesses an accident is a primary victim and may recover for nervous shock even though he suffered no physical injury during the rescue. *Hale v London Underground* (1992) 11 BMLR 81.

d. **Fear of contracting an illness** [493]

   (1) *Fletcher v Commissioners of Public Works* [2003] 2 ILRM 94 (SC). The Supreme Court refused to allow the plaintiff to recover damages for psychiatric injury resulting from an irrational fear of contracting a disease because of the plaintiff's negligent exposure to health risks by his employer, where the risk was characterised by medical advisors as being very remote.

6. **Present status of nervous shock in Ireland** [494]

  a. *Kelly v Hennessy* [1995] 3 IR 253. The plaintiff's husband and daughters were involved in a car crash. The husband and one daughter suffered brain injuries. The Supreme Court set out six principles to determine whether a plaintiff suffering nervous shock comes within the defendant's duty of care.

(1) Plaintiff must suffer a *recognised psychiatric illness*.
  (a) **Note**: Post traumatic stress disorder *is* a recognised psychiatric illness.
(2) Plaintiff's illness *must* arise from *shock*.
(3) It must be *foreseeable* that the defendant's act or the event *could cause* psychiatric injury.
(4) The illness must result from the *perception of actual injury* or a *risk of injury* to oneself or another person.
  (a) *Curran v Cadbury Ltd* [2000] 2 ILRM 343 (CC). The plaintiff sustained injury when she turned on a machine at work and thought that she had killed a co-worker who, unbeknownst to the plaintiff, was working inside the machine.
(5) If harm results from exposure to *aftermath*, there must be a *close personal relationship* between victim and plaintiff.
  (a) **Aftermath**: Continues as long as the victim remains in the state caused by the accident, i.e. until he receives immediate post-accident treatment. *Jaensch v Coffey* (1984) 54 ALR 417. (*Dicta*)
(6) There are *no public policy limits* on the recovery where the plaintiff establishes sufficient proximity and foreseeability by fulfilling the five criteria above.

7. **Present English approach**: The Hillsborough football stadium disaster cases.   **[495]**
  a. **Note**: Present English approach is a retraction from previous liability expansion for nervous shock, and generally more restrictive than the Irish approach.
  b. *Alcock v Chief Constable of South Yorkshire* [1991] 4 All ER 907. In 1989, ninety-five people were crushed to death and 400 were injured at a football match when police negligently allowed too many people into the stadium. The 150 plaintiffs were friends and family of the dead and suffered nervous shock.
    (1) Categories of perception by plaintiffs included:
      (a) **Direct.** Plaintiff at stadium and saw disaster occur.
      (b) **Televised**. Plaintiff saw disaster on television.
      (c) **Travelled to stadium.** Plaintiff went to the stadium to look for family member or friend and learned of death.

(d) **Told of death/injury**. Plaintiff told of the death of his family/friend by a third party.

(e) **Morgue identification**. Plaintiff had to identify family member or friend in temporary morgue at the stadium.

(2) **Reasonable foreseeability test**: Secondary victims must prove that psychiatric injury was a *reasonably foreseeable* consequence of the defendant's negligence.

(a) Psychological damage must be caused by the plaintiff suffering a sudden and unexpected shock. Excludes:

(b) Psychiatric illness as a result of grief; or

(c) Stress from looking after someone injured by the negligence of the defendant. **[496]**

c. *White and Others v Chief Constable of South Yorkshire* [1999] 1 All ER1. Same event as outlined above in *Alcock*, but this case dealt with the rescuers, i.e. secondary victims, required to meet *Alcock* test of reasonable foreseeability. Rescuers not in a special position regarding psychiatric damage must show objectively that he had been exposed to physical danger.

(1) *Alcock* **test explained**: For a bystander, foreseeability would occur when a person of *reasonable fortitude* would be likely to suffer psychiatric injuries.

(2) **Susceptibility to shock**: If a person suffers psychiatric injury because he is unusually susceptible to shock, reasonable foreseeability is *not* proved.

(a) **Egg shell psyche**: If bystander of normal fortitude would be likely to suffer psychiatric injury, it does not matter that the psychiatric injury is made *more serious* by the personal characteristics of the plaintiff.

(b) **Note**: This is *not* the same as the general egg shell rule that a defendant takes his victim as he finds him.

(3) **Psychological damage** must be a *recognised* psychiatric illness. **[497]**

(a) **Primary victim defined**: A person put in danger of physical harm, but actually suffers only psychiatric injuries.

(b) **Secondary victim defined**: A person not in danger of physical injury, but suffers psychiatric harm as a result of witnessing injury to another.

8. **American approach** [498]
  a. Generally, for the tort of negligent infliction of emotional distress, plaintiff must suffer some physical manifestation of emotional distress.
    (1) Recognised physical manifestation may vary from:
      (a) Miscarriages and heart attacks; to
      (b) 'Panic attacks' with extreme abdominal pain. *Olson v Connerly*, 445 NE2d 706 (Wis. 1989).
      (c) Must be shown by objective symptoms such as weight loss, loss of sleep, general physical deterioration. *Corrigal v Ball and Dodd Funeral Home Inc.*, 577 P.2d 580 (Wash. 1978).
  b. Some jurisdictions allow recovery without any 'physical manifestation of emotional distress'.
    (1) Erroneously reporting a close relative's death.
      (a) *Johnson v State*, 37 NY2d 375 (1975). The plaintiff recovered where a hospital advised her that her mother had died, when in fact she had not died.
    (2) Mishandling the corpse of a relative.
      (a) *Cohen v Groman Mortuary*, 231 Cal.App.2d 1 (1964). The defendants negligently caused the corpse of the plaintiff's husband to be mutilated in public.
    (3) **Rationale**: These cases involve a high likelihood of genuine and serious distress.
  c. **Fear of future harm** [499]
    (1) Used primarily in context of toxic or environmental exposure resulting in the plaintiff seeking damages for the mental anguish suffered for fear of contracting a disease in the future. Often referred to as 'cancerphobia'.
    (2) Most jurisdictions in the US are wary of permitting recovery because of:
      (a) The difficulty in measuring damages;
      (b) The potential of crushing liability (floodgates); and
      (c) The serious proof difficulties.
    (3) Two types of approaches used.
      (a) Without physical injury, recovery of damages for fear of cancer in a negligence action is *limited* to cases where the plaintiff proves that it is probable that he will develop cancer in the future due to exposure. *Potter v Firestone Tire and Rubber Co.*, 863 P.2d 795 (Calf. 1993).

(b) The plaintiff may recover for serious mental distress arising from the fear of developing cancer where the fear is *reasonable* and causally *related* to the defendant's negligence. *Hagerty v L. and L. Marine Services, Inc.*, 788 F.2d 315 (1986).

C. Death [500]

1. **Death of a party**
   a. **Traditionally**: Under the common law, the death of one of the parties ended all actions in personal torts.
   b. **Statutory exceptions** to the common law rule allowed actions for personal torts to continue.
      (1) **Examples**:
         (a) Section 117, Road Traffic Act 1961 regarding personal liability for negligent driving.
         (b) Section 23, Air Navigation and Transport Act 1936 for damages caused by aircraft to persons or property.
   c. **Civil Liability Act 1961 (CLA): Abolished the common law rule.** [501]
      (1) **General rule**: The death of either party does not extinguish the action.
         (a) **Transferred to estate of deceased: Section 7** provides that all tort actions are transferred to the estate of the deceased.
         (b) **No transfer: Section 6** excludes defamation, seduction and claims for worker's compensation.
         (c) **Damages: Section 7(2)** provides that damages are confined to economic losses and property damage. All personal damages (pain and suffering, etc.) are often said to have died with the plaintiff.
      (2) **Limitations**: With regard to death: [502]
         (a) **General rule: Section 9(2)** of the CLA 1961 provides that the ordinary limitation period applies. If the plaintiff fails to bring an action within the specified timeframe, no action may be brought. See [605] *et seq* for limitations. [503]
         (b) **Exception to general rule**: If the action was not pending at the time of death, it must be brought within the normal period or within two years of death, *whichever* is shorter.

        i. In *Moynihan v Greensmyth* [1977] IR 55, the Supreme Court upheld the constitutionality of this provision as reflecting a reasonable balance between the competing interests of the parties.

    (c) **Note**: The limitation period with regard to death does not apply to claims under the Liability for Defective Products Act 1991, see [306] and [323].

2. **Wrongful death**: The defendant wrongfully caused the death of another. **[504]**

    a. **Common law rule**: The death of a human being could not be the basis of a cause of action.

       (1) **Note**: Under the common law, it was cheaper to kill than to injure another.

    b. **Statutory reform: Civil Liability Act 1961** **[505]**

       (1) **Section 48(1)**: An action may be brought for the benefit of the dependants of the deceased against the person causing the death. (The plaintiff is the dependent of the deceased.)

       (2) The defendant's conduct must have been an actionable wrong against the deceased.

         (a) In other words, if the decedent had lived, he must have had an action against the defendant.

    c. **Section 48(2)**: Only *one action* is allowed.

       (1) **Example**: If a man is injured and dies because of the negligent acts of another, the deceased's four dependent children cannot each bring an action separately.

    d. **Section 47(1)**: A dependent is any member of the family of the deceased suffering injury or mental distress because of the death.

       (1) **Expansion** of dependent classes of persons was made under the Civil Liability (Amendment) Act 1996.

         (a) **Section 47(1)(b)**: A former spouse may be a dependent.

         (b) **Section 47(1)(c)**: A person in co-habitation with the deceased for three years prior to his death.

    e. **Special period of limitation** **[506]**

       (1) The action must be brought within *three years* from the death, Statute of Limitations (Amendment) Act 1991, section 6(1). See [623] and [624] for amendments.

    f. **Damages for wrongful death**: Section 49.

       (1) **Emotional distress**

(a) Has a recovery cap of £20,000 (1996 Act).

(b) Not available to former spouses.

(c) **Note**: A family member may still maintain their own action for nervous shock under proper circumstances. See [482].

(2) **Expenses**

(a) Costs of funeral.

(b) Medical bills related to death.

(3) Injury suffered.   [507]

(a) Loss of financial support due to the death. *Gallagher v ESB* [1933] IR 558.

(b) Loss of services for work in home. *Cooper v Egan* (1990) unrep. HC. Financial valuation made for work performed in the family home.

(4) **Damages calculated**: Without reference to the gain, e.g. insurance, or loss (except funeral costs) caused by the death.

6

BREACH OF THE DUTY OF CARE

Chapter synopsis

I.   General principles of breach
II. Act or omission (failure to act) by defendant
III. Determining unreasonable conduct
IV. *Res ipsa loquitur* (the thing speaks for itself)

I. General principles of breach   [508]

A. *Once it is found that the defendant owed a duty of care to the plaintiff,*

1. Then it must be shown that the defendant *breached* this duty through an act or omission (failure to act).
2. The breach must be unreasonable under the circumstances.

II. Act or omission (failure to act) by defendant   [509]

A. *The defendant's act must be a voluntary act by defendant. See [14].*

1. **Voluntary**: Meaning under defendant's conscious control.
   a. **Example**: A person whose hand is physically forced by another person to pull down a lever, allowing the escape of a dangerous substance, did not act voluntarily.

B. A **negligent** *act is said to be:*   [510]

1. Act or omission (failure to act) by the defendant;
2. With a duty of care owed to the plaintiff; and
3. Breach of that duty by defendant's unreasonable conduct.

C. **Omission**: *Or a failure to act may be the basis for liability in negligence.*   [511]

1. **Note**: Only when the defendant is under a duty to perform an act.
2. See affirmative duties [380] *et seq.*

III. *Determining unreasonable conduct*   [512]

A. **Balancing test:** *The defendant's act or conduct is not considered unreasonable if the* magnitude of the risk *involved to plaintiff is less than the* utility of the defendant's conduct.

Magnitude of risk to plaintiff	Utility of the defendant's act(s)
-likelihood of harm	-social value of the def.'s act(s)
-gravity of threatened harm	-cost of eliminating the risk

B. *Magnitude of risk*   [513]

1. **Likelihood of harm**: Generally, the less the risk of injury, the less the likelihood of liability.
   a. **Example**: *O'Gorman v Ritz (Clonmel)* [1947] Ir Jur Rep 35. The plaintiff stretched her legs under the seat in front of her. The occupant caused the plaintiff's leg to be cut by the seat. At trial, evidence heard that in the previous seven years nearly 1 million people had used the seats without injury or complaints. The trial court dismissed the action.
   b. **Injury not foreseeable**:
      (1) *Plunkett v St Lawrence Hospital* [1952] 86 ILTR 157. It was not foreseeable that a quiet patient, barely able to move due to a suspected spinal injury, would fall off of an X-ray table.
      (2) **Contrast with** *Walsh v Dublin Corp.* (1998) (HC). The plaintiff, a visitor to a flat owned by the defendant, suffered an injury to her thumb when a door slammed on it due to 'wind tunnel effect' in the flat. The case was dismissed, as such an injury could happen to anyone at any time.
   c. **Injury foreseeable**: Possibility of harm need *not* be *probable*, just *possible.*
      (1) **Example**: *Kelly v Governors of St Lawrence Hospital* [1988] IR 402. Liability imposed where patient admitted to hospital was taken off all drugs for epilepsy and was allowed to go to toilet unattended. The patient jumped from a window.

2. **Gravity of threatened harm**   **[514]**
   a. Where potential harm is great, the creation of the slightest risk to plaintiff may constitute negligence.
   b. For the defendant's acts or conduct to be reasonable, the defendant's conduct must meet the risk created.
      (1) **Classic example**: *Paris v Stepney Borough Council* [1951] 1 All ER 42. The plaintiff had only one good eye and was working as a welder for the defendant. Unfortunately, the plaintiff was blinded by a welding injury to his good eye in the course of his employment with the defendant. The court held that the defendant had failed to meet his duty of care toward the plaintiff. It ruled that the precaution expected for the plaintiff was higher than that expected for persons with normal vision.
   c. The nature and extent of the threatened harm significantly impacts on determining the standard of care owed.
      (1) *Fitzsimmons v Bord Telecom Eireann and the ESB* [1991] 1 IR 536. The plaintiff's spouse was electrocuted when he attempted to move a fallen telephone cable that came into contact with an electric cable.
   d. Once there is a foreseeable possibility of harm, the standard of care expected from a defendant owing a duty must be commensurate to the risk involved in order to be considered reasonable. *Kelly v Governors of St Lawrence Hospital* [1988] IR 402.

C. *Utility of the defendant's conduct*   **[515]**

1. **Social value of defendant's conduct**
   a. An act of high social utility or value will be regarded as reasonable.
      (1) **Example**: *Whooley v Dublin Corporation* [1961] IR 60 (HC). The plaintiff was injured when she stepped into an open fire hydrant box. She alleged the defendant was negligent in the easy access design. **Held**: Social purpose of easy access (quick response to fires) outweighed the protection of the public against malicious interference with the hydrants.
2. **Social value is not absolute**   **[516]**
   a. **Example**: Police driving in course of employment must still exercise reasonable care in the circumstances.
      (1) *Marshall v Osmond* [1983] 2 All ER 225. Police officer caused injury while in pursuit of a joy rider. While

officer's driving was held not to be negligent, court noted that similar driving by a civilian would be negligent.

(2) *Strick v Tracey* (1993) (HC). While escorting a civil defence fire tender to a fire, police entered an intersection well in front of the fire tender. A collision occurred between the tender and another vehicle. All three drivers held negligent. Police allowed too much space between emergency vehicles. Fire tender failed to take steps to halt traffic in intersection. Motorist negligent in assuming the emergency had passed.

3. **Acts with no social value or utility** are regarded as unreasonable, even if the risk of injury is small. [517]
   a. **Classic example**: There is a big difference between throwing a burning object from a house onto the street below for fun and throwing it in order to save the house from fire. (Fleming)

4. **Cost of eliminating the risk**: A slight risk is reasonable if the cost of eliminating it is high.
   a. **Example**: *O'Gormon v Ritz*, see [513]. All cinema seats could be made completely safe, but at what cost?

5. The cost of eliminating the risk is not limited to economic factors.
   a. **Example**: *Muldoon v Ireland* [1988] ILRM 367 (SC). The court found that while it would be possible to implement a system of security that would prevent prisoners from stabbing one another in a prison yard, the intrusion upon the civil rights of the prisoners by severe security means would not be proportionate to the objective of reducing risk to other prisoners. Therefore, it was held that there was no breach of duty as the present system of supervision of prisoners was reasonable.

6. Quill notes that the cost-benefit analysis has a recognised role in the setting of behavioral standards outside the US, but it is less developed. He points out that the cost-benefit analysis suffers from three major deficiencies:
   a. Economic values are not the only values that a society may want to pursue.
   b. Evidence of relevant economic facts may be difficult to obtain.
   c. Decision makers (judge or jury) may not be equipped to evaluate the evidence which is available, so that a fair result might not be obtained.

IV. Res ipsa loquitur *(the thing speaks for itself)*   [518]

A. *Types of evidence*

1. There are two basic forms of evidence that a plaintiff can use in attempting to establish negligence by the defendant:
   a. **Direct evidence**: Evidence that comes from personal knowledge or observation, such as from an eyewitness.
      (1) **Examples**:
          (a) A security camera captures a car crash on film.
          (b) An eyewitness to the defendant's acts.
   b. **Circumstantial evidence**: Is proof that requires inferences to be drawn from other facts.
      (1) **Examples**:
          (a) Hoof prints in the sand indicate that a horse walked across the beach earlier.
          (b) Skid marks at the scene of a car crash indicate that the driver braked.
2. There are some incidents or injuries that are of a type that normally do not occur without negligence.
   a. If this type of injury or incident occurs and there is no direct evidence, *res ipsa loquitur* may apply.

B. *Development of* res ipsa loquitur   [519]

1. First articulated in *Byrne v Boadle* [1863] 159 E R 299.
   a. Chief Baron Pollock stated in *Byrne* that 'There are certain cases of which it may be said *res ipsa loquitur*, and this seems one of them. A barrel could not roll out of a warehouse without some negligence, and to say that the plaintiff who is injured by it must call witnesses from the warehouse to prove negligence seems to me preposterous.' See [524] for facts.
   b. The fact that a particular harm occurs may tend to establish a breach of the duty of care.
2. ***Res ipsa loquitur* overview**   [520]

---

1. Incident or injury must be of a type that normally does not occur in the absence of negligence, and
2. The source of negligence must be within the scope of a duty that the defendant owes to the plaintiff.
3. The plaintiff must prove that the defendant had *sole control* of the incident.
4. That the defendant had *knowledge denied* to the plaintiff.

> 5. That the *damage* would *not normally happen* without some element of negligence by the defendant.
>
> **Procedural effect**: The onus or burden of proof shifts from the plaintiff to the defendant.

C. *Required elements of* res ipsa loquitur   [521]

1. The first two required elements for *res ipsa loquitur* were first articulated in *Scott v London and St Katherine Docks Co.* (1865) 159 ER 665. Bags of sugar fell from a hoist, injuring the plaintiff.
    a. Incident or injury must be of a type that normally does not occur in the absence of negligence, and
    b. The source of negligence must be within the scope of a duty that the defendant owes to the plaintiff.
2. The plaintiff must prove that the defendant had *sole control* of the incident.   [522]
    a. **Examples**:
        (1) Operation of vehicle. *Corcoran v West* [1933] Ir 210 (HC).
        (2) Operation of aircraft. *Fosbroke-Hobbes v Airwork Ltd* [1937] 1 All ER 108.
    b. Sole control has expanded to include management of the incident.
        (1) *Mullen v Quinnsworth* [1990] IR 59 (SC). Clear cooking oil on the defendant's store floor was held to be under the management of the defendant.
    c. **No control**: Where the defendant did not have the right to control at the time of the injury.
        (1) *Tracey v Hagen* (1973) unrep. (SC). The plaintiff was injured by a machine six months after it left the defendant's control. *Res ipsa* was denied.
3. That the defendant had *knowledge denied* to the plaintiff. [523]
    a. **Note**: This does not relieve the plaintiff of the onus of proving that the thing that caused the injury was under the defendant's control.
        (1) *Hanrahan v Merck Sharp and Dohme* [1988] ILRM 629 (SC). The plaintiffs brought a nuisance action premised on negligence claiming that emissions from the defendant's

factory were damaging their health and killing their cattle. *Res ipsa* **denied**: It does not apply only when the evidence is more accessible to the defendant. Plaintiff must prove that the thing that caused injury was under the defendant's control. See [280], [525] and [723].

(2) *O'Mahony v Tyndale* (2000) unrep. (HC). The plaintiff's injuries at birth were alleged to have occurred because of the negligence of the defendant. While defendant hospital had been found wanting, plaintiff did not prove that disabilities were caused by it.

4. That the damage would not normally happen without some element of negligence by the defendant. **[524]**

   (a) *Byrne v Boadle* [519]. A barrel of flour fell out of an upper-storey window of the defendant's warehouse. It landed on the plaintiff, causing serious injuries.

   (b) *Daniel v Heskin* [1954] IR 73 (SC). A needle broke while the defendant doctor was stitching the plaintiff. The court held that *res ipsa* did not apply. Evidence showed that while surgical needles usually broke because of improper technique by the doctor, in this case it could have broken because of a flaw in the needle.

5. **Causal connections** **[525]**

   (a) Traditionally, the successful plaintiffs have been able to show what caused the injury, e.g. *Byrne v Boadle* [519].

   (b) However, the Supreme Court decisions in *Hanrahan* [523] and *Lindsay v Mid-Western Health Board* [526] have cast doubt on the need to be able to identify what caused the injury.

D. *Procedural effect of* res ipsa loquitur   **[526]**

1. If *res ipsa* is granted, the onus or burden of proof *shifts* from the plaintiff to the defendant.

2. The defendant has the onus of proving that he did not act negligently.

3. However, the defendant is not required to prove what injured the plaintiff.

   a. *Lindsay v Mid-Western Health Board* [1993] 2 IR 147 (SC). After surgery, a child suffered seizures and lapsed into a coma. Court ruled that the defendant, to avoid liability, had to show that he exercised reasonable care. *Not required to show what caused the injury.*

E. Medical malpractice cases often cause difficulties   **[527]**

    1. **Experts**: Sometimes experts are needed to determine whether negligence can be inferred from the event or the plaintiff's injuries.

      a. **Reasoning**: Finder of fact not competent to infer negligence from the injury in the course of complicated medical treatment. *Lindsay v Mid-Western Health Board* [1993] 2 IR 147 (HC). 'Medical science is not an exact one.' See [526].

    2. **Exception**: Even in medical malpractice, expert testimony is not required where negligence is obvious. **Examples**:

      a. *Mahon v Osborne* [1939] 1 All ER 535. The plaintiff had a swab left in him after surgery.

      b. *Ybarra v Spangard* 154 P.2d 687 (Cal. 1944). The plaintiff's shoulder was injured while he was unconscious and undergoing an appendectomy. The plaintiff sued everyone who might be responsible and all defendants denied liability or knowledge of the cause of the injury. The court held all defendants jointly liable.

F. Factual defences to res ipsa locquitur   **[528]**

    1. Defendant may defeat *res ipsa locquitur* by showing that he:

      a. Exercised reasonable care; or

      b. There was no causal link between his act or conduct and the plaintiff's injury. *Lindsay* [526]–[527].

G. Criticism   **[529]**

    1. Many legal commentators criticise *res ipsa* because it treats circumstantial evidence differently than it would normally be treated.

    2. The Canadian Supreme Court and the Australian High Court have announced the demise of the doctrine.

      a. Negligence litigation is to be resolved on the weight of the evidence.

      b. McMahon believes that such a trend would clarify Irish law.

    3. In the US, the doctrine has been used as a means of assuring that a case gets before a jury.

      a. However, legal commentators there question the need for the doctrine, alleging that with modern rules of discovery there is less need for the doctrine than when *Ybarra* was decided.

7

CAUSATION

Chapter synopsis

[530]

Causation
1. Causation is *not* limited to negligence. Causation applies to other torts too, but it generally arises in neglignce.
2. Causation is concerned with the link between the defendant's act or conduct and the harm suffered by the plaintiff.
3. There are two types of required causation:
   a. Actual (sometimes called cause in fact), and
   b. Proximate cause (sometimes called legal cause).

I. Actual cause   [531]

A. In general

1. The defendant's negligent act must have been the factual cause of the harm suffered by plaintiff.
2. If the negligent act is not the cause in fact of the harm suffered, there is no liability.
   a. **Note:** Negligence is not actionable per se.
   b. If the plaintiff did not suffer any harm (injury, loss or damage), she cannot maintain a cause of action in negligence against the defendant, regardless of how negligent the conduct of the defendant.

B. *'But for' test* [532]

1. **Traditional approach**: The *'but for'* test requires the plaintiff to prove by a preponderance of the evidence that more likely than not, the defendant's conduct was the cause of the harm suffered by plaintiff.
Examples:
   a. *Barnett v Chelsea Kensington Management Committee* [1969] 1 QB 428. The plaintiff's husband, a night watchman, went to the hospital after drinking a cup of tea and becoming ill. He died shortly after leaving the casualty ward, where he was seen by a nurse who consulted with a doctor over the phone. The decedent died of arsenic poisoning. The court concluded that the doctor had negligently failed to see the decedent, but since the decedent would have died anyway the harm was not *'but for'* the doctor's negligence.
   b. *Kenny v O'Rourke* [1972] IR 339. The plaintiff was injured when he fell off of a defective ladder. The jury found that the plaintiff fell due to leaning over too far on the ladder rather than due to the ladder's defect. Could not say that *'but for'* the defect in the ladder the plaintiff would not have been injured.
2. **Criticism** of the 'but for' test: The test is *not* able to adequately deal with: [533]
   a. **Successive** causes of harm;
      (1) *Dillon v Twin State Gas and Electric Co.* [545].
   b. **Simultaneous** causes of harm; or
      (1) *Summers v Tice* [541].
   c. **Uncertain** causes of harm.

C. *Concurrent liability: Addresses some of the problems.* [534]

1. Under the common law, three types of situations were distinguished relating to the plaintiff's injuries, damage or loss.
   a. **Joint liability**: Where the plaintiff's injury is caused by the joint or concerted conduct of two or more persons.
      (1) **Example**: Two men attack the plaintiff with sticks.
   b. **Several liability**: Where the negligence of two or more persons combine to cause the plaintiff's injury.
      (1) **Example**: The plaintiff is a passenger in a taxi, and due to the negligence of the taxi driver and another driver, the plaintiff is injured.
      (2) Under the common law, all of the defendants are

severally liable to the plaintiff. In other words, the plaintiff could sue each defendant for all the damage; however, the plaintiff could not bring a joint action against all the defendants.

c. **Joint and several liability**: Under the common law, all the defendants are jointly and severally liable to the plaintiff. In other words, each defendant is liable for the total amount of damages.

   (1) Where there was joint and several liability, a judgment against one defendant discharged the other.

   (2) The release of, or accord with, one defendant discharged the others.

d. **Independent liability**: Where the plaintiff suffers two distinct injuries caused by the independent acts of two or more persons.

   (1) **Example**: The plaintiff is hit in the head by his arch enemy, and while being rushed to the hospital the ambulance driver negligently drives into a tree and the plaintiff suffers a broken leg.

   (2) Under the common law, if there is independent liability, each defendant is liable for the injuries he or she caused only.

2. Civil Liability Act 1961

   a. The distinction between joint liability and several liability has been largely abolished by the Civil Liability Act 1961 (CLA 1961).

   b. The CLA 1961 treats joint tortfeasors and several concurrent tortfeasors in a similar manner, under the heading of concurrent wrongdoers.

   c. **CLA 1961, section 11(3): Concurrent wrongdoers** [535]

      (1) **Definition**: Where two or more persons may be responsible for the plaintiff's damage but it is not possible to establish which caused the damage, both are concurrent wrongdoers.

      (2) CLA 1961 allows total recovery against any of the defendants, leaving it to the defendants to work out liability under rules of contribution per part III of the Act.

3. **Person may become concurrent wrongdoer by**: [536]

   a. Vicarious liability of another;

   b. Breach of a joint duty;

   c. Conspiracy or a concerted action to a common end; and

   d. If independent acts cause the same damage.

4. **Note**: Generally bringing an action against one concurrent wrongdoer does not bar the plaintiff from bringing a cause of action against the other wrongdoers.
   a. However, a plaintiff cannot recover more damages than what he suffered.
5. **Liability** [537]
   a. Each concurrent wrongdoer is liable for the entire amount of damages.
   b. Except where one person caused independent items of damage, the court may apportion the damages.
6. **Contribution**: Joint Tortfeasors Act 1951, section 5 [538]
   a. **No** contribution is allowed to be made to a concurrent wrongdoer from a person who is entitled to be indemnified.
   b. **Example**: An employer will not be able to claim contribution from an employee who would be entitled to indemnification.
7. **Release**: Satisfaction of judgment [539]
   a. Under the common law, the release of one joint tortfeasor released *all* the joint tortfeasors.
   b. Sections 17 and 18 of the CLA 1961 abolished the common law rule.
   c. **Release or accord** (agreement on settlement) with one concurrent wrongdoer does not discharge the others *unless* the release and accord reflects such an intention to release all of them.

D. *The material and substantial factor test* [540]

1. **Definition**: The defendant's conduct will only be treated as a cause of an injury if it is a material element and a substantial factor in bringing about the injury.
2. **Historically**: Jermiah Smith is credited with proposing this approach in 'Legal Cause in Actions of Tort', 25 *Harv L. Rev* 102 (1911).
   a. Used in the US as a *supplement* to the 'but for' test where multiple causes would preclude a recovery for a plaintiff under the traditional rule.
   b. This test was adopted by Laffory J. in *Superquinn Ltd v Bray Urban District Council and Others* (1998) unrep. (HC). See [238], [288], [564] and [732].
3. **Simultaneous causes of harm**: Where two or more acts cause the harm. If one act is tortious and the other is not, both may be held to be legally liable. [541]

a. **American approach**: Onus shifting.
   (1) *Summers v Tice* 33 Cal.2d 80 (Calif. 1948). The two
       defendants negligently fired shotguns in the plaintiff's
       direction. Plaintiff was hit in the eye by one pellet, but
       could not tell which defendant fired the shot. Under the
       traditional 'but for' analysis, the plaintiff could not prove
       that *either* of the defendants caused her injury. The court
       shifted the onus to the defendants to prove that they
       were not the cause of the plaintiff's injury. Both defen-
       dants were unable to exculpate themselves, thus both
       were found liable as joint tortfeasors. **Note**: Neither
       defendant was innocent of wrongdoing, but only one
       caused the injury.
       (a) *Summers* shifting onus was later adopted by 2nd
           Restatement, section 433B.
   (2) **Expansion of *Summers***: *Haft v Lone Palm Hotel*, 478 P.
       2d 465 (Calif. 1970). The onus of proof of causation was
       shifted to the defendant where a father and his child
       drowned in the defendant's swimming pool. The plain-
       tiff was able to prove that the defendant breached a
       California safety statute requiring lifeguards or warning
       signs indicating no lifeguard service was provided.
       Because the statute was violated and the violation made
       it difficult for the plaintiff to prove the cause of the
       drownings, the court shifted the onus onto the defen-
       dant.   **[542]**
b. **English approach**: Substantial contribution test provides that
   where a defendant's negligence makes a substantial contribution to the plaintiff's harm, the defendant may be held liable.
   (1) *Pride of Derby v Celanese Ltd* [1953] 1 All ER 179. Three
       different sources polluted a river and this combined to
       damage the plaintiff's rights. All of the defendants were
       held liable for the pollution.   **[543]**
   (2) *McGee v National Coal Board* [1972] 3 All ER 1008. The
       plaintiff suffered dermatitis and alleged that it was
       caused by his exposure to brick dust at work. The work
       he performed did carry the risk of dermatitis. His
       employers were found negligent in failing to provide
       showers which would have lessened, but not eliminated,
       the risk of dermatitis. The House of Lords held
       that where a defendant's negligence made a *substantial*

contribution to the harm suffered, the defendant could be liable. It is not necessary to show that defendant's negligence was the sole cause.

(3) *Page v Smith II* [1996] 1 WLR 855. The Court of Appeal upheld the trial court's use of the *McGhee* test allowing the plaintiff to recover. The plaintiff was not physically injured in the car crash, but argued that the disease of chronic fatigue syndrome was reactivated and made worse by the mental shock he suffered as a result of the crash. See nervous shock [482].

(4) No onus shifting: Onus remains on the plaintiff to prove causation.   [544]

    (a) *Pickford v Imperial Chemical Industries* [1998] 1 WLR 1189. The plaintiff, a secretary, suffered repetitive strain injury after her employers increased her amount of typing. Evidence concluded that condition could be caused by (1) physical or (2) psychological factors or (3) both. The plaintiff was held required to prove the condition resulted from typing. The court did not shift the burden onto the defendant to prove that the cause was psychological.

4. Successive causes of harm   [545]

a. Under the traditional 'but for' test, a plaintiff would not be able to recover for successive causes of harm.

    (1) For example, in *Dillon v Twin State Gas and Electric Co.* 163 A. 111 (N.H. 1932), the defendant electric company's liability was limited to the value of the pain suffered by a boy electrocuted after falling from a bridge. The court held that the boy's life expectancy was negligible due to the fact his death was inevitable from the high fall. **Note:** Under the traditional 'but for' test, the plaintiff would not have been able to recover.

b. Where a second tortfeasor caused the plaintiff some additional loss, this does not relieve the first tortfeasor of all liability.   [546]

    (1) *Baker v Willoughby* [1970] AC 467. The plaintiff's leg was damaged due to the defendant's negligence, but later the plaintiff was shot in that leg. The leg had to be amputated. While the defendants argued that the later injury superseded their wrongdoing and ended their liability, the House of Lords disagreed.

(2) However, *Baker* does not give rise to a rule of continuing liability in all cases of multiple potential causes. *Jobling v Associated Dairies* [1981] 2 All ER 752 (HL).   **[547]**

(3) Leading Irish case is *L v The Minister for Health and Children* [2001] 1 IR 745. The plaintiff was infected with hepatitis C when treated for moderate haemophilia. The infection hurt his career opportunities and left him with a lower income. Later he was involved in a road accident, and his right leg was amputated. The question raised was whether the liability of the defendant for loss of income resulting from the hepatitis should stop at the time the plaintiff lost his leg. It was held that there was continuing liability on the part of the defendant.

c. **Note**: When dealing with successive causes of harm, determine if the second cause is a *novus actus interveniens* [568] breaking the chain of causation between the defendant's act and the plaintiff's injury, loss or damage.

5. **Uncertain causes** (often arises in medical malpractice)   **[548]**

   a. **American approaches**

      (1) **Reduction in the chance of survival**: *Herskovitz v Group Health Coopertive of Puget Sound*, 664 P.2d 474 (Wash. 1983). The court allowed the plaintiff to recover for the wrongful death of the decedent against the doctor whose malpractice significantly reduced the decedent's chance of survival (39 per cent dropped to 25 per cent). It was held that the reduction of the chance of survival was sufficient evidence to allow the jury to determine whether the increased risk to the decedent was a 'substantial factor' in causing the death. This case has been seen as a relaxing of the causation requirement.

      (2) **Loss of opportunity to survive**. *Falcon v Memorial Hospital* 426 N.W.2d 44 (Mich. 1990). 'But for' the doctor's negligence, the plaintiff's decedent's chance of survival would have risen from 0 per cent to 37.5 per cent. The court awarded the plaintiff 37.5 per cent of the wrongful death damages on the theory that the decedent had lost a 'substantial' opportunity for survival. In *Falcon* the court refused to relax the causation requirement, but instead formulated a new cause of action.

         (a) **Note**: The use of statistics in trials has been criticised by many courts and legal commentators. It is argued that statistics are unreliable, misleading, easily manipulated and confusing to a jury. *Fennell v Southern Maryland Hospital Center, Inc.* 580 A.2d 206 (Maryland 1990). **[549]**

(3) **Market share liability** has been imposed in some jurisdictions on industry groups when it is impossible to know which defendant was responsible for the plaintiff's injury.

(a) **Example**: In the famous case of *Sindell v Abbott Labs*, 26 Cal.3d 588 (Calif. 1980), the daughters of women who took an anti-miscarriage drug (DES) developed reproductive diseases, including ovarian cancer, as a result of the defendant drug manufacturer's negligence. Because the health problems developed years after DES was taken, it was usually impossible to determine which manufacturer had supplied the drug taken by any particular woman. Several courts required all producers of DES unable to prove non-involvement to pay a proportion of their percentage of the market share.

(b) **Market share liability was rejected** for asbestos cases. *Goldman v John Mansville Sales, Corp.* 514 NE2d 691 (OH 1987). The Ohio court found that asbestos products are distinguishable from other asbestos products. However, the approach has been followed for blood-clotting protein for haemophiliacs in *Smith v Cutter Biological Inc.* 823 P.2d 717 (Hawaii 1991). **[550]**

b. **English approach**: The plaintiff must prove that the defendant's act was a material cause of the injury suffered by the plaintiff.

(1) **Material cause requires** that on the balance of probabilities, the defendant's act caused the harm to the plaintiff.

(2) The House of Lords decisions generally provide that causation requires a preponderance of the evidence of 51 per cent and have rejected loss of chance arguments concerning causation.

(a) **Example**: *Hotson v East Berkshire Health Authority* [1987] AC 750. A child released from the hospital without proper diagnosis and treatment developed serious complications. Experts concluded that the child had a 75 per cent chance of developing complications if the proper diagnosis and treatment had taken place. The plaintiff failed to meet the preponderance of the evidence requirement.   **[551]**

(3) **Possibility vs probability**: *McGhee v National Coal Board* [1972] 3 All ER 1008 (HL).

    (a) *McGhee* **facts**: The plaintiff worked in the defendant's brick kilns, where he was exposed to hot and dusty conditions. No washing facilities were available. The plaintiff contracted a skin disease and alleged that if the defendants had provided washing facilities, he would not have caught the disease.

    (b) **Held**: The plaintiff established only a possibility rather than a probability and should have lost. However, the House of Lords unanimously held for the plaintiff and refused to distinguish between *conduct materially increasing risk and conduct materially contributing to the injury.*

    (c) **Lord Wilberforce**: (Onus shifting) where a person creates a risk and injury occurs within that area of risk, the burden of proof reversed and the defendant has to prove that his negligence was not the cause of the injury.   **[552]**

(4) **Material contributory cause**: The House of Lords rejected onus shifting and held that the burden of proof for establishing causation remains on the plaintiff throughout the case. *Wilsher v Essex Area Health Authority* [1988] AC 1074.

    (a) *Wilsher* **facts**: The plaintiff was born prematurely and due to the admitted negligence of a doctor was given too much oxygen. The plaintiff became blind. The medical evidence noted that while excessive oxygen in premature babies did cause blindness, it was not the only factor.

    (b) **Held**: The plaintiff had to prove that the breach of duty was at least a material contributory cause of the harm suffered. A cause is a material one if either it was more likely the cause of the blindness was the defendant's breach of duty more than any of the other four causes put together, or the breach of duty was more likely to be the cause than any other single cause. **[553]**

(5) **One noxious agent distinction**: Recently the House of Lords have held that a modified approach to causation is justified and the principle in *McGhee* was to be regarded as a rule of law. *Fairchild v Glenhaven Funeral Service Ltd* [2003] 1 AC 32.

  (a) *Fairchild* **facts**: The plaintiffs developed mesotheolioma, a form of cancer, as a result of exposure to asbestos while working for a number of employers. The plaintiffs could not establish on the balance of probabilities that exposure to asbestos had caused the cancer or was the result of any employer's breach of duty.

  (b) **Held**: In the special circumstances of this type of case, the normal 'but for' rule would be relaxed. *McGhee* was upheld. No distinction was to be drawn between making a material contribution to causing the damage and materially increasing the risk to the claimant. A material increase in the risk should be treated the same as if it had materially contributed to the risk. *Wilsher* survives on its own facts because of the number of possible agents involved.

c. **Irish approach** **[554]**

  (1) *Best v Wellcome Foundations Ltd* [1993] 3 IR 421 (SC). O'Flaherty J. cited *Wilsher* and the *Wilsher* interpretation of *McGhee* with approval.

  (2) Quill does not predict whether the Irish courts will follow *Fairchild* or stick with *Best*.

II. Proximate cause (legal cause) [555]

A. General principles

1. **After** proving actual cause, the plaintiff *must establish* that the defendant's act or conduct was the *proximate* or legal cause of the harm.

2. **Note: Proximate cause** is seldom a factor in intentional torts.

  (a) **Example**: If I throw a stone at you, I am liable if I hit you, even if there is little chance of the stone actually hitting you.

3. Scholars argue that the proximate cause requirement is a *policy issue* rather than the application of legal rules.   **[556]**
   (a) A variety of factors influence this policy issue, including:
      (1) Foreseeability of injury,
      (2) Intervening acts,
      (3) Acts of God, and
      (4) General social and economic policy goals.
4. After proving actual causation, the plaintiff may still lose if: **[557]**
   (a) The damage, loss or injury suffered is considered too remote.
   (b) A *novus actus interveniens* occurred, breaking the chain of causation between the defendant's act(s) and the injury, loss or damage suffered by the plaintiff.
5. **Note**: The defendant will not escape liability if the type of injury suffered by the plaintiff is foreseeable, but the extent of the injury is not. See egg shell skull rule [581].

B. *Remoteness*   **[558]**

1. **General principles**
   a. Even when actual cause is proven, the court may not hold a defendant liable if the causal relationship between the defendant's conduct and the plaintiff's injury is remote.
   b. The question is where a line should be drawn relieving the defendant of liability. Remember Mrs Palsgraf? See [373] *et seq*
      (1) The majority opinion by Cardozo reflects a reasonable foreseeability approach.
      (2) The dissent opinion by Andrews reflects a direct consequence approach.
   c. Some legal commentators use the example of the Chicago fire whereby a cow kicked over a lantern negligently left on the floor near the cow. Within a day half the city had burned. At what point does the defendant's liability end? The immediate neighbours, all the damage caused by the fire, or somewhere in between?
   d. Generally, remoteness issues arise in three areas.   **[559]**
      (1) **Unforeseeable manner** in which damage occurred.
      (2) **Unforeseeable results**: Where the damage is different than anticipated.
      (3) **Unforeseeable plaintiffs**.
   e. Under the common law, two different approaches are used to deal with the issue of remoteness:

(1) **Direct consequence rule,** and

(2) **Reasonable foreseeability rule**. **[560]**

2. **Direct consequence rule**: Usually associated with the case of *Re Polemis* [1921] 3 KB 560.

   a. **The rule**: The defendant is liable for *all* the direct consequences of his actions.

   b. *Polemis* **facts**: The defendant's employees were unloading the plaintiff's ship. One employee negligently knocked a plank into the hold. The defendant's employees did not know that gas fumes were in the hold. The plank created a spark that ignited an unforeseeable fire that destroyed the plaintiff's ship. The defendant was liable under the theory that he should be responsible for all harm directly caused. The fact that the explosion and fire were different damages than what could reasonably be anticipated from dropping a plank into a hold was found not to be relevant.

   c. **Note**: The direct consequence rule *always* applies to intentional torts.

3. **Reasonable foreseeability rule**: Was established in the famous case of *Wagon Mound I* [1961] AC 388. Applies in negligence cases. **[561]**

   a. **The rule**: Provides that the defendant is only liable for the harm that is reasonably foreseeable.

   b. *Wagon Mound I* **facts**: The defendant negligently spilled oil into Sydney harbour. A large amount of oil settled near the plaintiff's wharf. The plaintiff's employees were using welding equipment on the wharf and stopped welding to make inquiries about the safety of working with the oil on the water. After inquiries, they resumed working and some hot molten metal ignited some debris, which ignited the oil. The wharf was damaged in the resulting fire. The Privy Council held that the consequence (damage to the wharf) was not reasonably foreseeable.

      (1) *Wagon Mound I* approved in Ireland in *Burke v John Paul and Co. Ltd* [1967] IR 277 (SC). For facts see [447].

   c. **Defining 'foreseeable' and 'reasonably foreseeable'**: *Wagon Mound II* [1967] 1 A.C. 617. **[562]**

      (1) *Wagon Mound II* **facts**: The court attempted to define foreseeable and reasonably foreseeable. The owner of another ship destroyed in the fire sued the same defendant for the negligent discharge of the oil. The plaintiff

argued that the fire was a foreseeable risk of the spilled oil. The court held that while probability of fire was relatively remote, foreseeable means that the likelihood need not be great if the magnitude of risk would be significant. This would be especially true if there was no justification to incur the risk. The court held that if it is clear that the reasonable man would have realised or foreseen or prevented the risk, then the defendant is liable.

    (a)   *Wagon Mound II* approved in Ireland in *Wall v Morressey* [1969] IR 10 (SC).   **[563]**

  d. **Note**: The reasonable foreseeability rule is used in negligence and may be used in nuisance.

  e. **Note**: The reasonable foreseeability rule was used by the House of Lords in a *Rylands v Fletcher* action entitled *Cambridge Water Co. v East Counties Leather plc.* [1994] 1 All ER 53. See [280] and [283].

    (1)   *Cambridge* was endorsed in Ireland in *Superquinn Ltd v Bray Urban District Council and Others* (unrep. HC 1998). See [283].   **[564]**

4. **Present foreseeability test**: Focuses on whether the defendant should have reasonably foreseen as a risk of his conduct the harm suffered by the plaintiff.

  a. **Foreseeable result**: Even if the result was foreseeable, there will be no liability if there is an intervening act or force which takes place after defendant's act.

    (1) **Intervening force**: Where a new force that joins with the defendant's act(s) to cause the plaintiff's injury.

       (a)   Intervening force: Can be human, animal, mechanical or natural, such as a change of wind. See [568].

  b. **Unforeseeable**   **[565]**

    (1) **Unforeseeable results**: The defendant is not liable for unforeseeable harm. *Wagon Mound I*, see [561].

    (2) **Unforeseeable extent**: So long as the type of harm or general consequence is reasonably foreseeable, the extent of the harm need not be foreseeable.

       (a)   *Condon v CIE* (1984) (HC). The plaintiff was employed by the defendant and suspected of being responsible for a train crash. After a statutory inquiry, the plaintiff sought damages from the defendant and costs for being represented at the inquiry. **Held**: The plaintiff's damages were a reasonably foreseeable result of the defendant's negligence. **[566]**

(3) **Unforeseeable manner**: While the consequences or type of harm must be reasonably foreseeable, the precise manner in which the harm occurs is not required to be foreseeable.

   (a) *Egan v Sisk* (1996) (HC). The plaintiff's warehouse was flooded, ruining business brochures due to the defendant's negligence. The plaintiff sought damages for lost profits as the brochures could not be reprinted in time. The claim was allowed. **[567]**

(4) **Unforeseeable plaintiffs**: A duty of care is owed only to those persons reasonably foreseen to be injured by defendant's acts or omissions (failure to act). See *Donoghue v Stevenson* [370] and *Palsgraf v Long Island Railway* [373].

   (a) *Turner v Irish Rail* (1996) (HC). The defendant's fence near houses was not maintained. The plaintiff was injured when she went through the hole in the fence to look for her child. Flood J. held that the plaintiff's injuries were a direct consequence of the defendant's failure to provide adequate fencing. McMahon and Binchy note that it is clear from the facts that Flood J.'s view of the facts was that the plaintiff's agitation and fall were entirely foreseeable.

C. Novus actus interveniens – *new intervening act* **[568]**

1. *Novus actus interveniens* occurs when new forces join with the defendant's negligence to injure the plaintiff.

   a. The intervening forces can be:
      (1) Human, e.g. an act by a third party or an act by the plaintiff,
      (2) Animal,
      (3) Mechanical, or
      (4) Natural, e.g. a hurricane.

   b. Intervening: Requires that the force occurred *after* the defendant acted, but *before* the plaintiff suffered injury, harm or a loss. **[569]**

2. **General rule**: The defendant will not be liable if the intervening act or force is the sole cause of the plaintiff's injury, harm or loss.

a. This is because the intervening force becomes the legal cause of the plaintiff's injury.
b. **Example**: *Conole v Redbank Oyster Co.* [1976] IR 191 (SC). The defendants were testing a boat. It was found that the boat was not safe. Despite orders to tie up the boat, one of the defendant's employees took fifty children out on the boat. The boat sank. It was held that the decision to use the boat after the defect was discovered was the legal cause of the injuries. The reckless decision broke the causal connection between the alleged negligence of the manufacturer for the defect and the injuries. **[570]**
3. **Exception to general rule**: However, if the defendant causes the new intervening force, he may still be liable.
   a. In *Doran v Dublin Plant Hire* [1990] 1 IR 88 (HC), it was held that:
      (1) If the plaintiff acts and injures himself or another, the defendant will not escape liability for his prior negligence if the defendant caused the plaintiff's act to be dangerous.
   b. Likewise, if the defendant could reasonably foresee the new intervening act, he may still be liable if:
      (1) The defendant intended for the plaintiff or third party to act,
      (2) The plaintiff or third party acted as an inevitable response to the defendant's unlawful act, or
      (3) It was likely that the plaintiff or the third party would act in response to the defendant's unlawful act.
         (a) **Example**: *Smyth v Industrial Gases* (1950) 40 ILTR 1 (SC). The plaintiff was seriously injured when another child threw lime putty in his eyes. Other child found the putty on the road after it leaked from the defendant's cart. It looked like snow. **Held**: That the defendant should have reasonably foreseen the intervention, i.e. child throwing putty. **[571]**
   c. **Note**: If the intervening force is human in nature, foreseeability is not the sole test. The court will examine the:
      (1) Nature of the act,
      (2) The character of the act, and
      (3) The mental state of the intervening person.
4. **The act of a third party**: May be an independent sole cause making the defendant not liable, or may combine with the

defendant's wrongful act, making the defendant and third party
concurrent wrongdoers. See [534]. **[572]**

a. If the intervening person's acts are foreseeable, but not probable or likely, the court will look at the nature of his acts.

b. If the acts are intentional, criminal or reckless, the conduct will
probably be considered to be *novus actus interveniens*. The chain
of causation linking the defendant's conduct to the plaintiff's
injuries will be broken. (The defendant will not be liable.)

   (1) Sometimes intentional wrongdoing by a third party does
not break the chain of causation between the defendant's
acts and the plaintiff's injuries. *Breslin v Corcoran and
MIBI* [2003] 2 ILRM 189 (SC).

     (a) However, the Supreme Court upheld the trial
court's finding that the first named defendant was
not liable. He had left his car unlocked with the
keys in the ignition. It was stolen and struck and
injured the plaintiff.

   (2) McMahon and Binchy suggest that foreseeability and the
mental attitude of the intervenor are the key features
used by the courts in determining whether the new act
breaks the chain of causation.

c. However, gross negligence by the intervening person is generally not enough to break the chain of causation to relieve the
defendant of liability. **[573]**

   (1) **Example**: *Connolly v South of Ireland Asphalt Co.* [1977]
IR 99 (SC). While driving, C hit and killed a man. The
asphalt company had made potholes next to the road.
The holes filled with water and splashed onto the road,
rendering the road dangerous. The court held that the
gross negligence of C was not a *novus actus* extinguishing
the negligence of the asphalt company in failing to maintain the road. Gross negligence, i.e. objective recklessness, is not enough to break the causal chain.

5. **The act of the plaintiff** **[574]**

a. **Contributory negligence**: Occurs if the plaintiff's act adds to
or joins with the wrongful act of the defendant to cause the
plaintiff's injuries. See [586].

6. **Factors not *novus actus interveniens*** **[575]**

a. **Pre-existing conditions**: If the plaintiff's condition *combines*
with the defendant's negligence to cause an unexpected injury,
this is not a *novus actus interveniens*.

(1) The defendant must take the plaintiff as he finds him. See egg shell skull rule [581].

b. **Force set in motion** by the defendant's conduct is not an intervening act.   **[576]**

　(1) **Example**: A motorist driving negligently runs into a parked lorry loaded with watermelons, causing the melons to fall off of the lorry and onto a pedestrian. The melons are set in motion by the motorist.

c. **Omission (failure) to act**: Generally, a third person's failure to act may contribute to the plaintiff's injury and this is not considered an intervening act.

　(1) **Example**: While negligently operating a motor boat, the defendant strikes a swimmer. A fisherman sees the incident, but idly stands by, watching the swimmer drown. The fisherman's refusal or failure to act, i.e. attempt to save the swimmer or summon help, is not an intervening act.   **[577]**

　(2) **Exception**: When the third party was required to act.

　　(a) *Crowley v AIB and O'Flynn* [1988] 1 ILRM 225 (SC). The plaintiff was injured when he fell from the roof of a bank. He sued the architect that designed the flat roof without a rail. **Held**: No nexus between the architect and the injury. The link was broken by the fact that the boys played on the roof and the bank failed to stop them. The omission of the bank was a *novus actus interveniens*.

　　(b) *Daly v Guinness Peat Aviation Ltd Eurosec Protection Ltd and Mid-Western Health Board* (HC) (1998) unrep. The plaintiff was injured through the negligence of the first and second named defendants. The third defendant failed to render proper medical treatment and this attributed to the plaintiff's injuries. The court held that all three defendants were concurrent wrongdoers because negligence does not constitute a *novus actus interveniens*.   **[578]**

7. **English approach**: Where a force, event or act breaks the chain of causation, the defendant will only be liable for such damage as occurred *up to* the intervening force, event or act.

　a. **Example**: *Baker v Willoughby* [1969] 3 All ER 1528. The plaintiff injured his left leg because of defendant's negligence. Later he was shot by an armed robber, and his left leg was amputated. The defendant successfully argued that his liability only extended to the time of the armed robbery.

b. *Jobling v Associated Dairies* [1982] AC 794. The plaintiff was injured at work in 1973, rendering him 50 per cent disabled. In 1976, the plaintiff was diagnosed with a medical condition that had no connection with the work injury. Due to the new condition, he was rendered 100 per cent disabled. The House of Lords applied the 'but for' test strictly. The risk of unrelated medical conditions is habitually taken into account when calculating damages for future loss of earnings; it should not be ignored when it is already present.

c. *Thompson v Blake-Jones* [1998] Lloyd's Rep Med 197. The defendant doctor advised the parents of a six-month-old child not to immunise the child against measles. The parents talked to other doctors, and when the child was eighteen months old they decided not to have her immunised. The child caught measles and developed a rare condition which caused brain damage. The Court of Appeal held that the advice given by the other doctors was an intervening event which broke the chain of causation. It showed the parents were not relying on the defendant's advice.

8. **American approach** [579]
   a. Generally, courts characterise intervening forces as:
      (1) Dependent or stimulated by the defendant's negligence; or
      (2) Independent or not stimulated by the defendant's negligence.
         (a) **Example**: If X negligently knocks Y onto a high ledge, a rescuer's efforts to save Y is stimulated by X's earlier negligence and therefore is a dependent intervening force. If a mountain climber collides with Y on the ledge, the climber's actions were not stimulated by X's actions and would be characterised as an independent intervening force.
   b. **Superseding forces**: Whether an intervening force or act will supersede the original negligence depends on how improbable the intervening force is.
      (1) Superseding: Allows the earlier tortfeasor to be relieved of further responsibility.
      (2) **Intervening natural forces**: Storms may be superseding, but if an extraordinary violent storm could be anticipated,

then the storm is foreseeable and not superseding. (2nd Restatement, section 451) **[580]**

(a) **Exception**: Car accidents and medical malpractice have been held not to be superseding, although the odds of their occurring might be slight.

(b) **Example**: *Pridham v Casy and Carry*, 359a.2d 193 (1976). The plaintiff suffered a serious injury due to the defendant's negligence. The plaintiff died when the driver of the ambulance suffered a heart attack and drove into a tree while rushing the plaintiff to hospital. The defendant was held liable.

D. *Egg shell skull rule (also known as the thin skull rule)* **[581]**

1. **General rule**: The defendant must take the plaintiff as he finds him.
   a. Generally, the type of injury is foreseeable but the extent of the injury is not.
   b. **Classic example**: A negligently hits B on the head. Normally B would only suffer a minor bump or bruise, but B has an egg shell-like head and the knock to the head results in a catastrophic brain injury. A is liable for all of B's brain injuries.
   c. Egg shell skull rule alleged to have originated in *Dulieu v White*, 2 K.B. 669 (1901). See nervous shock [482].
3. This rule has survived *Polemis* and the *Wagon Mound* cases. **[582]**
   a. This rule has reduced the practical differences between:
      (1) *Polemis* – defendant liable for all consequences of his act; and
      (2) *Wagon Mound I* – defendant liable for the damages that are reasonably foreseeable.
2. **Personal injuries**: **Once any personal injury is foreseeable**, the particular type of harm need not be foreseeable. **[583]**
   a. **Physical injuries**
      (1) *Burke v John Paul and Co. Ltd* [1967] IR 277 (SC). The plaintiff suffered a hernia while cutting steel bars. The plaintiff had complained without success about the dullness of the cutting machine to his employer, the defendant. The defendant argued that it could not reasonably foresee the plaintiff might develop a hernia. Medical evidence showed that to develop a hernia a person must have some congenital weakness. **Held**: The tortfeasor has to take his victim as he finds him. See [561].

b. **Psychological injuries** [584]
  (1) Controversial: Courts and jurisdictions divided on this issue. See nervous shock [482].
      (a) *Malcolm v Brodhurst* [1970] 3 All ER 508. No difference in principle between egg shell skull and egg shell psyche.
      (b) *McCarthy v Murphy* (1998) (HC). The plaintiff suffered whiplash in a minor car accident and developed a depressive reaction which was due in part to an underlying depression condition. The egg shell skull rule was applied.

4. **Criticism** of the egg shell skull rule: [585]
  a. Many legal commentators believe that the application of the rule can be very harsh.
  b. A defendant can be held liable for injuries that were not foreseeable.

8

DEFENCES, LIMITATIONS AND DAMAGES

Chapter synopsis

Negligence defences
II. Limitations of actions
III. Damages

I. Negligence defences

A. Contributory negligence [586]

1. **Definition**: Contributory negligence is an act or failure to act by a plaintiff that is a contributing cause to her damage, injury or harm, and the act or failure to act falls below the required standard of reasonable care.
   a. The same act can be negligence and contributory negligence.
      (1) **Example**: See rescuers [376].
   b. Distinguished from negligence.
      (1) Negligence: The defendant owes a duty of care to others.
      (2) Contributory negligence: The plaintiff owes a duty to exercise reasonable care for his own protection.
   c. **Prior to Civil Liability Act 1961 (CLA 1961)**, contributory negligence afforded a complete defence to the defendant.
2. **CLA 1961, section 34(1)** [587]
   a. **General rule**: Damages must be *apportioned* between the parties where the damage suffered by the plaintiff results partly from the defendant's wrongful act and partly from the plaintiff's own negligence.
      (1) Apportionment based on fault is deeply rooted in civil law jurisdictions and admiralty law.
   b. **Exceptions to general rule** [588]
      (1) **Equal apportionment** will be made if it is not possible to establish the different degrees of fault.

(2) **Waiver**: Contributory negligence will not apply if the plaintiff agreed to waive his legal rights prior to the act.

    (a) Consent or voluntary assumption of the risk would apply instead. **[589]**

(3) **Note**: Any limitations imposed by contract or legislative enactments would still apply under waiver.

    (a) **Example**: If Fred agreed to waive his rights before he got into Ashley's rally car, he cannot defeat the defence of voluntary assumption of the risk by relying on contributory negligence apportionment.

c. **Defendant's onus**: Defendant must show that the plaintiff was negligent, i.e. the plaintiff's negligence caused some of the plaintiff's loss.

3. **Negligence of the plaintiff** **[590]**

a. **Principles of standard of care** are the same as those in negligence.

    (1) Did the plaintiff exercise reasonable care?

b. **Contributory negligence** is concerned with the plaintiff's contribution to his injury, not to the incident that caused the injury. **[591]**

c. **Test** for reasonable care is the objective reasonable person standard.

    (1) Would a reasonable person, under the same or similar circumstances, behave like the plaintiff?

d. **Causation**: The defendant's negligence must be at least part of the factual and legal cause of the plaintiff's injuries. This often raises the dilemma principle. **[592]**

    (1) **Dilemma principle**: This occurs where the defendant's negligence placed the plaintiff so that to avoid a greater inconvenience he chose to run a slight risk of injury or damage.

        (a) **Example**: *Sayers v Harlow UCD* [1958] 2 All ER 342 (CA). A woman locked in a lavatory was injured while trying to escape.

        (b) McMahon: Since apportionment, contributory negligence applies. **[593]**

4. **Duty to mitigate damages**: The plaintiff has a duty to take reasonable steps to reduce the loss resulting from the injury suffered.

a. **Failure to mitigate damage**: will lead to apportionment of the additional loss suffered under section 34(2b) of the CLA 1961.

b. **Examples**:
   (1) Failure or refusal to return to work.
   (2) Failure or refusal to undergo necessary medical treatment. **[594]**
5. **Imputed contributory negligence: Section 35(1)** of the CLA 1961 makes the plaintiff responsible for the conduct of others in certain circumstances, and the plaintiff's conduct is treated as contributory negligence.
   a. There are three basic areas where imputed contributory negligence arises:
      (1) Persons for whom the plaintiff is vicariously liable,
      (2) Cases where the plaintiff is not the immediate victim of the wrong, and
      (3) Cases involving concurrent wrongdoers.
   b. In order to establish that the plaintiff was contributorily negligent under this section, the defendant must show that the plaintiff or the person the plaintiff is responsible for was negligent and this negligence caused some of the loss.

B. Volenti non fit injuria *(voluntary assumption of the risk)* **[595]**
   1. **Traditional general rule**: If the plaintiff consented to the defendant's actions or conduct, the defendant may have the defence of consent (or as it was called in negligence, voluntary assumption of the risk).
   2. **After the CLA 1961, section 34(1)(b)**
      a. The plaintiff's consent to the risk created by the defendant's act(s) will not automatically evoke contributory negligence.
      b. However, the action *must* be dismissed if the defendant can show that:
         (1) The parties entered into a contract to exempt; or
         (2) The plaintiff agreed to waive his legal rights. *O'Hanlon v ESB* [1969] IR 75 (SC).
   3. **Waiver of legal rights**: Requires some sort of communication. *O'Hanlon*. **[596]**
      a. Communication requires more than mere notice.
         (1) **Example**: *McComsikey v McDermott* [1974] IR 75 (SC). The parties were together in a rally car. The plaintiff was navigating and the defendant was the driver. The plaintiff was injured when the rally car crashed. The issue of waiver was raised because of a notice on the dash that stated that passengers travelled at their own risk. The

notice was in the car when the defendant bought it, the parties joked about it and the court held that there was no real communication regarding the waiver. The defence was not available.

C. *Illegality (wrongful conduct)* [597]

1. *Ex turpi causa non oritur actio* defence: No action can be founded upon a wicked act.
2. The defence of illegality is based on the public policy objection to allowing a person engaged in an illegal activity from maintaining a lawsuit when injured during the course of the illegal activity.
   a. **Example**: *Ashton v Turner* [1981] QB 137. The plaintiff was injured while a passenger in a getaway car speeding away from a burglary he committed. The plaintiff sued the driver of the getaway car, but his claim was dismissed. English law refuses to recognise the existence of a duty of care owed by one participant in a crime to another in respect of an act done in furtherance of the crime.
3. **Scope of defence in Ireland** is not clear. [598]
   a. **Section 57(1) of the CLA 1961** provides that it is *not* a defence to *merely* show that the plaintiff was in breach of a civil or criminal law.
      (1) **Note**: Therefore, not every illegal act will bar the claimant from recovering in negligence.
      (2) **Example**: Dan is driving to work. Dan is not aware that the fuse that controls his brake lights has failed. Dan is driving in violation of the traffic regulations. If Sandra negligently drives into the side of Dan's car, his illegal act (driving with non-functioning brake lights) will not bar him from seeking damages from Sandra.
4. **English approach** [599]
   a. **General rule**: *Ex turpi* will apply to situations where the plaintiff, while engaged in a crime, is negligently injured by the defendant, who was not engaged in the crime.
   b. **Exception to general rule**: The only exception is for trespassers. [600]
      (1) **Example**: *Revill v Newberry* [1996] QB 567. R, an elderly man, slept in his garden shed to safeguard his possessions. N, with another man, tried to break into the shed while on a crime spree. R shot N with his shotgun

through the door of the shed. R was acquitted of wounding N. N then sued R and was awarded damages. The court relied on the duties imposed by the occupiers' liability statute on R, the occupier, to N, the trespasser. **[601]**

c. **Note**: There has been no expansion for failure to care cases.
  (1) **Example**: *Clunis v Camden and Islington Health Authority* [1998] 3 All ER 180 (CA). The plaintiff stabbed a man to death on the platform of the underground. The plaintiff had a long history of mental illness, and was convicted of manslaughter on the ground of diminished responsibility. He sued the defendant, alleging that the Health Authority had failed to care for him, and this failure caused him to kill, be convicted and incarcerated. His claim was dismissed.
  (2) *Worral v British Railways Board* (1999) unrep. (CA). The plaintiff alleged that he committed a number of sexual assaults because he had suffered a personality change due to the defendant's negligence. He sought damages for his imprisonment. His claim was dismissed. **[602]**

5. **Joint illegal enterprise**: Where one criminal makes a civil claim against another.
  a. Courts have had great difficulty in assessing when illegality will act as a bar.
    (1) English approach: English law refuses to recognise the existence of a duty of care owed by one participant in a crime to anther in respect of any act done in furtherance of the crime.
      (a) *Asherton v Turner* [1981] QB 137. The plaintiff was injured while a passenger in a getaway car speeding away from a burglary he committed. The plaintiff sued the driver of the getaway car, but his claim was dismissed. **[603]**
  b. Some courts have employed one of the following tests regarding joint illegal enterprise:
    (1) **Public conscience test**: Would it shock the public conscience if the plaintiff were allowed to recover?
      (a) Test rejected in England: *Tinsley v Milligan* [1994] 1 AC 340.
    (2) **Australian approach**: Considers whether there would have been a cause of action had there not been a joint

enterprise. *Jackson v Harrison* (1978) 138 CLR 438.

D. *Not valid negligence defences* [604]

1. It is not a valid defence to allege in a negligence cause of action:
   a. Necessity,
   b. Mistake, or
   c. Inevitable accident.
2. **Necessity**: The commission of a tortious act to prevent a greater evil where there is no reasonable alternative. See [85].
   a. **Necessity**: Only applies to intentional damage. It does not apply in negligence.
3. **Mistake**: Does not generally apply because of the emphasis on the standard of the reasonable person.
4. **Inevitable accident**: Is not relevant in negligence. See [87].
   a. In negligence, the burden is on the plaintiff to prove the defendant's fault.
   b. However, Winfield argues that it should apply in *res ipsa loquitur* because the defendant bears the burden of proof regarding whether he acted negligently.

II. *Limitations of action*

A. *General principles* [605]

1. The **Statute of Limitations 1957 (SOL 1957)** (as amended) sets forth the time limits within which all tort actions must be brought.
2. If an action is not brought within the specified timeframe, it cannot be brought and is said to be *statute barred*.
3. **Section 11(2)(a) of the SOL 1957** provides that tort actions shall be brought within *six years* of the date on which the cause of action *accrued*.
4. A cause of action accrues: [606]
   a. Once the tort is complete, or
   b. When all the elements required to establish the tort have come into existence.
      (1) **Example**: *Hegarty v O'Loughran* [1990] 1 IR 148 (SC). The cause of action accrued only when the personal injury manifested itself. The statute begins to run then.
         (a) Quill cites this case as being the leading Irish case.
            [607]

c. If the tort is actionable per se, the cause of action accrues (and the statute of limitations begins to run) at the time of the act.
d. If the tort is continuing in nature, a new cause of action accrues every day, i.e. continuing trespass.
e. If the tort is not actionable per se, the cause of action accrues when the damages occur.

B. *Personal injuries before 31 March 2005*   **[608]**

1. **Statute of Limitations Amendment Act 1991 (SOLAA 1991)**: Section 3 amended section 11(2)(a) of the SOL 1957. See [605].
2. Under the SOLAA 1991, the limitation period for personal injuries caused by negligence, nuisance or breach of duty is *three years* from the date of the accrual of the cause of action *or* later where relevant information was not known to the plaintiff. See SOLAA 1991 chart [623].
   a. **Section 2(1)**: If relevant information is not known, the statute begins to run from the date of the knowledge.
   b. **Note**: The extension of the limitation period for late discovery of vital knowledge *only* applies to *personal injuries*.
      (1) The extension does not apply to property damage or economic loss. *Touhy v Courney* [1994] 2 ILRM 503.

C. *Personal injuries after 31 March 2005*   **[609]**

1. **Civil Liability and Courts Act 2004 (CLCA 2004)**: On 21 July 2004 the CLCA 2004 was enacted, amending the SOLAA 1991. See CLCA 2004 chart [624].
2. **Section 7 CLCA 2004**:
   a. Amends section 3 of the SOLAA 1991: The limitation period for personal injuries is *two years* from the date of the accrual of the cause of action *or* later where relevant information was not known to the plaintiff.
   b. Became effective on 31 March 2005.   **[610]**

D. ***Date of knowledge:*** *Occurs when a person has under section 2(1) SOLAA 1991:*

1. **Knowledge of his injury**.
   a. **Example**: *Behan v Bank of Ireland* [1998] 2 ILRM 507 (SC). The plaintiff alleged that he had received bad advice from his bank. The plaintiff suffered a nervous breakdown because of the advice. The court held that the statute began to run on the

date on which he suffered the nervous breakdown, or was aware that the defendant's conduct has been harmful.

2. **That his injury is significant**.
   a. This is a subjective test.
   b. **Example**: *Gallagher v Minister for Defence* (1998) (HC). Army deafness claims.
3. **The injury was attributable** to the defendant's act or omission.
4. **Knowledge of the identity of the defendant**.
5. **Knowledge of the identity of any other person** who performed the act or omission along with the additional facts supporting the action against the defendant.
   a. **Example**: Vicarious liability, see [262] *et seq*.

E. Presumed knowledge [611]

1. The SOLAA 1991, section 2(2) presumes that a person:
   a. Will have knowledge of fact observable or ascertainable.
   b. Will have knowledge from facts ascertainable with the help of medical or other expert advice that is reasonable to seek.

F. Fraud [612]

1. **SOL 1957, section 71(1)** provides that the period of limitations does not begin to run until the plaintiff *has, or with reasonable diligence could have discovered*, the *fraud* of the defendant.
2. This provision could arise because the right of action is based on the defendant's fraud, or essential facts may have been concealed by the defendant from the plaintiff.
   a. **Example**: *Heffernan v O'Herlihy* (1998) unrep. (HC). A solicitor failed to inform his client that no proceedings had been instituted, and this was held to be a fraud under section 71(1). The court rejected the argument that the client could have discovered facts by searching the Central Office of the High Court.
   b. **Example**: *Tierney v Midserve Ltd and Genport Ltd* [2002] 3 IR 90. It was held that the failure to disclose a change of corporate ownership of a business constituted fraud. The business had been transferred from the first defendant to the second defendant without the statutory requirements having been met. The plaintiff was injured and the plaintiff's solicitor could not identify the second defendant. The second defendant was not allowed to claim that the action was statute barred.

G. Death [613]

1. **SOLAA 1991, section 6(1)** requires an action under section 48(1) of the CLA 1961 (wrongful death [504]) shall not be brought after the expiration of *three years* from the date of death or the date of knowledge of the person for whose benefit the action is brought, whichever is later.

2. **Deaths or accrual of action after 31 March 2005** [614]
   a. **CLCA 2004, section 7(e)** requires that an action under section 48(1) of the CLA 1961 shall not be brought after the expiration of two years from the date of death or the date of knowledge of the person for whose benefit the action is brought, whichever is later.

3. **Deaths or accrual of action before 31 March 2005** [615]
   a. **CLCA 2004, section 7(d)** requires that for any actions for fatal injuries, if the relevant date in respect of the cause of action falls before 31 March 2005, the action must be brought two years from 31 March 2005 or three years from the relevant date, whichever occurs first.

4. **Death of party and no case pending at death:** [616]
   a. **CLA 1961, sections 8 and 9** provide that in other actions, i.e. not involving fatalities, if a party dies and a case is not pending, it must be brought within two years of the date of death or within the statute of limitations, whichever is shorter.
      (1) **CLA 1961, section 8** provides that no causes of action can be maintained against the estate of a deceased unless the action was brought within the period of limitation and was pending at the time of his death; or pursuant to section 9.
      (2) **CLA 1961, section 9**: The action was brought within the first to expire of:
          (a) Two years from the date of his death, or
          (b) Within the required limitation period.

H. Disability [617]

1. **SOL 1957, section 49(1)** provides that the limitation period does not begin to run until the end of the disability or the death of the disabled party.

2. Disabilities may include:
   a. Persons under age;
   b. Persons of unsound mind;

(1) **Example**: A person suffering brain damage in an accident. *Rohan v Bord na Móna* [1991] ILRM 123.

c. A convict without an administrator or curator.

3. **Sexual abuse: The Statute of Limitations (Amendment) Act 2000** [618]
   a. **Section 2** added a fourth disability for victims of sexual abuse who are suffering from consequent psychological injury.
   b. **Section 3** allows the court to dismiss the action on the grounds that the interests of justice would not be served due to the delay.

I. Property damage and economic loss: Six years [619]

1. Defective buildings are difficult when attempting to determine when the cause of action accrued.
   a. *Pirelli General Cable Works Ltd v Oscar Faber and Partners* [1983] 1 All ER 65. The House of Lords found that the action accrues when the physical deterioration first occurs.
2. *Pierelli* approach adopted by Herbert J. in *O'Donnell v Kilsaran Concrete Ltd* [2002] 1 ILRM 551.

J. Various limitation periods [620]

1. **Contribution actions**: Case between two defendant wrongdoers, see [538].
   a. **CLA 1961, section 31** provides that a case may be brought:
      (1) Within the limitation period applicable to the plaintiff, or
      (2) Within two years after the liability of the claimant is ascertained, or
      (3) Within two years after the damages are paid, whichever is greater.
2. **Admiralty actions**
   a. **CLA 1961, section 46(2)** provides that all actions for damage or injury caused by the sole or concurrent fault of a vessel to another vessel, or to person or property on a vessel, must be brought within two years.
3. **Products' liability** [621]
   a. **Liability for Defective Products Act 1991, section 7** provides that an action must be brought within three years.
   b. The cause of action accrues on the date the plaintiff became aware, or should have been aware, of the damage, defence and the producer's identity, whichever is later. See [323].

4. Judicial discretion   [622]
  a. **SOL 1957, section 5** provides that the courts retain the power to refuse relief even if the case is brought within the prescribed time period.

Statute of Limitations (Amendment) Act 1991   [623]

S. 3	Personal injuries caused by negligence, nuisance or breach of duty (contract or under statute) shall be brought within three years of the date of injury. **See [608].**
S. 4	If an injured person under section 3 dies before the expiration of the three-year period, an action may be brought for the estate within three years from the date of death or the date of the personal representative's knowledge, whichever is later. **See [501]** *et seq.*
S. 5	**Extension of limitation period for disabilities:** An action under section 3 or under section 48(1) of the CLA 1961 (wrongful death), the person having the right to bring the action is under a disability at the time when the right accrued or at the date of his knowledge, the action may be brought at any time before the expiration of three years from the date when the disability ended or the person died, whichever event occurred first. **See [617].**
S. 6	**Period of limitation in case of fatal injuries:** An action under section 48(1) of the CLA 1961 shall not be brought after three years from the date of death or the date of knowledge of the person for whose benefit the action is brought, whichever is the later. **See [613].**

Civil Liability and Courts Act 2004   [624]

S. 7(a)	The Statute of Limitations (Amendment) Act 1991 is amended in section 3 with 'two years' for 'three years'.
S. 7(b)	…is amended in section 4 with 'two years' for 'three years'.
S. 7(c)	…is amended in section 5 with 'two years' for 'three years'.
S. 7(d)	…is amended in that if the relevant date of injury or discovery of knowledge falls before the commencement of section 7 of this Act (the Act was enacted on 21 July 2004), an action under sections 3, 4, 5 or 6 must be brought before

	the expiration of two years before the commencement of the Act or three years from the relevant date, whichever occurs first.
S. 7(e)	…is amended in section 6 with 'two years' for 'three years'.

III. Damages

A. Negligence is not actionable per se. **[625]**

1. **The plaintiff must prove an injury, loss or damage to his person or property.**
   a. **Person**: Includes both physical and/or mental injuries. See nervous shock [482] *et seq*.
   b. **Property**: Includes chattels and land.
      (1) Expansion: Has occurred for foreseeable pure economic losses. See [466].

B. Basic purpose of damages in negligence is compensatory. **[626]**

1. **Purpose**: To restore the plaintiff, as far as possible, to the condition the plaintiff was in prior to the injury, loss or damage.
2. Additional purposes:
   a. Vindication of rights.
   b. Deterrence.
   c. Public censure of tortious behaviour.

C. Types of damages **[627]**

1. There are three main types of compensatory damages:
   a. Special damages,
   b. General damages, and
   c. Aggravated damages.
2. There are also:
   a. Exemplary or punitive damages,
   b. Nominal damages, and
   c. Contemptuous damages.

D. Compensatory damages **[628]**

1. **Special damages**: The plaintiff is entitled to all economic losses and expenses incurred as a result of the injury. This would include:
   a. Medical costs,
   b. Lost wages,

    c. Business profits, and

    d. Property damages.

        (1) For destruction of personal property. Generally, property damage is measured by the:

           (a) Fair market value;

           (b) Cost of reproduction or replacement; or

           (c) Value to owner, excluding unusual sentimental value.

        (2) **Exception for impecunious (penniless) plaintiffs**

           (a) While a person acting reasonably in mitigating damages may take out a loan to repair a car, the cost of the loan may not be recoverable unless the plaintiff's impecuniosity is itself foreseeable. *Doran v Delaney II* [1999] 1 ILRM 225.

2. **General damages**: Or damages inherent to the injury itself. **[629]**

    a. Pain and suffering (past, present, future).

    b. Disfigurement.

    c. Disability.

    d. Quill has noted that in exceptional cases, future loss of income can be included as general damages if they are sufficiently unpredictable to be special damages. *Rossiter v Dun Laoghaire-Rathdown County Council* [2001] 3 IR 578.

3. **Aggravated damages**: Damages awarded in exceptional cases to compensate the plaintiff for any additional harm suffered. **[630]**

    a. Additional harm is harm that is not normal for the tort.

    b. Additional harm may be due to the manner in which the harm was inflicted.

    c. Additional harm may be due to the defendant's conduct towards the plaintiff after the tort.

E. In addition to compensatory damages, there are also: **[631]**

1. Exemplary or punitive damages,

2. Nominal damages, and

3. Contemptuous damages.

1. **Exemplary or punitive damages**   **[632]**

    a. The purpose of exemplary damages is to censure or punish the defendant, and to act as a deterrent for the defendant and others.

    b. Exemplary damages are rarely awarded and only in exceptional cases.

(1) *Conway v INTO* [1991] ILRM 497 (SC). Exemplary damages were awarded against the defendant union for interfering with the right to primary education of a group of pupils in the course of an industrial dispute.

(2) *Crawford v Keane* (unrep. HC 2000). Exemplary damages were awarded against the defendant, who drove into the back of the plaintiff's car and then falsely alleged that the plaintiff had reversed into him and smelled of alcohol.

(3) *Crofter Properties Ltd v Genport Ltd* [2002] 3 IR 94. Exemplary damages were awarded for a false allegation of serious criminal activity made against the plaintiff to the English police.

2. **Nominal damages**   [633]
   a. Nominal damages are generally regarded as a token sum awarded where the plaintiff has established a right, but has not suffered harm.
   b. The recognition of the plaintiff's rights is vindication enough, i.e. no need for significant damages.
   c. The plaintiff's costs should be awarded against the defendant.

3. **Contemptuous damages**   [634]
   a. Contemptuous damages are generally regarded as a token sum awarded where the plaintiff has established a technical wrong, but is found not to have a sufficient reason for bringing the case.
   b. In other words, the plaintiff has suffered no material harm and has no significant interest to protect. *Reynolds v Times Newspapers Ltd* [2001] 2 AC 127. (Overturned on appeal.)
   c. The plaintiff's costs are not awarded generally against the defendant.
   d. The court may also award contemptuous damages against a plaintiff who has acted improperly in the course of litigation. *Fagan v Wong* (unrep. HC 1995).

Chapter 8 Questions

1. Peter negligently drove his petrol tanker too fast around a bend. The tanker toppled over, sending hundreds of gallons of petrol down the main street of Ballyrose. The street was closed for three days while the clean-up took place. Margaret has a café in Ballyrose, and due to the spill no one could enter her café. Nicola was crushed to death in the tanker crash. Andy, an ambulance driver, suffered recurring

nightmares after removing Nicola's mangled body from under the tanker. Nicola is survived by her husband and three adult children.

(a) What type of damage, if any, has Margaret suffered?

(b) Will Margaret be able to maintain a negligence suit against Peter for her losses?

(c) Assuming that Andy is suffering from post-traumatic stress, can he maintain a cause of action against Peter?

(d) Under what statute can Nicola's husband bring a cause of action against Peter?

(e) What is the name of the type of action Nicola's husband can bring for her death?

(f) When will Nicola's husband be statute barred from bringing a cause of action?

(g) Can each of Nicola's children, if dependent, bring a cause of action against Peter?

2. Tony negligently drove his car into the side of Mary's car. Mary has an unusual medical condition that makes her bones very brittle. Mary suffered two broken legs, a broken arm, a fractured skull and a broken neck in the minor crash. The impact from the crash caused Mary's boot to fly open and her suitcase was thrown onto Paul, who was out riding his new motorcycle. Neither Paul nor his motorcycle was injured when hit by the suitcase, but his passenger, Shelly, was injured by it. David witnessed the crash. He was standing on the corner talking to his friend on his mobile and he saw the entire incident. When Tony rushed over to David and asked to use the mobile phone to call an ambulance, David refused.

(a) Is Tony liable in negligence for all of the injuries suffered by Mary in the minor crash?

(b) Is Tony liable in negligence to Paul?

(c) If Mary suffers further injuries because of the delay in being transported to the hospital, can she maintain a cause of action in negligence against David?

(d) Can Tony claim *novus actus interveniens* with regard to the injuries suffered by Shelly?

(e) Assuming that Mary's boot was securely shut, can Shelly maintain a cause of action in negligence against Mary for the injuries she suffered?

3. Tom is being bullied by other students at his school. One day while walking home from school, he noticed that Elmer Fudd's window was open. He climbed through the open window and began to search the house. Tom knew that Elmer Fudd is an avid rabbit

hunter. Eventually, Tom located Elmer's gun safe and continued searching until he found the key to the safe hidden in another room. Tom stole one of Elmer's shotguns and shells for the gun. Tom hid the gun in the garden and retrieved it after dark. Once he had it home, he sawed off the barrel so it could be easily hidden under his coat. The following day at school, Tom shot Richard, one of the students who has made Tom's life a living hell. Richard was severely injured. Richard's parents want to bring a negligence action against Elmer Fudd because they believe that any person who owns a gun should be legally responsible for injuries caused by that gun.

(a) To bring a successful negligence action, what are Richard's parents required to prove?

(b) Will Elmer have the defence of contributory negligence because Richard bullied Tom?

(c) Richard's parents believe that Elmer Fudd was negligent in (i) leaving his window open and (ii) leaving the keys to the gun safe in his home. For each allegation, determine if there is actual causation.

(d) Assume that Tom is also injured due to the poor job he performed in sawing off the gun barrel. Can he maintain a cause of action against Elmer Fudd?

4. Stephen had a terrible toothache while on holidays. He went to the local dentist, who informed Stephen that he had an impacted wisdom tooth that needed to be removed immediately. Stephen agreed to the removal of the tooth and was put under anaesthetic. When Stephen awoke, the wisdom tooth had been pulled, but his chest was very sore. Stephen went to the local doctor the following morning because he was having difficulty breathing. When the doctor removed Stephen's shirt he was amazed to find a fresh bruise, in the shape of a foot, on Stephen's chest. The doctor informed Stephen that he has two broken ribs at the exact location of the bruise. Stephen was not bruised prior to his visit to the dentist, and he incurred no injuries after his visit.

(a) What duty of care, if any, did the local dentist owe to Stephen?

(b) Assume that impacted wisdom teeth are difficult to remove, and that most dentists refer such patients to oral surgeons. Has the local dentist breached the duty of care he owed to Stephen merely because he did not send him to an oral surgeon?

(c) Will the doctrine of *res ipsa loquitur* apply to the injuries Stephen sustained to his chest?

5. Anthony is a television producer. He has just come up with an idea for a new programme based on real Dublin crimes. He employs Daniel to act in the programme. Anthony gives Daniel his costume and an authentic-looking handgun prop. On the day of the filming, Daniel decides to have a little fun. In the taxi on the way to the filming, Daniel takes the handgun out of his briefcase and begins to polish it. Daniel never says a word, even though he knows that the taxi driver has seen the gun in the mirror and is frightened. The taxi driver is sweating profusely and shaking when Daniel exits the taxi and pays the fare.

   (a) Has Daniel committed an assault?

   (b) Can the taxi driver bring an action against Anthony as Daniel's employer?

   (c) Assume that Daniel first went to the wardrobe department and was travelling in the taxi from wardrobe to the location of the filming on a back street in Dublin. Can the taxi driver bring an action against Anthony as Daniel's employer?

6. 'Biker Gang Sues Harrah's Over Fatal Brawl' (Las Vegas, Findlaw, 26 September 2003) 'Nine members of the Mongols motorcycle gang are suing Harrah's Entertainment, claiming the company's hotel casino in Southern Nevada failed to provide adequate security during a biker rally last year that erupted in violence. Two Hells Angels and one Mongols motorcycle gang member died, and at least twelve people were injured during a brawl involving guns and knives inside Harrah's casino in Laughline, about 100 miles south of Las Vegas…In the federal suit…the Mongols are seeking unspecified damages for injuries suffered during the melee for "anguish, despair and emotional distress." The lawsuit says hotel security knew the Hells Angels would be at the rally…and should have known there was a good chance of trouble. The suit says Harrah's employees saw Hell Angels coming through the doors with guns, knives and various other weapons but did nothing to stop them.' Assume that these events took place in Dublin.

   (a) Would the fact that the plaintiffs are members of a motorcycle gang impact on their ability to pursue an action for nervous shock?

   (b) Did the defendant hotel/casino owe the plaintiffs a duty of care, and what duty, if any, was owed?

   (c) Would the surviving members of the Mongols motorcycle gang be able to maintain a wrongful death action against the (i) defendant hotel/casino and (ii) the surviving Hells Angels that participated in the violence?

(d) Assume that both motorcycle gangs willingly participated in the violence and do so whenever and wherever the two gangs meet. May the defendant hotel/casino avail of the defence of *ex turpi*?

7. Dr Quack has come to you for advice. Last week he had difficulty reading his own notes and performed a vasectomy on a young man when he should have performed an appendectomy. What duty and standard of care, if any, did Dr Quack owe to:

(a) His patient?

(b) His patient's wife or partner?

8. On 1 August 2003 Peter was a passenger in his friend Susan's car. On that date Susan died in a crash and Peter was seriously injured because of the negligence of David. Peter was taken to the local hospital. His mother, Breda, rushed to the hospital, where she found Peter in a terrible state. For two years Breda stayed by Peter's side, hoping that he would come out of the coma. Unfortunately, Peter died on 3 June 2004 from his injuries. Breda was always prone to depression and the trauma of Peter's injuries, care and death caused Breda to lapse into a deep depression where she could not manage her affairs.

(a) Assume that on 24 December 2005 no actions have been brought against David. As of 24 December 2005, is an action brought by Susan's husband for her death statute barred?

(b) As of 24 December 2005, is an action brought by Breda for the death of her son Peter statute barred?

(c) As of 24 December 2005, is an action brought by Breda for nervous shock statute barred?

9

STATUTORY FAULT-BASED TORTS

Chapter synopsis
I. Statutory standard of care
II. Occupiers' Liability Act 1995

I. Statutory standard of care

A. General principles [635]

1. **Statutory duty**: Some statutes impose a duty, and liability may be imposed by breach of that duty.
2. **Negligence per se**: A breach of a statutory duty is often referred to as negligence per se.
   a. **Note**: Like all common law negligence actions, a breach of a statutory duty requires damage, injury or loss.
   b. **Not actionable per se**: Negligence per se is *not* actionable per se. [636]
3. Not all statutory duties can be enforced through a tort action.
   a. A statute may:
      (1) Contain *all* elements necessary for action.
         (a) **Example**: Occupiers' Liability Act 1995.
      (2) Contain *provisions* governing actionability; [637]
         (a) Either allowing civil actions, e.g. Data Protection Act 1988, or
         (b) Refusing to allow civil actions.
      (3) Have *no express* provision governing actionability.
4. **Statutes with no express provision**: Where a statute that imposes a duty of care but is without an express provision regarding whether a tort action can be brought to enforce the duty, the issue of actionability is left to judicial interpretation.
5. **Liability based on fault** (negligence). [638]
   a. **Statute imposing liability based on fault** may only require exercise of reasonable care in the circumstances.
   b. Same as duty of care in common law negligence action.

(1) **Example**: Safety, Health and Welfare at Work Act 1989.
c. **Note**: Statutes may impose strict liability (no fault required). See Chapter 3.
   (1) **Example**: The Liability for Defective Products Act 1991.

B. *Determining legislative intent* [639]

1. **Sets standard of care**: To determine legislative intent, a number of factors are examined to determine whether the statute sets a standard of care in a particular case.
   a. **Statutory interpretation techniques**: Over the years, statutory interpretation techniques have been developed by the courts to help them decide such things as the harm the statute was designed to protect.
   b. These statutory interpretation techniques include: [640]
      (1) Examining the preamble of the Act;
      (2) Examining other sections of the Act to determine if an intention to create civil liability for breach may be inferred;
      (3) Look to previous statutory enactments on the subject; and
      (4) Look to the previous status of the common law.
2. Once it is decided that the statute does impose a duty of care, the court must determine: [641]
   a. **What type of *harm* the statute was designed to protect.**
      (1) **Classic example**: *Gorris v Scott* [1874] LR 9 Exch 25. The plaintiff sued when his animals were washed overboard while being transported on the defendant's ship. In his negligence action, the plaintiff tried to use as the standard of care a provision of a Contagious Disease Act that required animals on ships to be kept in pens. The court refused to use the provision in the Act instead of the reasonable person standard because the Act's purpose was to prevent the transmission of disease, not to prevent their death from drowning.
   b. **Was the plaintiff within protected class?** [642]
      (1) If the plaintiff relies upon a duty imposed by a statute, to prevail, the plaintiff must be within the class or persons the statute is tying to protect.
         (a) **Example**: The Control of Bulls for Breeding Act 1985. This Act provides that all purebred bulls must be registered. Failure to register such bulls could result in a fine, castration or slaughter of the bull. A

plaintiff suffering personal injury by an unregistered bull could not use the Act as imposing an actionable standard of care. The injured person is not within the class of persons the statute is trying to protect, i.e. breeders.

3. **Availability and suitability of other remedies** [643]
   a. **The inadequacy of criminal penalties** has been used as a ground for allowing tort actions (*obiter* by Hanlon, J. *Parsons v Kavanagh* [1990] ILRM 50).
   b. **Adequacy of alternative remedies** may provide grounds for rejecting claim. *ILSI v Carroll* [1995] 3 IR 145.

C. *Breach of actionable duty* [644]

1. **Breach of statute**: The defendant *must* be in breach of the statute in order for the plaintiff to rely upon the statute in imposing a duty of care.

D. **Causation**: *The defendant's breach must be the cause of the plaintiff's harm or injury, loss or damage. See causation [530] et seq.* [645]

E. *Statutory defences* [646]

1. The statute may provide special defences:
   a. For duties imposed by statute, or
   b. May restrict the application of general defences.
   c. **Examples**:
      (1) **Contributory negligence**: Courts are reluctant to allow contributory negligence for breaches of statutory duties, especially under occupational and safety statutes.
      (2) **Voluntary assumption of the risk**: Courts are also reluctant to allow this defence under occupational and safety statutes.
   d. **Rationale**: These types of defences would reduce the effect of the statutes.
2. **Contributory negligence**: Generally is *not* the same for a breach of a statutory duty as it has in a common law negligence action. *Stewart v Killeen Paper Mills Ltd* [159] IR 436 (SC). [647]
   a. **Rationale**: The policy of the statutory protection is to protect workers, e.g. from their own carelessness.
   b. Plaintiff's required care is less under statutory duties.
      (1) A plaintiff's carelessness, inattention or forgetfulness does not rise to contributory negligence.

(2) However, if a plaintiff is negligent or careless in a positive manner, this does rise to contributory negligence. *Kennedy v East Cork Foods Ltd* [1973] IR 244 (SC).

F. Damages [648]

1. **Proof of damages**: Required in an action for damages.
2. **Proof of risk of harm or damage**: Required in action for injunctive relief.
3. **All damage threatened or suffered**: Must be of the type the statute was designed to prevent. *Gorris v Scott* [1874] LR 9 Exch. 125.

II. Occupiers' Liability Act 1995 (OLA 1995) [649]

A. In general

1. **OLA 1995 replaced the common law rules** that concerned the occupiers' duty owed to entrants based on the condition of his land or premises.
2. **Note**: The Act only applies to harm caused by dangerous condition of premises.
   a. The Act does not affect other duties owed for harm occurring on the premises, i.e. activity duties. [650]
   b. **Example**: Tilly was visiting her friend, Betty. Betty was frying chips. Betty negligently poured water into the hot oil, causing it to splatter and burn Tilly. The Act does not apply, and it does not affect the common law negligence duty owed to Tilly.
   c. **Example**: While trespassing, Theresa was injured when the occupier negligently discharged his shotgun while trying to clean it. The Act does not apply, and it does not affect the common law negligence duty owed by the occupier to Theresa.
3. **Occupier** [651]
   a. There may be more than one occupier on the premises.
   b. An occupier is *not* necessarily the owner.
   c. **Independent contractors** [652]
      (1) OLA 1995, section 7: An occupier is not liable to any entrant for injury or damage caused to the entrant or his property because of a danger on the premises caused by the negligence of an independent contractor hired by the occupier.

    (2)   However, an occupier cannot avoid liability by assigning all tasks to an independent contractor, especially those things that an occupier is competent to do, such as menial tasks. *Crowe v Merrion Shopping Centre Ltd* [1995] 15 ILT (CC).

    (3)   Also, an occupier cannot escape liability if he or she knows or should know that the work was not properly done.

        (a)   Reasonable care requires that an occupier should verify that the independent contractor was competent to do the work.

4. **Premises**:   **[653]**

   a. Includes land, water, fixed or moveable structures and means of transport.

    (1)   A caravan could be a movable structure.

    (2)   A means of transport could be a train.

   b. **OLA 1995, section 8(b)**: Does not lower or affect the duties owed by three classes of persons:

    (1)   Commercial carriers (the operators of trains, planes, ships, etc.),

    (2)   Commercial bailees, and

    (3)   Employers with regard to the duties owed to their employees.

5. **Entrants** under the Act are broken down into three primary groups: **[654]**

   a. **Visitors**

   b. **Recreational users**

   c. **Trespassers**

6. **Note**: Common law principles apply to: **[655]**

   a. Causation, see [531] *et seq.*

   b. Remoteness, see [558], and

   c. Defences, see [586] *et seq.*

7. **Damages**   **[656]**

   a. **OLA 1995, section 1** provides that injury includes:

    (1)   The death of the entrant, or

    (2)   Physical person injuries to the entrant, and/or

    (3)   Mental injuries to the entrant.

   b. Damages include: **[657]**

    (1)   The loss of property, which includes all chattels in the possession or control of the entrant while on the premises.

        (a)   This could include an injury to an animal belonging to the entrant.

(2) The Act is silent regarding pure economic loss.

(3) Quill notes that the definition of damage is not exhaustive in the Act; economic loss could arise under it.

B. *Duty owed to a visitor* [658]

1. **OLA 1995, section 1(1)**: A visitor is a lawful entrant who enters:
   a. As a right,
   b. Under a contractual provision,
   c. By invitation of, or with the permission of, the occupier,
   d. As a member of the occupier's family,
   e. At the express invitation of a member of the occupier's family,
   f. Or for social purposes connected with the occupier or one of the family members. [659]

2. **Duty owed to visitor**: The OLA imposes a common law duty in negligence.
   a. **OLA 1995, section 3(2)** requires an occupier to take reasonable care in the circumstances to ensure that a visitor does not suffer any injury or damage because of any *danger or unsafe condition* on the premises.
   b. **OLA 1995, section 3**: The factors for determining what is reasonable under the circumstances include:
      (1) The level of care the visitor can be expected to take for his or her own safety, and
      (2) The level of supervision and control a visitor can exercise over another visitor.
         (a) **Examples**: Supervised school groups, parent and child. [660]
   c. **OLA 1995, section 5**: The duties imposed by the Act on an occupier for visitors may be extended or restricted or excluded by:
      (1) **Express agreement**; or
      (2) **Notice** given by the occupier.
         (a) **OLA 1995, section 6**: Strangers to any agreement to restrict or exclude the duty of care owed to entrants is not binding on strangers to the agreement.
         (b) **OLA 1995, section 5(2)(b)(ii)**: Any modification to the duties owed must be reasonable in all the circumstances.
         (c) **OLA 1995, section 5(3)**: Any restriction or exclusion cannot allow the occupier to intentionally or recklessly cause injury or damage to a visitor.

(3) **Notices**: To restrict or exclude liability, a notice must be reasonable and must be reasonably brought to the attention of the visitor. **[661]**

    (a) **Presumed reasonable**: A notice will be presumed reasonable if the occupier prominently displayed it at the normal place of entry.

(4) **OLA 1995, section 5: Adequacy of the warning** must enable a visitor to avoid injury and damage.

    (a) *O'Donoghue v Green* [1967] Ir 40. A person was injured while on premises to use the toilet facilities.

C. Duty owed to a recreational user [662]

1. **OLA 1995, section 1(1)**: A recreational user is a person who is present on the occupier's premises to engage in recreational activity with or without the occupier's consent.

    a. A recreational user is *not* a: **[663]**

        (1) Member of the occupier's family;

        (2) An entrant at the express invitation of the occupier or a member of his family;

        (3) An entrant whose recreational activity is in connection with the occupier or a member of his family; or

        (4) A person who has paid an admission fee to enter the premises.

    b. **Note**: A recreational user may be charged a reasonable amount for car parking.

    c. The distinction between a social guest and recreational user is that the social guest is a person whose presence is desired by the occupier or a member of the family.

2. **Recreational activities** [664]

    a. **OLA 1995, section 1(1)**: Recreational activities include open-air activities such as:

        (1) Sport,

        (2) Nature studies (such as exploring caves), or

        (3) Visiting sites and buildings of importance:

            (a) Historically,

            (b) Architecturally,

            (c) Traditionally,

            (d) Artistically,

            (e) Archaeologically, or

            (f) Scientifically. **[665]**

3. **Duty owed to recreational user**: Generally, the Act imposes a duty on an occupier not to intentionally injure or damage the recreational user's property, or to act with reckless disregard for the recreational user's person or property.
   a. **Reckless disregard**: See [673].
   b. **Note**: No common law duty in negligence is imposed by the OLA 1995 for recreational users.
   c. In other words, no liability is imposed on an occupier due to the dangerous state of the land or premises for injuries to the recreational user due to the dangerous condition.   **[666]**
      (1) Legal commentators are critical of this provision, especially with regard to children.
         (a) McMahon: Refers to the adventurous urban child.
         (b) This provision overturns *McNamara v Electricity Board* [1975] (SC). An eleven-year-old climbed over a fence around an electricity station and while attempting to slide down a drain pipe came into contact with a high tension cable. The occupier was held to owe a duty to take reasonable care to foreseeable trespassers.   **[667]**
   d. **OLA 1995, section 4(4)**: Provides that structures provided for recreational users must be maintained in a safe condition.
      (1) Example: Playground equipment.
      (2) This special duty under section 4(4) does not include entry structures such as gates or stiles.
   e. **Agreements or notices**: The duty owed to a recreational user cannot be reduced by agreement or notice, but the duty can be increased.
4. **Right of entry for recreation users?**   **[668]**
   a. Quill notes that the Act does not address the issue of an entrant who enters for recreational purposes against the express wishes of the occupier. Is such a person a recreational user or a trespasser?
      (1) If the entrant is a recreational user, the occupier cannot rely upon section 8. See [675].
      (2) Quill submits that the courts would find that an occupier has a right to determine entry and persons denied entry would be trespassers.

D. Duty owed to a trespasser   **[669]**

1. **OLA 1995, section 1**: A trespasser is any person entering who is not a visitor or recreational user; or any person entering without legal authority and for reasons other than recreational activities.
2. **Note**: A trespasser is not a criminal entrant.
   a. A criminal entrant is a person who enters land to commit an offence, or a person who while on the premises commits an offence.
3. **Duty owed to a trespasser**: Generally, the Act imposes on the occupier a duty not to intentionally injure or damage a trespasser's property, or to act with reckless disregard for a trespasser's person or property.   **[670]**
   a. **Note**: A common law duty in negligence is not imposed.
   b. Legal commentators are critical of this provision, especially with regard to children. See [666].
   c. Therefore, no liability can be imposed on an occupier due to the dangerous state of the land for injuries suffered by a trespasser due to the dangerous state.
   d. Duties imposed by the Act on an occupier may *not* be restricted or excluded.
      (1) However, duties imposed by the Act on an occupier may be increased or extended by:
         (a) Express agreement; or
         (b) Notice given by the occupier.   **[671]**
      (2) **OLA 1995, section 4(3)(a)**: **Criminal entrants** are *not* owed the non-reckless duty.
         (a) McMahon notes that 'occupiers are now free to act reckless' toward criminal entrants.
         (b) However, immunity toward criminal entrants is not absolute.   **[672]**
         (c) **OLA 1995, section 4(3)**: In the interests of justice, an occupier may owe a duty not to act reckless.
   e. **Note**: Occupier always under a duty not to intentionally injure the entrant or his property.
      (1) However, an occupier is entitled to use reasonable force for self-defence and the defence of her property. See [675] *et seq*.
4. **OLA 1995, section 4(2)**: Factors for determining intentional or reckless disregard: **[673]**
   a. Whether the occupier knew, or had reasonable reason to

know, that a *danger existed* on the premises;
   (1) **Example**: An open well.
   b. Whether the occupier knew, or had reasonable reason to know, that the recreational user/trespasser or his *property* was, or was likely to be, on the premises;
   c. Whether the occupier knew, or had reasonable reason for believing, that the recreational user/trespasser or his property was *near* or likely to go near the area of the *danger;*
   d. Whether the *danger* was such that the occupier should provide protection;
   e. The *burden* of eliminating the danger or providing protection;
   f. The *character* of the premises;
      (1) **Example**: Traditional hill walking path or mass path.
   g. The conduct of the person entering and the level of care that could reasonably be expected of persons entering regarding their own safety;
      (1) Distinguishes between innocent (children) and bad trespassers (burglar).
   h. The nature of any warnings given by any person regarding the danger;
   i. The expected level of supervision by persons entering in the company of others.
      (1) **Examples**: Parents with children, teachers with pupils.
      [674]
5. **Objective test**: To determine recklessness, the courts use an objective test. *Weir-Roger v The S.F. Trust Ltd* (2005) (SC).
   a. ***Weir-Roger* facts**: The plaintiff fell down the edge of a cliff in Donegal on land owned and occupied by the defendant. The plaintiff alleged that she was misled as to the nature of the cliff and claimed that the defendant was negligent in failing to fence off the area and/or failing to erect a warning notice on the land. **Held**: The Supreme Court held that the defendant was not liable. The defendant was not being unreasonable in not fencing off the area nor putting up warning notices given the obvious danger of the cliffs on the land. Even if the plaintiff had been a visitor, the defendant would not be liable for her injuries.

E. *Defence of self and property* [675]

1. **OLA 1995, section 8(a)**: Preserves the common law rules regarding the defence of persons or property. See [96].

2. Thus, while an occupier is always under a duty not to intentionally injure any entrant or his property, an occupier is entitled to use reasonable force for self-defence and the defence of her property.

Occupiers' Liability Act 1995 chart   [676]

S. 1(1)	Premises	Includes land, water and any fixed or moveable structures thereon and also includes vessels, vehicles, trains, aircraft and other means of transport. **See [653].**
S. 1(1)	Occupier	A person exercising control over the state of the premises that it is reasonable to impose upon that person a duty towards entrants. **See in general [651].**
S. 1(1)	Danger	In relation to a danger existing on premises, means a danger due to the state of the premises. **See [649].**
S. 1(1)	Visitor	A lawful entrant who enters: • As a right, • Under contract, • By invitation of, or with permission of, the occupier. • Family member of occupier, • At express invitation of occupier's family member, or • For social purposes with occupier or family. **See [658].**
S. 3(2)	Duty owed to visitor	Requires that an occupier must take reasonable care in the circumstances to ensure that a visitor does not suffer any injury or damage because of any danger of unsafe condition of the premises. **See [659].**
S. 3	Reasonable care	Factors for determining what is reasonable under the circumstances include: • The level of care the visitor can be expected to take for his/her own safety, and • The level of supervision and control a visitor can exercise over another visitor. **See [659].**

S. 1(1)	Recreational user	A recreational user is a person who is present on the occupier's premises to engage in recreational activity with or without the occupier's consent. A recreational user is not: • A member of the occupier's family. • Entrant at the express invitation of the occupier or his or her family. • Entrant whose recreational activity is in connection with the occupier or his or her family. • Entrant who paid an admission fee to enter the premises. **See [662].**
S. 1(1)	Recreational activities	Open-air activities such as sport, nature studies or visiting sites and buildings of importance: • Historically • Architecturally, • Traditionally, • Artistically, • Archaelogically, or • Scientifically. **See [664].**
S. 1(1)	Trespasser	An entrant who is not a visitor or recreational user. **See [669].**
S. 4	Duty owed to recreational user and trespasser	The Act imposes a duty on an occupier not to intentionally injure or damage the recreational user's/trespasser's property or to act with reckless disregard for the recreational user's/trespasser's person or property. **See [665] and [669].**
S. 4(2)	Determining reckless disregard	In determining whether an occupier has acted with reckless disregard, whether the occupier knew or had reasonable grounds to believe: • That a danger existed on the premises. • That the plaintiff was or was likely to be on the premises. • That the plaintiff was in, or was likely to be near, the place where the danger existed. • That the danger was such that the occupier would be expected to provide

		protection for the plaintiff or his property. • The cost of eliminating the danger. • The character of the premises. • The conduct of the plaintiff. • The nature of any warnings given to the plaintiff. • The extent of supervision and control another entrant might exercise over the plaintiff. **See [673] and [674]**.
S. 5	Notices	• 5(1): An occupier may by express agreement or notice extend the duty owed to entrants under sections 3 and 4. • 5(2)(a): An occupier may by express agreement or notice restrict, modify or exclude the duty towards visitors under section 3. • 5(2)(b): The restriction, modification or exclusion is not binding unless it is reasonable, and the occupier has taken reasonable steps to bring the notice to the attention of the visitor. **See [660]** *et seq*.
S. 8	Self-defence	Nothing in this Act affects the right of an occupier to use self-defence, defence of another or the defence of property. **See [675]**.

Chapter 9 Questions

1. Georgia was invited to her friend Penny's house to go swimming. Is Georgia a recreational user under the Occupier's Liability Act 1995?
2. Tina was injured when a table in the dining car of the Waterford to Dublin train collapsed onto her legs. Can Tina bring an action under the Occupier's Liability Act 1995?
3. The Having Fun Amusement Company opened a haunted castle in Cork City. Because of the nature of the activities, i.e. scaring patrons, the company erected a large notice inside the first haunted room. When the room is entered by the patrons it is very dimly lit and then goes completely dark.

(a) If Sally takes her two daughters to the fun house, what type of entrants are they?

(b) What duty of care is owed to them?

(c) If the notice restricts or excludes liability for all injuries on the property, is the notice valid?

4. Hillary, a hillwalker, attempted to enter the lands of Finbar by climbing an old stone stile. Unfortunately, the stones in the stile gave way and Hillary fell to the ground, injuring her foot. Limping across Finbar's field, Hillary came upon Finbar's bull, Jean Luke. Jean Luke became aggressive and began to chase Hillary. While limping away from the bull, Hillary slipped in some wet cow manure and fell, breaking her arm.

(a) What type of entrant was Hillary?

(b) What type of duty, if any, does Finbar owe to Hillary?

(c) Assume that Finbar did not know that Hillary was on his land. Can Finbar be held liable for entrants he did not know were present on his land?

(d) Under the OLA 1995, will Finbar be liable for Hillary's injury to her foot?

(e) Under the OLA 1995, will Finbar be liable for Hillary's broken arm?

5. Tom is being bullied by other students at his school. One day while walking home from school he notices that Elmer Fudd's window is open. He climbs through the open window and begins to search the house. Tom knows that Elmer Fudd is an avid rabbit hunter. Eventually, Tom locates Elmer's gun safe and continues searching until he finds the key to the safe hidden in another room. Tom steals one of Elmer's shotguns and shells for the gun. Tom hides the gun in the garden and retrieves it after dark. Once he has it home, he saws off the barrel so it can easily be hidden under his coat. The following day at school, Tom shoots Richard, one of the students who has made Tom's life a living hell. Richard is severely injured. Assume that Ireland has enacted a statute that makes it a criminal offence to fail to keep guns locked in an approved gun safe when not in use. The statute is silent as to whether a person can bring a cause of action against any person violating the statute. The legislative intent of the statute is to keep legally held guns from falling into the hands of criminals to be used in robberies and other violent crimes.

(a) What factors will a court weigh to determine whether the statute sets a standard of care?

 (b) Is Richard within the class sought to be protected by the statute?

 (c) Has Elmer Fudd breached the statute?

 (d) Can Richard maintain a cause of action against Elmer Fudd pursuant to this statute?

6. Ben invited Jerry to visit his home to play tennis. Assume that while playing tennis Jerry tripped over his open shoelace and fell, injuring his shoulder.

 (a) What type of entrant is Jerry?

 (b) What duty of care does Ben owe to Jerry as an occupier?

 (c) Will Ben be liable under the OLA 1995 for Jerry's injury?

7. Ben took Jerry to Home Hospital. Jerry was taken in a wheelchair to radiology for an X-ray of his injured shoulder. Unfortunately, the front wheel of Jerry's wheelchair caught in a small gap between the lift and the floor. Jerry was thrown from the wheelchair and broke his front teeth.

 (a) What type of entrant is Jerry?

 (b) What duty of care does Home Hospital owe to Jerry?

 (c) Will Home Hospital be liable under the OLA 1995 for Jerry's injury?

SECTION IV:
MISCELLANEOUS TORTS

10

NUISANCE

Chapter synopsis

I. General principles   [677]

A. Nuisance
1. **Definition**: Nuisance is an act or omission that amounts to an
   unreasonable interference with, disturbance of or annoyance to
   another person in the exercise of his rights.
   a. Historically, nuisance dates back to the Middle Ages.
      (1) It was connected to land.
   b. Today it is important as a tool of environmentalists.
      (1) Generally, no connection to land is required.   [678]
2. **Continuing wrong**: Nuisance is generally regarded as a continuing wrong and is divided into two categories:
   a. **Private nuisance**; and
      (1) **Definition**: If the rights relate to the ownership or occu-
          pation of land, or of some easement, profitor other right
          enjoyed in connection with land, then the acts or omis-
          sions amount to a private nuisance. *Connolly v South of
          Ireland Asphalt Co.* [1977] IR 99 (SC).
   b. **Public nuisance**.
      (1) **Definition**: If the rights interfered with belong to the
          person as a member of the public, the act or omission is
          a public nuisance. *Connolly v South of Ireland Asphalt Co.*
3. Distinguished from trespass   [678a]

a. **Similarities**: Many acts may be both a trespass and a nuisance.
   (1) Both trespass and nuisance protect possession rather than ownership of land.
   (2) Both protect against physical damage to land.
   (3) A direct interference with land may be a trespass as well as a nuisance.
       (a) **Example**: Excavations on the defendant's land near the plaintiff's home may cause vibrations which crack the foundation of plaintiff's home, which is a nuisance, but at the same time the excavating may cause stones to land in plaintiff's garden, which is a trespass.
b. **Differences**   [679]
   (1) **Nuisance**: Usually said to be more concerned with the interference with the use or enjoyment of land.
       (a) **Note**: Nuisance is not generally actionable per se, therefore proof of damage is required. See [709] for exceptions.
   (2) **Trespass**: Is more concerned with physical invasion of land.
       (a) **Note**: Trespass is actionable per se, therefore *no* proof of damage required.
4. **Compared with negligence**   [679a]
   a. **Negligence**: The conduct of the defendant is of central consideration.
      (1) **An objective analysis** is made of the defendant's actions.
   b. **Nuisance**: Involves a balancing process between the competing interests of the plaintiff and the defendant.
      (1) **Analysis** is of an objectively reasonable plaintiff at the time of the invasion or interference.
   c. Quill has noted that private and public nuisance straddle the boundaries between strict and fault-based liability.
      (1) Some interference will be actionable despite the exercise of reasonable care by the defendant.
      (2) While in some cases the taking of reasonable pre-causations will protect the defendant.   [680]
5. **Liability**: As a general rule, the defendant's liability for nuisance may arise because the defendant's action or omission is intentional, negligent or because it is imposed by strict liability.
   a. Classification of the type of liability is important to determine what defences are available to the defendant.
   b. **Intentional**: Liability may be imposed where the defendant has intentionally or wilfully failed or refused to abate a nuisance.

    (1) **Examples**: Hosting weekly wild parties knowing that the noise generated disturbs the other occupants in the apartment building.

    (2) **Note**: Reasonable care is not a defence to an intentional nuisance.

  c. **Negligent or fault based**: Liability may be imposed where the defendant has failed to exercise due care to abate a condition under his or her control.

    (1) **Example**: Allowing manure to become heaped on the defendant's land near the plaintiff's home, thus exposing the plaintiff to a constant stench of rotting manure.

    (2) **Note**: Fault-based nuisance tends to involve omissions.

[681]

  d. **Strict liability**: Liability may be imposed where the law (statutory or common law based) imposes liability without either intent or fault on the defendant's part.

    (1) **Example**: Vicarious liability. Liability may be imposed on an employer for nuisances caused by the employer's employees, or a landlord may be held vicariously liable for nuisances created by tenants.

B. Required elements for nuisance

---

1. Act by the defendant   **[682]**
2. Invasion or interference
3. Intent, negligence or strict liability
4. Unreasonable and substantial harm
5. Causation

II. Public nuisance   **[683]**

A. **Definition**: *If the rights interfered with belong to the person as a member of the public, the act or omission is a public nuisance.* Connolly v South of Ireland Asphalt Co. *[1977] IR 99 (SC)*

B. **The essence of a public nuisance** *is injury to the reasonable comfort and convenience of the public.*   **[684]**

C. *Standing to sue*   **[685]**

  1. **General rule**: Only the attorney general can bring a civil action for a public nuisance.

a. This requirement avoids a multiplicity of actions against the defendant arising from the same event.

2. **Special damage requirement**: A private individual may maintain an action only if a special, particular or peculiar damage is suffered by him and his damage must be more serious than the damage suffered by the general public.

   a. **Special, particular or peculiar damage** may consist of injury to plaintiff's pecuniary interests where his person or property is damaged or it may include the deprivation of the opportunity to earn a living.

      (1) **Note**: A personal injury *is* a particular or special damage.
      [686]

   b. **No interest in land necessary**: A person suffering a particular or special damage as a result of a public nuisance is not required to have an interest in land to bring an action.

      (1) **Example**: *Boyd v Great Northern Ry.* [1895] 2 IR 555. The plaintiff was a doctor who was delayed twenty minutes at a level crossing due to the fault of the defendant's agents. The court found that the plaintiff had a huge practice, so his time was of pecuniary value. He was found to have suffered an appreciable damage peculiar to himself beyond that suffered by other members of the public ordinarily using the road. Accordingly, the plaintiff was awarded ten shillings.

      (2) **Example**: *Smith v Wilson* [1902] 2 IR 45. The plaintiff, an elderly man, walked to town on a public road until the defendant obstructed the road by removing a bridge and erecting a fence. As a result of the obstruction, the plaintiff had to take a much longer route, and sometimes had to hire a car to drive him. The plaintiff was awarded damages for his peculiar damage. **[687]**

3. **Breach of planning law**: Local Government (Planning and Development) Act 1976, section 27.

   a. Any person has standing to go to the High Court if an activity constitutes a breach of the planning law to seek an injunction.
   [688]

D. **Onus of proof:** *Once a public nuisance is proved by the plaintiff and the defendant is shown to have caused it, the onus is shifted onto the defendant to defend his actions. See defences [724].*

E. *Public nuisances on the highway*   **[689]**

1. **Note**: Public nuisance can arise in any number of contexts. Public nuisance on the highway is the most common, but not the only public nuisance.

2. **Obstructions**
   a. Generally, any obstruction on the public highway is a public nuisance. *Cunningham v McGrath Bros.* [1964] IR 209 (SC).
      (1) **Exception**: Not every obstruction creates a cause of action for a person injured or inconvenienced. *McKenna v Stephens and Alexander E. Hull and Co.* [1923] 2 IR 112 (SC).   **[690]**
         (a) **Temporary blocking**: Generally of streets or footpaths for the unloading of goods does not create a nuisance.
         (b) **Building or renovation**: Generally, the blocking or closure of a footpath in front of buildings being built or renovated to protect the public from falling building materials does not create a nuisance.   **[691]**
   b. **Temporary obstructions which may constitute nuisance**:
      (1) Allowing picketers or queues to form across footpaths or streets so as to cause an obstruction. *Boyd v GN Ry Co* [1895] 2 IR 555.
      (2) Allowing animals to obstruct the highway. *Gillick v O'Reilly* [1984] ILRM 402 (HC).
         (a) **Note**: Lawfully driving animals on a roadway is not an obstruction. See generally cattle trespass [257].
      (3) Allowing a ladder to remain on a public footpath for an unreasonable period of time.
      (4) Allowing railway gates to remain closed for longer than is reasonable and necessary. *EI Co. Ltd v Kennedy* [1968] IR 69 (SC).
   c. **Permanent obstructions which may constitute nuisance**:   **[692]**
      (1) Digging a trench in the highway. *Wall v Morrissey* [1969] IR 10 (SC).
      (2) Building a structure that obstructs a road. *AG v Mayo Co. Council* [1902] 1 IR 13

3. **Dangers on a highway**: A nuisance may consist of anything that makes the use of the highway unsafe or dangerous to the public, whether temporary or more permanent in nature.   **[693]**
   a. **Temporary dangers**: Rendering roadway hazardous.

(1) Placing dangerous material on or about a roadway.
  (a) **Example**: Diverting water onto the roadway in freezing weather.
(2) Inappropriate use of road.
  (a) **Example**: Holding unauthorised motor rallies on unsuitable roads.
b. **Permanent dangers**: Rendering roadway hazardous.
  (1) Damaging the road surface.
    (a) **Example**: Digging up the road.
  (2) Excavating near a road or footpath, causing the surface of the road or footpath to collapse. *Baker v Alliance and Dublin Consumers' Gas Co.* [1946] Ir Jur 48 (CC).
4. **Special consideration for misfeasance/nonfeasance**:   [694]
  a. **Common law**: A road authority may be liable in misfeasance but not nonfeasance.
    (1) **Nonfeasance**: There is no legal duty to act.
      (a) In other words, the road authorities are under no legal duty to maintain or repair roads, however negligent that failure may be.
    (2) **Misfeasance**: If a road authority decides to perform maintenance or repairs on roads, it has a *legal duty* not to negligently maintain or repair the roads.
  b. County councils are not liable in public nuisance for permitting extensive development without the necessary road infrastructure. *Convery v Dublin Co. Council* [1996] 3 IR 153 (SC).

III. Private nuisance   [695]

A. **Definition:** *If the rights relate to the ownership or occupation of land, or of some easement, profit or other right enjoyed in connection with land, then the acts or omissions amount to a private nuisance.* Connolly v South of Ireland Asphalt Co. *[1977] IR 99 (SC).*

B. *Act or omission by defendant generally required*   [696]

1. Who is liable in nuisance?
  a. **Creator**
    (1) **Person creating** the nuisance is liable for it.
      (a) This is true even if he is not in occupation of the land.
    (2) Person allowing a nuisance to continue.
      (a) **Example**: A builder constructs a building that constitutes a nuisance. The builder will be liable, and

will continue to be liable, even where he has no power to abate it. *Thompson v Gibson* (1841) 151 ER 845.

b. **Occupier**   **[697]**

(1) **Personal creation**: An occupier will be liable if he personally creates a nuisance.

(2) **Authorised creation**: An occupier may be liable where he *authorises* its commission *or* where his servants, and in some circumstances, his invitees or licensees, create the nuisance. *Daly v McMullan* [700].

   (a) **Example**: *Tetley v Chitty* [1986] 1 All ER 663. The defendant council allowed a club to use its land. The neighbours complained regarding the noise and dust generated by the go-karts. **Held**: Permitting the use of the land by the club amounted to authorisation of the nuisance.

(3) **Adopts or fails to reduce**: An occupier may be liable when he begins occupation and adopts or fails to take reasonable steps to reduce the interference created by the nuisance of another such as the previous occupier. *Penruddock's Case* (1597) 5 Co Rep 1006.   **[698]**

   (a) **Expansion**: If the nuisance is created by a stranger, trespasser or from natural causes, the occupier will be liable if he fails to take reasonable steps to stop it within a reasonable time. *Sedleigh-Denfield v O'Callaghan* [1940] AC 880.

   (b) *Vitalograph Ltd v Ennis UDC and Clare Co. Council* (1997) unrep. (HC). An injunction was issued restraining the defendants from allowing a group of Travellers, creating a nuisance, from remaining on the defendant's land near the plaintiff's business. **Held**: The county council adopted the nuisance by failing to take steps within a reasonable time to stop it.

   (c) *Lind v Tipperary Council* (1998) unrep. (HC). An injunction was granted against the local authority for intensifying a nuisance that already existed by providing an inadequately supervised halting site.

c. **Landlord**   **[699]**

(1) **General rule**: A landlord will not be liable for a nuisance on the demised premises unless he is an occupier.

(2) **Exception to general rule**: Where the landlord has authorised the creation or continuation of the nuisance, she may be held liable.

   (a) **Example**: *Goldfarb v Williams and Co.* [1945] IR 433 (HC). Liability was imposed on the defendant lessors because they let premises to a social club. The social club operated dances and other activities causing a noise nuisance to neighbours in the building. During lease negotiations, dancing was specifically mentioned as an activity the club was going to engage in. **Held**: The lessors were responsible as having authorised the nuisance. Landlords are presumed to know the characteristics of their buildings, such as for soundproofing. **Rationale**: The nuisance was inevitable if the premises were used as intended.

2. Act or omission [700]

a. See [509] regarding act(s) and omissions.

b. **Traditional rule**: A person is under no duty to avoid harm to neighbours from natural conditions.

   (1) **Exception for failure to repair or maintain property to prevent or minimise risk**: Persons in control of property will be liable in nuisance if they do not reasonably prevent or minimise the risk of *foreseeable damage* where they know, or should know, that something on the land has or will encroach on neighbouring land.

   (a) *Leakey v National Trust* [1980] QB 485. The defendant occupied land which was a large naturally occurring mound known as the 'Burrow Mump' located at the rear of the plaintiff's home. The topsoil began to slide onto the plaintiff's property due to the weather, causing damage and creating a significant risk of further damage.

   (b) *Leakey* approach followed in *Daly v McMullan* [1997] 2 ILRM 232 (CC). See [697]. [701]

   (c) *Holbeck Hall Hotel v Scarborough Borough Council* [2000] 2 All ER 705. The plaintiffs had a hotel on a cliff overlooking the sea. The land between the hotel and the sea was owned by the defendant. The land eroded and in 1993 the hotel became undermined and had to be demolished. The Court of

Appeal held that there was no difference between withdrawal of support and any other type of nuisance which resulted from natural forces. Liability denied, as the defendant had no knowledge of the danger and had done nothing to create it.

(d) *Maric v Thames Water Utilities Ltd* [2004] 2 All ER 385. The plaintiff brought an action in private nuisance and for breach of section 8 ECHR on the basis that his home was repeatedly flooded as a result of the defendant's sewage system being defective during heavy rains. The Court of Appeal held the defendant liable in nuisance. **Held**: The House of Lords held that the defendant's conduct was not a nuisance. The sewage system was not adequate due to increased use. Remedial work could remedy the problem, but under the defendant's prioritising work, the remedial work would be done sometime in the future. **[702]**

(2) **Exception for trees adjoining roadways or neighbouring land**: A landowner with trees adjoining the roadway or his neighbours' land must take reasonable care to guard against damage from his tree falling.

    (a) Reasonable care does *not* mandate that an expert inspect the trees for the occupier. *Gillen v Fair* (1956) 90 ILTR (HC).

    (b) *Lynch v Hetherton* [1991] 2 IR 405 (CCA). The plaintiff's car was damaged in a crash with a tree that fell from the defendant's land onto the road. **Held**: The landowner must exercise reasonable care.

    (c) **Note**: What is reasonable is subject to change. *Lynch v Dawson* [1946] Ir 504 (HC). Liability was imposed on the defendant landowner for allowing a tree branch to project onto the highway. The top of a turf lorry hit the branch, causing an injury to the plaintiff. **Rationale**: Changing times require changes in the level of vigilance required.

C. Interference with plaintiff's interests   [703]

1. **Standing to sue**
   a. **Traditional rule**: Any person with a proprietary interest in the affected land had the right to bring an action in nuisance.

b. **Expansion**: To include the rights of occupiers with no proprietary interest, such as mere occupation of a home.
   (1) Family members of an owner or occupier. *Hanrahan v
       Merck, Sharp and Dohme* [1988] ILRM 629. See [723].
   (2) Personal harassment, not connected with land.
       Khorasandjian v Bush [1993] 3 All ER 669 (CA).
       (a) *Khorasandjian* facts: A teenager broke up with her
           twenty-one-year-old boyfriend. He took the break-
           up badly and for months was violent and threaten-
           ing towards the girl. He followed her and made
           repeated menacing phone calls to her home, where
           she lived with her parents. After he threatened to
           kill her he was jailed, but continued to harass her.
           She successfully sued him for private nuisance
           despite the fact that she had no traditional propri-
           etary interest in the family home.
       (b) *Khorasandjian* may no longer be relevant since the
           enactment of the Protection from Harassment Act
           1997 in England.
c. **Retreat to traditional rule?**   **[704]**
   (1) **English approach**: *Hunter v Canary Wharf* [1997] AC
       655 (HL). Hundreds of residents sued for the interfer-
       ence caused to their television reception due to the con-
       struction of the huge Canary Wharf tower in East
       London. **Held**: The House of Lords rejected the claim,
       relying on old cases where it was held that the obstruc-
       tion of a person's view was no grounds for a nuisance
       action. Further, only plaintiffs with a right in land can
       sue in private nuisance. This limits actions to those who
       own or rent land, or have exclusive possession of it.
       Rationale: There needs to be a clear distinction between
       nuisance and negligence. Nuisance is limited to protect-
       ing a person's right to the use and enjoyment of land,
       and negligence is limited to protecting a person's bodily
       security.
   (2) **Irish approach**: Not settled, but the High Court does
       not appear willing to follow *Hunter*.   **[705]**
       (a) *Royal Dublin Society v Yates* (1997)(HC). Shanley J.
           observed that the Supreme Court in *Hanrahan*
           [723] was more flexible regarding the standing to
           sue than the House of Lords in *Hunter*.

    (b) *Molumby v Kearns* (1999) (HC). A legal interest over and above being in occupation of land is not necessary.

2. **Interference** may consist of: **[706]**
  a. **Physical injury to the land**.
    (1) **Examples**: Blasting, vibrations, dust, sewage and smoke.
    (2) *Halpin v Tara Mines Ltd* [1976-7] ILRM 28. It was held that cracks in a building due to vibrations was actionable. The plaintiff failed, as he did not prove the required causal link between the damage he suffered and the activities of the defendant.
  b. **Substantial interference with the use and enjoyment of land.**   **[707]**
    (1) **Definition**: Personal inconvenience or interference with one's enjoyment, quiet, freedom or anything that injuriously affects the senses or the nerves. *St Helens Smelting Co. v Tippin* (1865) 11 HLC 642.
      (a) **Examples**: Noise, loud music, strong odours.
      (b) **Note**: The term 'land' refers to more than the real estate; it also refers to buildings, minerals, fixtures and the air space above the land. See [103] *et seq.*
  c. **An interference with servitudes.**   **[708]**
    (1) **Example**: Air, or right to sunlight blocked by a neighbour's new twenty-foot garden wall.
  d. **Personal injury.**
    (1) **Irish approach**: Personal injury is sufficient material damage to allow a claim in private nuisance. *Hanrahan v Merck, Sharp and Dohme.* See [723].
    (2) **English approach**: Nuisance only applies to property damage, and negligence is the tort for personal injuries caused by a neighbour's activities. *Cunard v Antifyre Ltd* [1933] 1 KB 551.

D. *Harm must be unreasonable and substantial*   **[709]**

1. **General rule**: Nuisance is not actionable per se, the plaintiff must prove actual damage.
  a. **Exceptions to general rule**: There are three exceptions where the plaintiff is not required to prove actual damage:
    (1) The court may infer damage if to require the plaintiff to prove damage would be superfluous. *Fay v Pentice* (1845) ICB 828.

(2) No damages required where the plaintiff is seeking damages for interference with an easement or profit *a prendre*.

(3) An injunction may be granted where harm is reasonably feared to be imminent. **[710]**

2. In deciding whether an interference is unreasonable, the court will take into account all of the circumstance, including:
   a. The locality of the area, and
   b. The duration and cause of the nuisance.

3. **Two strand competing interest test**: Weighs the competing interests of the parties. **[711]**
   a. The **utility of the defendant's conduct**, and
   b. The **gravity of the harm** resulting or likely to result from it to the plaintiff's interests.

4. **Substantial**
   a. **General rule**: The interference to the plaintiff's interest must be something that a reasonable person would take offence at, rather than a mere annoyance.
   b. **Sensitivity of the plaintiff** **[712]**
      (1) **Reasonable person**: The interference must be something that a reasonable person would take offence at, rather than a mere annoyance.
      (2) **Standard**: Nuisance is based on reasonable give-and-take between neighbours, and the standard of tolerance is that of the normal neighbour.
         (a) **Unduly sensitive plaintiffs**: Will not be able to compel his neighbour into accommodating his own unusual needs.
      (3) **Usual characteristics**: Some characteristics of a plaintiff will not be deemed unusual.
         (a) **Example**: *O'Kane v Campbell* (1985) (HC). The defendant was enjoined from twenty-four-hour trading. Elderly people may sleep more lightly than young people, but they are not abnormal for that and are entitled to their night's sleep.
      (4) **Sensitivity may be taken into account**: If the sensitivity was caused by the defendant's earlier nuisance. *Mullin v Hynes* (1972) unrep. (SC). **[713]**
   c. **Gravity of harm resulting or likely to result from defendant's conduct.**
      (1) **General rule**: An injury must be of a substantial character, *not* fleeting or unlikely to recur. See duration [718].

(a) **Allowances** must be made for the incidents of neighbourly relations.

(2) **Exception to general rule: Material injuries.** If an injury is of a material nature, the courts will *not* have regard to competing considerations, such as public benefit or the character of the neighbourhood.

    (a) **Material** means not trivial, fanciful or just exaggerated inconvenience.

    (b) **Interference**: Generally must cause damage that is a *discomfort or inconvenience*. There is *no* requirement of actual injury to land.

    (c) **Personal injuries**: Are always material. *Hanrahan v Merck, Sharp and Dohme.* See [723].

    (d) **Damage to chattels**: May be material. **Examples**:

        i.   *Halsey v Esso Petroleum Co. Ltd* [1961] 2 All ER 145. Damage to laundry on a line held to be material harm.

        ii. *Hanrahan* [723]. Damage to farm animals.

        iii. *St Helens Smelting Co. v Tippin* (1865) 11 ER 1483. The owners of copper smelting works were held liable in nuisance for damage done to trees and shrubs from fumes.

5. **Unreasonable: Utility of the defendant's conduct**   **[714]**

  a. **General rule**: Where an intentional or negligent nuisance is alleged by the plaintiff, the defendant's conduct must be unreasonable for liability to attach.

    (1) **Example**: *Baxter v London Borough of Camden* [1999] 1 All ER 237 (CA). The defendant council converted a house into flats. The plaintiff lived in one of the flats. She sued the council, claiming that the building was poorly soundproofed and she suffered from the everyday noise generated by the other occupants of the flats. **Held**: The ordinary use of residential premises could not amount to a nuisance because there was nothing unusual about the way the building had been converted and the noise was normal for the residential use of the building.

  b. **Utility of the defendant's conduct**. See [515] generally. **[715]**

    (1) **General rule**: Allowances may be made for the social and economic contexts in which the interference takes place.

    (2) **Exception to general rule: Public convenience or benefit.**

(a) A court is not entitled to take the public convenience into consideration when dealing with the rights of private parties, or to deprive the plaintiff of his legal rights because of public convenience. *Bellew v Cement Ltd* [1948] IR 61 (SC).

(b) ***Bellew* facts**: The only cement factory in Ireland was forced to close for causing a nuisance, even though cement was desperately needed for new building projects.

(3) **Possible exception to general rule**: Public interest.**[716]**

    (a) *Clifford v Drug Treatment Centre Board* (1997) (HC). The High Court declined to enjoin the defendant drug treatment centre for the nuisance created by its patients because it would be against the public interest in having the addicts treated. The court did enjoin further expansion of the centre.

(4) **No allowances for malice**: The court will take into account the defendant's intention of causing annoyance to his neighbour, or use of his property in an unneighbourly fashion.

    (a) **Classic example: *Christie v Davey*** [1893] 1 CH 316. The defendant, upset by the noise from music lessons given late at night by the plaintiff, wrote a letter asking the plaintiff to stop. When this letter was ignored, the defendant resorted to making noise by performing a 'mock concert' to annoy the plaintiff. **Held**: The defendant committed a nuisance.

    (b) *Hollywood Silver Fox Farm Ltd v Emmett* [1936] 2 KB 468. The defendant's farm bordered the plaintiff's fox farm. The defendant, knowing that noise near the breeding pens would put the vixens off mating, began shooting on his own property near the mating pens. The noise caused the vixens to stop mating and some killed and devoured their young. Liability was imposed against the defendant.

    (c) **Note**: Malice is not relevant if the plaintiff does not have a protectable interest. *Bradford v Pickles* [1895] AC 587.

c. **Suitability of locale.** [717]

(1) What may be acceptable in one part of a city may be unacceptable in another.

      (a) Courts often give more weight to the demands of a neighbourhood with a fixed character over the demands of a neighbourhood in change.

      (b) This is referred to as 'judicial zoning' in the US.

  (2) Difficulties may arise in mixed-use areas.

      (a) *O'Kane v Campbell* [1985] IR 115 (HC). The defendant, a shop owner on the corner of the intersection of a wide, busy street and an old established residential street, began trading twenty-four hours a day. The increase in his operating hours caused the neighbours to be disturbed at night by the defendant's customers. The court enjoined the defendant from opening his business between midnight and six a.m.

d. **Duration of nuisance.**   **[718]**

  (1) **General rule**: The longer the interference continues, the more likely it is to be considered unreasonable.

      (a) However, there is no requirement that a nuisance must last a long time. *Crown River Cruises v Kimbolton Fireworks Ltd* [1996] 2 LR 533. It was held that a twenty-minute fireworks display could amount to a nuisance.

  (2) **Single act**: While nuisance is generally regarded as a continuing wrong, an action will lie where damage results from a single act such as the escape of gas.

e. **Utility may also be relevant in determining the proper remedy**.   **[719]**

  (1) **Recreation and innocent amusement**: *New Imperial and Windsor Hotel Co. v Johnson* [1912] 1 IR 327. The plaintiff hotel sought an injunction against the defendant, who operated a tea room and restaurant across the street. The defendant held dances and other entertainment at night, disturbing the guests sleeping in the plaintiff's hotel. The court held that one of the necessary incidents of the social life of the industrial city is a certain amount of recreation and innocent amusement. A limited injunction was granted ordering the defendant to keep his windows shut after midnight and to prevent patrons from making undue noise as they entered or left.

  (2) **Sunday recreation**: *Dewar v City and Suburban Racecourse Co.* [1899] 1 IR 345. The defendants organised

race-meetings on Sundays to take place in a residential area. The area residents complained that it interfered with the ordinary comfort and enjoyment of the property users and with religious services in an adjacent church. The court granted an injunction prohibiting the Sunday races.

(3) **Twenty-four-hour trading**: See *O'Kane* [717].

IV. Causation   [720]

A. Intentional nuisance

1. **Causation** is basically the same as for other intentional torts such as battery.
2. **General rule**: The intentional wrongdoer is liable for the direct and indirect consequences of his acts, whether or not the harm is foreseeable. See causation [530] *et seq.*
   a. **Harm**: The injury or damage to the plaintiff's interest must be caused by the defendant's act or omission, or brought about by some force that the act or omission set in motion.
   b. **Defendant's conduct**: Causation is satisfied if defendant's conduct directly or indirectly results in the injury.
      (1) **Example**: The defendant drives piles into his land. The resulting noise may be a nuisance to plaintiff and it is a direct result of the act. If the vibrations disturb the plaintiff, this, too, is a direct result. However, if the vibrations cause structural damage to the plaintiff's home, this is an indirect result of the defendant's act.   [721]

B. Negligent nuisance and nuisance predicated upon principles of strict liability

1. **Requires** that the defendant's act(s) be the *cause* of plaintiff's injuries for liability to be imposed.
   a. The courts use a **two-strand test**.   [722]
      (1) **Actual cause**: Whether defendant's conduct was the actual cause or the cause in fact of the plaintiff's injuries.
         (a) **Example**: 'But for' the defendant burning tyres on his land, the plaintiff, a weaver, would not have been forced to rewash all his linen due to the smoke and soot drifting into his shop from the fire.
      (2) **Proximate cause**: Whether the defendant's conduct was the proximate or legal cause of the plaintiff's injuries.
         (a) **Proximate cause** deals with the defendant's liability

for unforeseeable or unusual occurrences or consequences of defendant's act. See [558], remoteness.

2. **Onus on the plaintiff to prove causation.**   [723]

   a. *Hanrahan v Merck, Sharpe and Dohme* [1989] ILRM 629
   (SC). The plaintiff argued that to prove causation was harsh
   and amounted to a failure of the state to fulfil the constitutional mandate under article 40.3 to vindicate the personal
   rights of the citizen. The plaintiff had alleged that emissions
   from the defendant's neighbouring chemical factory caused a
   variety of illnesses suffered by the plaintiff, and death of plants
   and animals on the plaintiff's farm. The plaintiff argued that
   the defendant had the capacity to prove or disprove causation
   better than the plaintiff. The Supreme Court rejected the
   plaintiff's argument to place the onus of proving causation on
   the defendant. See [280], [523], [525], [703], [708] and [713].

V. *Defences to nuisance*   [724]

A. Contributory negligence
B. Assumption of the risk
C. Inevitable accident
D. Prescription
E. Legislative authority
F. Act of stranger
G. Act of God
H. Non-valid defences

A. *Contributory negligence, see [586].*   [725]

1. **General rule**: Any negligent act on the part of the plaintiff will
   afford the defendant a defence in an action for nuisance, based
   on the defendant's negligence for failure to exercise due care to
   abate a condition under his control.

   a. Civil Liability Act (1961): Apportionment principles apply.

2. No defence available for contributory negligence based upon
   plaintiff 'coming to the nuisance'.

   a. **Example**: The plaintiff bought property knowing that it was
   subjected to a nuisance from the neighbouring property. The
   defendant does not have a valid defence merely because the
   plaintiff bought the property knowing of the nuisance.

B. Assumption of the risk, see [595]. **[726]**

    1. **Consent,** see [72].

        a. **General rule**: If the plaintiff consented to the act giving rise to nuisance, *knowing* that it would create a nuisance, the defendant may have a good defence to the nuisance.

        b. **'Coming to the nuisance'**: The fact that an activity creating a nuisance existed before the plaintiff came within its scope is ordinarily not a defence.

    2. **Civil Liability Act 1961, section 34(1)(b)**: Apportionment principles apply. See [587]. **[727]**

C. Inevitable accident: Injury could not be avoided by taking ordinary and reasonable precautions. See [87].

    1. Only available as a defence where liability in nuisance is based on negligence.

    2. **Onus** of proof is on the defendant.

D. Prescription: A defendant may acquire a right to commit a private nuisance by prescription. **[728]**

    1. Prescription applies where it can be shown that the nuisance has been actionable for at least twenty years, and that the plaintiff was aware of this fact during the relevant time.

    2. **Note**: The fact that the nuisance has existed for twenty years is not enough.

        a. It must have been a nuisance to the plaintiff or his predecessors on the land.

           (1) Defendant throughout period had to act openly with the knowledge of the plaintiff or his predecessors.

           (2) It is not enough that it may have been a nuisance to other neighbours.

        b. Prescription period runs from date nuisance began. **[729]**

    3. **Classic example**: *Sturges v Bridgman* (1879) 11 Ch D 852. The plaintiff, a doctor, built a consulting room at the end of his garden. Nearby the defendant had used heavy machinery for over twenty years. The noise from the machinery constituted a nuisance to the room, but prescription did not apply because no nuisance existed until the room was built.

    4. **Note**: Prescription does not apply to all types of nuisance. **[730]**

        a. Prescription is *not* a defence to public nuisance

        b. Prescription has been successfully applied to:

(1) Discharging water from eaves onto neighbours' land; and
  (a) **Example**: *Harvey v Walters* (1873) LR 8cP 162.
(2) Sending smoke through flues in a party wall.
  (a) **Example**: *a.G. v Copeland* [1902] 1 KB 690.

E. Legislative authority   [731]

1. **General rule**: Legislation may either in express terms or by implication authorise the commission of what would be a nuisance at common law.
   a. **Example**: Legislation creating a transit authority to develop and run commuter trains through the city cannot be sued in nuisance for the normal noise generated by the commuter trains.
2. **Exception to general rule**: The person or authority so acting under legislation creating a nuisance cannot be negligent in the exercise of the statutory duty or power.
   a. **Classic example**: *Smith v Wexford Co. Council* [1953] 87 ILTR 98. The defendants, who had a statutory duty to keep rivers clean, deposited large amounts of soil and vegetable matter on the plaintiff's land. Some of his cattle ate the roots, which were poisonous, and died. It was held that the defendant could not have reasonably foreseen the poisonous nature of the roots. Statutory authority was a good defence.   [732]
   b. *Superquinn v Bray UDC* (1998) (HC). The defendant local authority had a statutory duty to drain the area. The court held that the defendant was not negligent in the exercise of that duty. Liability denied. See [283], [540] and [564].
3. **Defence limited**: The statutory authorisation to commit a nuisance extends only to its delegated function.
   a. **Example**: *Kelly v Dublin Co. Council* (1986) (HC). The defendant had statutory authority to maintain and construct roads. In furtherance, the defendant built a depot for vehicle and materials. This depot was a nuisance to the plaintiff, as it caused noise, dust and fumes close to his home. **Held**: The defendant exceeded the function of the authority granted.
4. **Planning**   [733]
   a. Is treated similarly to statutory authority.
     (1) The grant of planning permission does not make the planning authority responsible for authorising the creation of a nuisance. *Convery v Dublin County Council* [1996] 3 IR 156.

b. Planning permission can only be taken as authorising a nuisance if the effect alters the character of the locale, so now after the change the nuisance is reasonable.
   (1) *Wheeler v JJ Saunders* [1995] 3 WLR 466. The defendants were granted planning permission to build two pigeries close to the plaintiff. The strong pig smells affected the plaintiff. **Held**: The planning permission did not alter the character of the locale.
   (2) *Hunter v Canary Wharf* [704] *obiter*: The fact that a building is part of an enterprise area does not mean that the legislators intended such developments to have blanket immunity for nuisance.

F. Act of stranger [734]

1. **General rule**: If a person acting independently, and over whom the defendant had no control, causes the nuisance, the defendant will not usually be liable.
   a. **Example**: A trespasser at night dumps several loads of slurry on defendant's land next to plaintiff's water well. The well becomes polluted from the slurry.
2. **Exception to general rule**: If the defendant's land is a well-known illegal dumping site, it could be said that the pollution of the well was a foreseeable consequence of the defendant's failure to secure his land against the act of the stranger.
   a. Or if the defendant fails to remedy the situation within a reasonable time. See [697] and [698].

G. Act of God [735]

1. **Definition**: Is an event which 'no human foresight can provide against, and of which human prudence is not bound to recognise the possibility.' *Tennent v Earl of Glasgow* (1864) 2 M (HL) 22.
   a. **Examples**: Extraordinary and unprecedented floods, storms and other weather conditions.
   b. **Note**: This defence has seldom been used successfully.

H. Non-valid defences [736]

1. **Exercise of reasonable care and skill**: Generally it is not a defence in nuisance to allege that the defendant used due care and skill to avoid committing a nuisance.

a. **Exception**: Where the defendant pleads statutory authority, he must exercise reasonable care and skill.
2. **Public convenience or benefit**: Traditionally the defendant that created a nuisance to benefit the public did not have a valid defence. See [715]–[716].

VI. Remedies   [737]

A. ***Damages:*** *Compensatory damages may be awarded for the interference with plaintiff's interests.*

B. ***Injunctions:*** *Equitable remedies, therefore discretionary on the court as to whether or not to grant.*

1. ***Quia timet* injunction**: If nuisance is of a recurring nature, an injunction against future nuisance may be sought.
   a. May be granted where damage is imminent, but has not yet occurred.
2. **Prohibitory or mandatory injunctions**: May be sought to stop current nuisances.

C. *Self-help*   [738]

1. **Abatement of the nuisance** is an ancient principle.
2. **Note**: This remedy is *not* favoured by the law and is usually not advisable. *Sedleigh-Denfield v O'Callaghan* [1940] AC 880.
   a. **Confined**: Today, abatement of the nuisance is generally confined to:
      (1) **Simple cases** such as an overhanging branch, or an encroaching root, which would not justify legal proceedings; and
      (2) **Urgent cases** requiring an immediate remedy.
         (a) **Example**: *Burton v Winters* [1993] 3 All ER 847. The plaintiff failed to obtain a mandatory injunction requiring the defendant to remove a garage wall built on the plaintiff's land by a predecessor in title. Later, the plaintiff was restrained from retaliating by attempting to build on the defendant's land and was found to have damaged the garage several times. **Held**: Courts have confined remedy of self-redress to simple cases and urgent cases.
3. **Traditional common law rule**: The plaintiff may take action to terminate or stop the nuisance.   [739]

a. **Examples**:
   (1) Cut off the overhanging branches of a neighbour's tree. *Lemmon v Webb* [1895] AC 1.
   (2) Sever roots from neighbour's tree entering the plaintiff's land. *Butler v Standard Telephone* [1940] 1 KB 399.

4. **Exception**: The plaintiff can only enter land of another to abate the nuisance:
   a. In cases of an emergency where the nuisance risks immediate harm to persons or property. *Lemmon v Webb* (above).
   b. **After notice**: The plaintiff may enter the land of another to abate a nuisance if the plaintiff has given notice of his intention to abate, and the notice has been ignored. *Lemmon v Webb* (above).
   c. A proper abatement will give the plaintiff a valid defence to any action of trespass brought by the defendant for the entering of his land.

5. **Retaliation by abatement**   [740]
   a. **Unnecessary damage**: Any damage done while abating a nuisance is an actionable wrong against the plaintiff. *Roberts v Rose* (1865) 4 H and C 103.
   b. **Malicious retaliation** to the nuisance can itself be a nuisance, making the initial victim the wrongdoer. See *Christie* [716].
      (1) However, there is no nuisance if the malicious behaviour does not infringe on any legally protected right. *Bradford Corporation v Pickles* [1895] All ER Rep 984. See [716].

6. **Alternative and exclusive remedy**: If the plaintiff chooses to abate the nuisance, he cannot seek damages for the injury suffered. *Baten's Case* (1610) 9 Co Rep 53b.

Chapter 10 Questions

1. Glow in the Dark Chemical Company manufactures various weed killers. Recently it has been discovered that a leak in the plant has allowed various chemicals to enter the local river, killing all the fish.
   (a) Assume that Erica, an environmentalist, sues Glow in the Dark on behalf of humanity for the pollution. Will Erica be able to maintain a nuisance action against Glow in the Dark?
   (b) Felix, a fisherman who earns his living by fishing in the affected river, sues Glow in the Dark in nuisance. Will Felix be able to maintain his action against Glow in the Dark?

   (c) Fred, a farmer, uses the river water for his cattle. He pumps the water to his land. The chemicals in the water poisoned several of Fred's cattle. Will Fred be able to maintain a cause of action in nuisance against Glow in the Dark?

2. Kevin is a secondary school student who dreams of becoming a great chemist. Recently he found a 'recipe' for making stink bombs on the internet. Carefully, while his parents were at work, Kevin constructed a stink bomb in a jam jar in his kitchen using common household products. When he went to take it outside to test it, he tripped in the hall of the apartment complex and dropped the stink bomb in the hall next to Clean Jean's front door. Clean Jean's apartment soon smelled like rotten eggs. The stench only lasted for ten minutes, but it turned the walls, furniture and floors a dirty brown.

   (a) Can Kevin's single act be a nuisance?

   (b) Assuming that there was no permanent damage to Clean Jean's apartment or furnishings, is the ten minutes of unpleasant odours enough to amount to a nuisance?

   (c) Can Kevin's parents be held responsible for any torts committed by Kevin?

   (d) Assume that Clean Jean is fastidious about her appearance and cleaning her apartment. Does this make Clean Jean an unduly sensitive plaintiff?

3. In 1980, Tony began repairing lawnmowers, chain saws and bicycles in his garage. In 1998, James moved next door to Tony and found the noise generated by Tony's repair business a disturbance to his use and enjoyment of his home.

   (a) Will the defence of prescription apply?

   (b) Does Tony have a valid defence that his business existed long before James bought his home?

   (c) Assume that James was fully aware of Tony's business and the noise it generated before James bought his house. Will Tony be able to plead contributory negligence?

   (d) Would it make any difference that in 1980 James obtained planning permission to convert his garage into a repair shop?

4. 'Flatulence Spray Clears Supermarket' (Hozaifa Cassubhair, Court TV, 28 March 2002, Franklin, NJ) 'The supermarket stinks! Or it did one day early this month when two middle-aged pranksters released an unpleasant odor in the produce aisle. Geremino Ranallo, 65, and Warren Jacoby, 50, were arrested last year after they allegedly polluted a suburban ShopRite supermarket with flatulent spray. The aging pranksters were convicted of disorderly

conduct on March 19, fined $500 and given the option of spend-
ing a month in jail or performing 90 days of community service...Authorities said the putrid stench, described as being like
sulphur or rotten eggs, drove away dozens of customers last May
and even caused a store clerk to vomit. Employees were able to
track the noxious gas to the produce aisle where the nonchalant
duo were found carrying several cans of "fart spray" and a "fart
machine". "I don't want to be known as the fart guy," Ranallo said
after Judge Steinhardt sentenced the two.'

(a) Have Ranallo and Jacoby committed a nuisance?

(b) If so, what type of nuisance have they committed?

(c) What defence(s) may apply?

5. Bertie and Cecelia come to you for advice about their neighbours.

(a) Brenda, who lives in the apartment above Bertie and Cecelia,
pulled up her carpeting and put down a timber floor. Bertie
and Cecelia can now hear every step that Brenda takes and are
kept awake many nights when Brenda practises ballroom
dancing with her partner on the new wooden floor.

(b) Charles, who lives next door, is keeping his sister's dog Honey
while his sister is in the hospital for a required major surgery.
Unfortunately, Honey is not happy and whines and barks all
night long, keeping Bertie and Cecelia awake.

(c) The neighbour who lives on the other side of Bertie and
Cecelia is Carmel. Carmel is a dedicated Irish cook and cooks
cabbage almost every day. Often Bertie and Cecelia complain
to the landlord concerning the other tenants cooking cabbage.
Bertie and Cecelia hate cabbage and the smell of cooked
cabbage.

(i) Is Brenda committing a nuisance?

(ii) Is Charles committing a nuisance by keeping Honey for
his sister?

(iii) Is Carmel committing a nuisance by cooking cabbage?

11

DEFAMATION

Chapter synopsis

I. Historical background
II. Present status of defamation
    Libel
    Slander
    Slander per se
III. Defences
IV. Remedies
V. Proposals for change

I. Historical background   [741]

A. Development of defamation

1. All commentators agree that the tort developed in a haphazard fashion.
   a. 'It contains anomalies and absurdities for which no legal writer ever has had a kind word...' (Prosser)
   b. 'The law went wrong from the beginning in making the damage and not the insult the cause of action.' (Pollock)
   c. 'It was...marred in the making.' (Winfield)

B. Slander originally applied to spoken words.   [742]

1. **Seigniorial courts**: Originally, defamatory utterances were dealt with in the local courts of the feudal lord.
2. **Ecclesiastical courts** dealt with slander when the local seigniorial courts went into decline.
   a. **Sin**: Ecclesiastical courts generally regarded slander as a sin and punished it with penance.
3. **Common law courts**: In the sixteenth century, as ecclesiastical courts lost power, slander began to appear in common law courts.

a. **Conflicts** developed between the Church and the common law courts over jurisdiction of the slander cases.
b. The common law courts held that:
(1) **Temporal damage,** or secular damage, was to be heard by common law courts; and
(2) **Spiritual damage** was to be heard by the Church courts.

C. *Libel* [743]

1. **Star Chamber Court** at the start of the fourteenth century began to *punish political* libel.
   a. **Star Chamber Court** was an administrative court which was *outside* the common law system.
   b. Used as a tool of the monarchy to persecute perceived enemies of the throne.
   (1) **Political libel**: Seditious publications. These types of publications had become widespread with the printing press.
   (2) Expansion of role: Later, the role of the Star Chamber Court extended to non-political libel. Damages provided a legal substitute for duelling.
   c. Decisions of the Star Chamber Court were arbitrary and without a jury.
   d. It was abolished in the eighteenth century.
2. **Common law courts** gained jurisdiction over libel. [744]
   a. **Note**: The common law courts already had slander.
   (1) Continued to recognise differences between:
   (a) Criminal libel,
   (b) Tortious libel, and
   (c) Slander.
   b. Present distinctions between libel and slander survives.

D. *Synopsis of common law defamation* [745]

1. **Strict liability**
   a. **No fault necessary**: The plaintiff could recover without proving any fault on the part of the defendant.
2. **Falsity of statement** was presumed.
3. **Damages** were presumed.
4. Plaintiff had to prove:
   a. **Defamatory statement**:
   (1) Was *made* by the defendant;

    (2) Was *about* the plaintiff; and

    (3) Was *published* to a third party.

II. Present status of defamation [746]

> **Definition**: The wrongful publication of a false statement about a person:
>
>   1. Which tends to lower that person in the eyes of right-thinking members of society, or
>   2. Tends to hold that person up to hatred, ridicule or contempt, or causes that person to be shunned or avoided by right-thinking members of society. *Berry v Irish Times* [1973] IR 368.
>
> **Defamation requirements** [747]
>
> 1. Defamatory communication
> 2. Published to third person
> 3. Causation
> 4. Damages

A. In general [748]

    1. **Defamation Act 1961**: Generally *supplements* common law defamation.
       a. **Controversial retention**: Irish law retains the common law presumption of falsity.
          (1) A statement is presumed false and the defendant bears the onus of proving that his statement is true.
    2. Defamation deals with *competing interests*: [749]
       a. The defendant's *right of free speech* (article 40.6.1) vs.
       b. The plaintiff's right *to preserve his 'good name' or reputation* (article 40.3.2).
          (1) All legal commentators question whether the balance between the two competing interests is presently proper.
          (2) 'Whatever is added to the field of libel is taken from the field of public debate.' *New York Times v Sullivan* 376 U.S. 254 (1964) (SC).
          (3) The criticism of the public conduct of a government official has caused dilemmas in many jurisdictions. [750]
             (a) **US approach**: *New York Times v Sullivan*. No libel without 'actual malice' or 'reckless disregard' for the truth.

(b) **English approach**: *Reynolds v The Sunday Times* [1999] 4 All ER 609 (HL) rejected the recognition of a political information category of information that would always be entitled to qualified privilege, regardless of the circumstances. It was accepted that a newspaper could raise queries or call for an investigation and not adopt allegations as statements of fact.

(c) **New Zealand approach**: *Lange v Atkinson and Australian Consolidated Press* [1998] 3 NZLR 424 (CA). No libel unless the statements were motivated by ill will or to take improper advantage.

(d) **Irish approach**: The Supreme Court declined to address defamation in light of the Constitution and the European Convention on Human Rights in *De Rossa v Independent Newspapers plc* [1999] 4 IR 6. It was alleged that the plaintiff supported anti-Semitic conduct, violent communist oppression and that he was involved in or tolerated criminal activities.

(e) **ECHR**: The European Court of Human Rights has recognised the distinction between public and private plaintiffs. *Lingens v Austria* (1986) 8 EHRR 407.

3. Defamation is still divided into two primary torts, libel and slander.

B. Standing to sue [751]

1. **Person defamed**: Only a living person is able to bring and maintain an action.

2. **Legal persons** such as a company or incorporated body may bring defamation actions.

   a. *Upjohn v BBC and Others* (1994) unrep. The plaintiff, as the manufacturer of 'halcion', was accused that it had concealed the dangerous side effects of the drug for over twenty years.

   b. McLibel case: *McDonalds Corp. v Steel* [1995] 3 All ER 615. The defendants unsuccessfully argued that there is a public interest in free speech concerning the activities of huge multinational corporations such as McDonalds, rendering such businesses unable to sue for libel.

3. **Local authorities** in Ireland may bring an action for defamation.

[752]

a. Local authorities in England may not sue in defamation.
   (1) *Derbyshire Co. Council v Times Newspapers Ltd* [1993] AC 534 (HL). A local authority was denied the right to bring an action for defamation. **Reasoning**: It would inhibit freedom of speech and be contrary to article 10 of the European Convention on Human Rights.
   (2) However, individual members may bring an action if they are identifiable as individuals.

4. **Trade unions** [753]
   a. Can sue in defamation. *ATGWU v Cork Examiner* (1987) unrep. (HC).
   b. But a trade union cannot be sued in tort. (Section 4, Trade Dispute Act 1906 and Industrial Relations Act 1990.)

C. False statement [754]

1. **Required**: Defamation *requires* a false statement that is *not* an expression of opinion.
   a. **Statement**: Includes any manner of communicating.
   b. Oral,
   c. Written, or
   d. **Defamation Act 1961, section 14(2)**: By visual images, gestures and other methods of signifying meaning.
      (1) **Examples**: Photos, drawings, cartoons, films, music, satire.
      (2) **By act(s)**: Such as by challenging persons suspected of shoplifting. *McEntee v Quinnsworth* (1993) (SC).
2. **False fact(s)**: About the plaintiff: [755]
   a. Could include inaccurate information or errors.
      (1) Transcription errors: *Clarke v Independent Newspapers* (1991) unrep. (HC).
      (2) Printing wrong photo of man: *O'Kelly v Evening Press* (1992) unrep. (HC).
   b. **Must** be defamatory in nature, causing others to avoid the person.
      (1) **Objective standard**: Would statement cause a reasonable person to form a negative or adverse view of the plaintiff's reputation?
      (2) **Speaker's intent** is not relevant regarding the issue of whether his statement is defamatory.
         (a) **Example**: *McDonagh v News Groups* (1993) unrep. (SC). The Supreme Court upheld jury finding in

respect of a libel alleging that the plaintiff, a prominent barrister, was a terrorist sympathiser.

(1) **Mere abuse** such as foul language or common name-calling is not defamatory. **[756]**

   (a) **Rationale**: It has no effect on reputation because people generally recognise it for what it is.

   (b) **Example**: Calling a person a 'Dutch bastard' is not defamatory. *Harberagen v Koppens* [1974] 2 NXLR 597.

   (c) **Example**: Calling a woman a 'bitch' at a public meeting, though abusive, was not defamatory. *Ward v Zelikovsky* 643a.2d 972 (NJ 1994).

c. **Allegations of crime** not required. **[757]**

(1) Alleging that the plaintiff is a criminal is clearly defamatory.

(2) However, there is no requirement that the allegation must concern a crime to be defamatory.

   (a) *Reynolds v Malocco* [1999] 2 IR 203 (SC). The defendant described the plaintiff as a 'gay bachelor'. The plaintiff is not a homosexual, and while the court noted that homosexuality is no longer a crime, this does not necessarily mean that the statement could not be defamatory.

   (b) **Example**: Per Kelly J. (HC) in *Reynolds*, adultery is no longer a crime, but an allegation of adultery could be defamatory. To lie is not a crime, but calling someone a liar is defamatory.

D. Publication   **[758]**

1. **Definition**: A communication made to a third party.

2. **General rule**: The defamatory statement must be published to a person other than the plaintiff.

a. **Rationale**: Falsely accusing the plaintiff of being a thief will not injure the plaintiff's reputation or good name unless the statement is made to someone other than the plaintiff.

3. **Acts of publication**   **[759]**

a. **Making a statement**.

(1) Speaking in a loud voice, allowing others to overhear. *White v JF Stone* [1939] 2 KB 827.

(2) Allowing an unauthorised defamatory statement to remain on the premises. *Byrne v Deane* [1937] 1 KB 818.

b. **Distribution of a statement.**   **[760]**
   (1) **General rule**: The person making an alleged defamatory
       statement will only be liable if he could have *reasonably
       foreseen* the particular publication.
   (2) **Foreseeable publications**: Circumstances where it
       would be likely to be seen by a third party.
       (a) Placing a defamatory statement in a letter and
           addressing the letter to the wrong person. *Hebdith v
           MacIlwaire* [1894] 2 QB 54
       (b) A clerk opened a letter for the employer. *Pullman v
           Walter Hill and Co. Ltd* [1891] 1 QB 524.
       (c) Addressing a letter to 'M. Paul' when it is known, or
           should be known, that two Mr Pauls live at the
           address. *Paul v Holt* (1935) 69 ILTR 157.
       (c) Making a defamatory statement on the envelope
           and sending it through the mail. *Hinderer v Cole*
           (1977) unrep. See [765] for facts.

c. **Dissemination of a statement.**   **[761]**
   (1) **General rule**: A person who did not author the alleged
       defamatory statement may be held liable in defamation
       for *disseminating* the statement.
   (2) Everyone in publication *process* is technically liable:
       (a) **Example**: Reporters, sub-editors, editor, newspaper
           owner, printer and distributor.
       (b) *Berry v Irish Times* [1973] IR 368. The defendant
           printed a photo of a placard containing a false state-
           ment about the plaintiff.   **[762]**
   (3) **Exception to general rule: Innocent dissemination.**
       No liability if:
       (a) The defendant did not know about the defamatory
           nature of the publication;
       (b) There was nothing in the publication or circum-
           stances that gave the defendant grounds to *suspect*
           the defamatory nature of the publication.
       (c) The defendant was not negligent in *failing* to dis-
           cover the defamatory nature of the publication.
           Fitzgibbon v Eason and Son (1910) 45 ILTR 91.
                                                       [763]
   (4) **Onus** is on the defendant to prove the exception. *Ross v
       Eason and Son and The Winning Post* (1911) 45 ILTR 91.
   (5) Exception successfully applied to:

(a) Retailers; and

(b) Libraries.

(6) Exception does not apply to:

(a) Media organisations; and

(b) Printers.

d. **Repeating a statement to a third party.** [764]

(1) **Repetition**: Every act of repeating the statement is a new publication.

(2) **Repetition by another person:** The original person making the statement is not liable for the statement later repeated by someone else. *Ward v Weeks* (1830) 7 Bing 211.

(3) Making a statement *likely* to be repeated: The original person making the statement may be liable for the statement later repeated.

(a) **Example**: *Slipper v BBC* [1991] 1 All ER 165. The defendant was held liable for the original statement made in a television broadcast, and later he was also held liable for the newspaper articles reporting on the statement.

4. *Not* **acts of publication** [765]

a. Making a statement to a person about themselves.

(1) In person: So long as no one else can hear the statement.

(2) Via telephone: So long as it is a private call.

(3) In letter: So long as it is done in a private letter.

b. **Accidental publications**: Where the defendant was not negligent regarding the communication of a false statement to a third person, he is not liable. *Paul v Holt* (1935) 69 ILTR157 (NICA).

c. If the *plaintiff* shows the defamatory statement to someone else.

(1) The plaintiff has published the statement, not the defendant.

(2) **Example**: *Hinderer v Cole* (1977) unrep. The plaintiff was sent a letter by his brother-in-law. In the letter, the defendant assassinated the character of the plaintiff. The plaintiff showed the letter to other people, so plaintiff published the contents, not the defendant. The plaintiff did obtain nominal damages of £75 because the defendant had addressed the letter in a defamatory manner which was or could have been seen by others. [766]

d. **Spouses**: A statement made by a person to his spouse is *not* a publication. *Wennhak v Morgan* (1888) 20 QBD 635.

    (1) However, a statement made by the defendant to the plaintiff's spouse is a publication. *Wenman v Ash* (1853) 148 ER 1432.

E. Referring to the plaintiff [767]

1. **General rule**: The plaintiff must be able to show that the defamatory statement refers to the plaintiff.
   a. However, the plaintiff is not required to show that his name was used.
   b. Identification of the plaintiff may be inferred from the surrounding circumstances. [768]
2. **Identification can be inferred**: All the plaintiff must show is that anyone who knows him knew that the statement refers to him.
   a. The statement would lead a reasonable person acquainted with the plaintiff to believe that he was the person referred to in the published statement. *Knupffer v London Express Newspaper Ltd* [1944] AC 116.
   b. **Fictitious name**: Even if the article claims to use a fictitious name, this will not stop a real person from succeeding in showing that the article referred to him and was false. *Murphy v Times Newspapers Ltd* [2000] IR 552 (SC).
      (1) Also, more than one real person may succeed in showing that the article referred to him and was false.
   c. That plaintiff belonged to a limited class of persons. [769]
      (1) **Example**: The defendant alleged that a female member of the county council was working as a prostitute. The plaintiff is one of the two female members of the county council.
      (2) **Example**: *Doyle v The Economist Newspaper* [1981] NI 171 (HC). The defendant stated that a recent Catholic appointee was considered a 'token' by his peers.
3. **Extrinsic facts**: Often extrinsic facts can be admitted to establish the link between the plaintiff and the published statement, such as evidence concerning the reaction of third parties. [770]
   a. **Example**: *Fulham v Associated Newspapers Ltd* [1955-6] IR Jur Rep 45. Evidence of jeering crowds greeting the plaintiff after the publication of the statement was admitted.
4. **Unintentional reference to the plaintiff** [771]
   a. **Common law**: Identification of the plaintiff, whether intentionally or negligently published, was actionable.
   b. **Defamation Act 1961, section 21**

(1) A *defence* is available for unintentional identification.
  (a) Reasonable care and offer of amends, see [802].
(2) **Example**: *Hill v Cork Examiner* [2001] 4 IR 219 (SC). The Supreme Court upheld an award of £60,000 where a photograph of the wing of a prison where sexual offenders are housed was placed beside a story of a man convicted of unrelated offences.

F. **Innuendo**: *If a statement has two meanings, one innocent and one defamatory.* [772]

1. Onus: The plaintiff must prove that the statement has a secondary meaning that makes it defamatory.
2. **Proof of second defamatory meaning**: From words themselves, or extrinsic information.
   a. **Example**: *The Irish People's Assurance Society v The City of Dublin Assurance Co. Ltd* [1929] IR 25 (SC). The defendant took figures out of context from the plaintiff's balance sheet concerning amounts the plaintiffs owed to their bank. The plaintiff successfully claimed that the defendant's statement was intended to represent that the plaintiff was in financial difficulties.

G. *Right-thinking members of society* [773]

1. Often it is not easy to determine the right-thinking members of society.
   a. **Example**: *Byrne v Deane* [1937] 1 KB 818. A golf club was raided by the police. The police removed an illegal gambling machine, and a poem appeared on the club notice board with a line, '…he who gave the game away may he byrne in hell…'. The plaintiff sued the club, alleging that the line accused him of being the police informer. It was held that the statement might lower the plaintiff in the eyes of the club members, but not in the eyes of right-thinking members of society. Right-thinking members would be against crime.
2. Appears to require the application of community norms. *Quigley v Creation Ltd* [1971] IR 269 (SC).
   a. **Example**: *McDonagh v News Group Newspapers Ltd* (1993) unrep. (SC). The Supreme Court upheld the decision of the High Court for the libel of the plaintiff. The plaintiff, a barrister, was appointed by the Irish government to represent it

at an inquest. The defendant published an article entitled
'Leftie Spies Pack Gov Inquest'. The jury found that it falsely
meant that the plaintiff was a terrorist sympathiser and
lacking in integrity.

H. Injury   [774]

1. **Statement must ruin reputation**: A statement will not be
   defamatory if it does not injure the plaintiff's reputation or 'good
   name'.
   a. A statement merely causing anger or upset is not enough.
      (1) **Example**: *Berkoff v Burchill* [1996] 4 All ER 1008 (CA).
          The plaintiff was called ugly by the defendant, a journalist.
          The defendant argued that the statement was not defama-
          tory. The court generally agreed, but because the plaintiff
          was an actor, the words were likely to lower him in the eyes
          of the public or make him the object of ridicule.
   b. The plaintiff must have a reputation or name to ruin. [775]
      (1) At common law, a plaintiff whose reputation is so bad
          that a false statement could not hurt it could not recover
          more than nominal damages.
          (a) **Example**: A convicted multi-murderer's libel action
              was dismissed when he attempted to sue over the
              false statement that he had also raped his victims.
              Jackson v Longcope, 476 N.E.2d 617 (Mass. 1985).
      (2) **Irish approach**: No Irish case regarding bad reputation
          before alleged false statement was made.
          (a) In 1991, the Law Reform Commission recom-
              mended that evidence of the bad reputation of the
              plaintiff should be allowed for mitigation of dam-
              ages purposes.
          (b) *Beverly Cooper Flynn v RTÉ, Charlie Bird and James
              Howard* [2004] IESC 28. The defendants proved the
              truth of one allegation, that the plaintiff had advised
              a number of investors to participate in an investment
              scheme, the alleged purpose of which was to evade
              taxes. The jury did not find that RTÉ had discharged
              the onus of proof in relation to another allegation
              that the plaintiff had encouraged the third named
              defendant. The jury decided that the unproven alle-
              gation did not materially damage the plaintiff's rep-
              utation given the allegations proven.

(3) **English approach**: Defamation Act 1996, section 13 allows the plaintiff's bad reputation to be used for mitigation purposes only and not as a defence.

I. Malice [776]

1. **Definition**: A defamatory statement published with spite, ill will or recklessness.
2. **Malice destroys** the defences of justification and fair comment.
   a. **Example**: *Halpin v Oxford Brookes University* [1995] QBENF 94/0863 (CA). The plaintiff was the subject of several memos. He alleged that the writer had acted out of malice. **Held**: Malice proved if it is shown that the writer knew that what he was publishing was not true, or he was reckless as to its accuracy, or in the case of qualified privilege, where he said it out of spite rather than in order to perform the alleged duty to inform others.

J. Limitations: Statute of Limitations 1957, section 11 [777]

1. A plaintiff has up to six years after the publication to bring an action for defamation. See limitations [605].

Libel [778]

A. **Definition**: *A defamatory statement that is in some permanent form.*

1. **Examples**:
   a. A defamatory statement contained in a letter.
   b. A defamatory statement contained in a book.
   c. A defamatory statement contained in a newspaper article.
2. **Expanded definition: Defamation Act 1961, section 15**
   a. Libel includes defamatory statements contained in radio or television broadcasts.

B. *In general, libel is:* [779]

1. Actionable per se.
2. A crime as well as a tort.
3. Forever a libel.
   a. Once a libel is made, it remains forever a libel.
   b. **Example**: *Forrester v Tyrrell* (1983) 9 TLR 257. A defamatory script was read to an audience, and was held to remain a libel.

C. Forum **[780]**

1. Due to the increase in international communications, more foreign communications are heard in Ireland than ever before.
   a. **Examples**: The internet, satellite television and radio.
2. EU communications: **Brussels Convention, section 5(3)**
   a. Forum proper either where:
      (1) The tort was committed.
         (a) **Note**: The plaintiff entitled to all damages suffered within that jurisdiction.
      (2) Where the defendant is domiciled.
         (a) **Note**: The plaintiff entitled to all damages suffered within the signatory states of the Convention.
   b. A tort is committed: **[781]**
      (1) Either where the damage occurred, or
      (2) Where the event causing the damage occurred.
   c. **Example**: *Ewins v Carlton UK Television Ltd* [1997] ILRM 223 (HC). The plaintiff sued under libel for two documentaries concerning the IRA that were made by the British defendant and published in Britain and Ireland. **Held**: The plaintiff could choose whether to sue in Britain or Ireland for defamation.

Slander **[782]**

*A. **Definition**: A defamatory statement which is transitory in nature.*

B. In general

1. Not a crime; slander is only a tort, not a crime.
2. Not actionable per se: Damages must be proved.
   a. **Example** of damages:
      (1) Loss of material benefit of friends.
      (2) Loss of a contractual or other tangible business advantage.

Slander per se **[783]**

*A. **Definition**: The law finds that certain transitory statements are defamatory without proof of damages.*

B. Four categories were developed in the common law.

1. **Imprisonable offence**: Where there is an imputation that the plaintiff has committed an imprisonable offence.

a. **Specific criminal offence required**: Not a vague reference to wrongdoing.

b. **Example**: Imputation that the plaintiff stole. *Corcoran v W. and R. Jacob Ltd* [1945] IR 446.

2. **Socially undesirable disease**: Where there is an imputation that the plaintiff is suffering from a socially undesirable disease.

a. **Examples**: Venereal diseases, AIDS, Ebola.

3. **Unchaste females**: Where there is an imputation that a female has committed adultery or otherwise behaved in an unchaste fashion.   **[784]**

a. Adopted by **Defamation Act 1961, section 16**.

b. **Allegations of lesbianism**: Included in the term 'unchaste'. *Kerr v Kennedy* [1942] 1 All ER 412.

c. Legal commentators agree that this provision would not survive a constitutional challenge based on unequal protection.

4. **Unfit in job**: Where there is an imputation that the plaintiff is not fit in his trade, profession or calling.

a. **Common law requirement**: The statement must disparage the plaintiff in the way in which he exercises his profession or job.

(1) **Example**: *Hopwood v Muirson* [1945] 1 KB 313. Allegations that a headmaster had committed adultery was not actionable per se. Could have been if the adultery had been alleged with a student or teacher at his school.

b. **Defamation Act 1961, section 19**: Slander may be about anything regarding the plaintiff's character so long as his 'commercial reputation' is affected.

III. Defences   **[785]**

There are five common law defences to defamation that have been expanded by the Defamation Act 1961.

A. Consent
B. Justification
C. Fair comment
D. Absolute privilege
E. Qualified privilege

A. Consent   **[786]**

1. **General rule**: A person who consents to the actual publication of a defamatory statement about himself cannot later bring an action for defamation.
   a. Consent must be to the actual publication itself.
      (1) **Example**: *Green v Blake* [1948] IR 242. The plaintiff, a racehorse owner, sued the defendant, *Racing Calendar*, for printing the decision of a complaint made against the plaintiff. The plaintiff argued that the entry of his horse in a race did not amount to consent to the publication of the decision of a complaint about the race. It was held that the publication was defamatory – the mere submission to a set of rules was not sufficient consent for the publication of the decision of the racing board.
   b. **Civil Liability Act 1961, section 34(1)(d)**: As interpreted by *O'Hanlon v ESB* [1969] IR 75. The plaintiff cannot complain if he consented under contract to the publication or he agreed to waive his legal rights.

B. Justification   **[787]**

1. **Traditional common law rule**: Truth is an absolute defence to defamation.
2. **General rule**: If the statement is *true in substance*, justification is a valid defence.
   a. **Justification does not require**:
      (1) That every detail of the statement is true.
      (2) That the defendant acted with malice.
      (3) That the defendant believed the statement to be false at the time he made the statement.
   b. **Justification requires** the statement to be true in *substance*.
      (1) **Example**: *Alexander v N.E. Railway Company* (1865) 122 ER 1221. While on the defendant's train, the plaintiff failed to pay his fare and was convicted. The defendant published a poster stating that the sentence given to the plaintiff for his failure to pay his fare was a fine or three weeks' imprisonment. The alternative to the fine was two weeks' imprisonment. **Held**: The inaccuracy was minor. The statement was true in substance and the defence of justification prevailed.   **[788]**
3. **Partial or literal truth (half-truths)**: If the defendant fails to

prove the truth of significant parts of his allegations or statement, he will be liable.

  a. **Example:** *Irish People's Assurance Society v City of Dublin Assurance* [1929] IR 25. Figures taken out of context from the plaintiff's balance sheet were true figures, but out of context gave the appearance that the plaintiff was in poor financial condition. Defence of justification denied.

  b. **Example:** *Lewis v Daily Telegraph* [1964] AC 234. Stating that the fraud squad was investigating the plaintiff was held not to infer guilt.

  c. **Example:** *Beverly Cooper Flynn v RTÉ, Charlie Bird and James Howard* [2004] IESC 28. The defendants proved the truth of one allegation, that the plaintiff had advised a number of investors to participate in an investment scheme, the alleged purpose of which was to evade taxes. The jury did not find that RTÉ had discharged the onus of proof in relation to another allegation that the plaintiff had encouraged the third named defendant. The jury decided that the unproven allegation did not materially damage the plaintiff's reputation given the allegations proven.

4. **Expansion: Defamation Act 1961, section 22**   **[789]**

  a. **Multiple allegations:** The *falsity* of *some* allegations will be *excused* if the *effect* on the reputation caused by the publication is merited.

  b. **False minor allegations:** May be excused if the more serious allegation is proved to be true, and

    (1) The main allegation does not materially injure the plaintiff's reputation, and

    (2) The minor false allegations are not a bar to the defence.

5. Onus of proving justification rests on the defendant.   **[790]**

  a. Justification is seldom used.

  b. If the defence of justification fails:

    (1) The court may award exemplary damages.

    (2) This is due to the fact that each repetition of the statement throughout the trial is a new publication of the defamatory statement.

  c. According to Marie McGonagle, *Media Law*, 2nd ed., justification is only pleaded in 5 per cent of the cases.

C. Fair comment   [791]

1. **General rule**: A statement of opinion, made in good faith on a matter of public interest, is protected by the defence of fair comment.
2. Onus is on the defendant to prove:
   a. That the statement of opinion was fair;
      (1) Fair comment only applies to opinions or comments; it does not apply to statements of fact.
      (2) **Fair**: As in honest or capable of being honestly held by a rational person in light of the facts, which are either true or privileged. *Stopes v Suterland* [1925] AC 47.
         (a) Generally, fair does not mean reasonable.
   b. That the statement was made in *good faith* and was *not* motivated by malice;
   c. That the statement of opinion concerned a matter of public interest or concern.
      (1) Public matters relating to the government, the administration of the state or any body which occupies a position of prominence in the state or in state affairs.
         (a) **Examples**: The conduct of politicians or judges, or the treatment of victims of violent crimes.
      (2) Matters of literary, artistic, etc. submitted to the public for approval.
         (a) **Examples**: Book, art and restaurant reviews.
         (b) **Note**: To avail of the defence, the review should not exceed the public aspect of the work.   [792]
   d. Under the common law, the defendant was required to prove that all of the facts which the opinion or comment was based upon were true.
      (1) **Defamation Act 1961, section 23**: The defence will not fail simply because the facts upon which the opinion is based are not true, but the opinion or comment *must* be fair.
         (a) *Foley v Independent Newspapers* [1994] 2 ILRM 61. The defence of fair comment failed because the defendant failed to report in its commentary criticising the fees paid to the plaintiff that the fees had been negotiated in advance.
3. **Difficult** to determine what is a fact or opinion.
   a. *Lingens v Austria* [1986] 8 ECHR. The European Court of Human Rights held that there is a difference between fact and opinion.

(1) Facts are susceptible to scientific proof.
(2) Opinions are not susceptible to scientific proof.

D. *Absolute privilege* [793]

1. Is generally granted in the limited circumstances where complete freedom of expression is of paramount importance.
2. **Constitution provisions**
   a. **Article 13.8.1: Presidential privilege.**
      (1) The President has absolute privilege for the exercise of any official functions or powers.
   b. **Article 15.13: Parliamentary privilege.**
      (2) Members of the Oireachtas: No defamatory action can be brought for any utterances in either house.
      (2) **No extension to tribunals**: *AG v Hamilton II* [1993] 3 IR 227 (SC). During the Beef Tribunal, an argument was made that parliamentary privilege should extend to statements made to the Tribunal because it was an agent of the Oireachtas. The argument was rejected.
      (3) **Article 15.12**: Parliamentary privilege extends to official reports and publications of either house.
   c. **Expansion: Committees of the Houses of the Oireachtas (Privilege and Procedure) Act 1976, section 2**
      (1) Privilege extended to:
          (a) Statements made before committees of the Oireachtas by members of either house,
          (b) Utterances of members, advisors, officials and agents of the committees, and
          (c) Documents and reports of the committees.
3. **Common law provides**: [794]
   a. **Judicial privilege**: No defamatory action can be brought for any statements made in the course of judicial proceedings by judges, counsel or witnesses.
   b. Judges
      (1) **Judicial privilege exception**: A judge of an inferior court may lose the privilege if she acted outside her jurisdiction. *Desmond and MCD Management Services v Riordan* (1999) (HC). Relied upon *Sirros v Moore and Ors* [1975] QB 118 holding that a superior court always has the power to determine the limits of its own jurisdiction. A wrong conclusion as to jurisdiction is merely an abuse of its jurisdiction and not an act outside it.

c. **Coroners**
   (1) **Judicial privilege extended** to coroners acting under the Coroners Act 1962. There is absolute privilege, unless the coroner acts without jurisdiction and is aware of it. *Desmond.*

d. **Witnesses** [795]
   (1) **Privilege absolute**: *Looney v Bank of Ireland and Morly* [1996] (HC). The plaintiff claimed he had been libelled in an affidavit made by Morly, an employee of the defendant bank. **Held**: Witness privilege is absolute.
      (a) Relied upon *Kennedy v Hilliard* (1859) 10 IR CLR 195. Discussing wide-ranging immunities for material statements made by witnesses and parties.
   (2) **Privilege not absolute**: *In re Haughey* [1971] IR 217 (SC). Ignored *Kennedy* and found that that immunity for witnesses does not exist to benefit the witness, but for the administration of justice. Immunity would apply only to material statements.

e. **Trial statements**: No defamatory action can be brought for statements made in connection with a trial. **Examples**:
   (1) **Court pleadings** and documents prepared for trial.
   (2) **Reports of court proceedings.**
      (a) **Exception**: A spectator's accusation that the witness testifying was committing perjury was not protected when reported by the defendant. *Lynam v Gowing* (1882) 6 LR IR 259.
   (3) **Expanded: Defamation Act 1961, section 18(1)**
      (a) Reports of court proceedings that are a fair and accurate report published in a newspaper or broadcast in Ireland or Northern Ireland are absolutely privileged.
      (b) Statutory provisions apply only to media in Ireland and Northern Ireland.
      (c) Blasphemous or obscene matters are not covered.
[796]

f. **Inter-spousal communications**: Absolute privilege applies to communications between spouses.

E. *Qualified privilege* [797]

1. Under the common law, qualified privileges exist to encourage a person to speak.

a. Unlike an absolute privilege, qualified privileges can be lost through malice or abuse.
b. **The communication**:
   (1) **Must not** be wider than is necessary.
   (2) **Must not** be motivated by malice.
2. **An honest but mistaken belief** by the speaker that the person receiving the statement had an interest in receiving the statement is *not* privileged.
   a. **Example**: *Hynes-O'Sullivan v O'Driscoll* [1988] IR 436. A fee dispute between the plaintiff, a psychiatrist, and the defendant, a solicitor, over the plaintiff's fee resulted in the plaintiff making a complaint to the Law Society about the defendant's conduct. The defendant then made complaints to the Medical Council and the Irish Medical Association about the plaintiff. The plaintiff was not a member of the Irish Medical Association and had no interest in the statement made by the defendant. Statement held not privileged. **[798]**
3. **Duty to report**: The defence applies to statements made under some duty to make a communication to a person who has some corresponding interest in receiving it. The duty may be:
   a. **Legal**;
      (1) *Kirkwood Hacket v Tierney* [1952] IR 185 (SC). While it is defamatory to accuse a student of receiving money by false pretences, the President of UCD had a legal duty to investigate the matter. **Held**: The alleged statement made in front of the College Secretary was privileged in the absence of malice.
      (2) *Hartley v Welltrade* [1978] ILRM 38 (HC). Accusing police of assault and brutality is defamatory, but in making it in a complaint to police about investigating it, it was privileged.
   b. **Social**; or
   c. **Moral**. **[799]**
      (1) **Protections for Persons Reporting Child Abuse Act 1998**: Provides statutory protection to certain specified categories of people who report child abuse in good faith.
4. **Protection of interests**: A defendant is conditionally privileged to defame another if there is:
   a. **Protectable personal interests**. The defendant must have a reasonable belief that some important personal interest is threatened:

    (1) **To a person;**
       (a) **Example**: Calling the police to report a domestic disturbance in a neighbouring flat.
    (2) **To property.**
       (a) Investigation of wrongfully obtained money was privileged. *Kirkwood Hacket v Tierney*. See [798].
       (b) Statement made to suspected shoplifter is conditionally privileged. *Coleman v Keans Ltd* [1946] IR Jur Rep 5.
       (c) Complaint to police regarding possible blackmail is privileged. *Hartery v Welltrade*. See [798].
       (d) Accusation of theft made against an employee by the employer was conditionally privileged. *Hyland v Cleary Ltd* (1964) (SC).   **[800]**

b. **Protection of public interests**: A defendant is conditionally privileged to defame another if the defendant reasonably believes that his statement is necessary to protect a legitimate public interest.
    (1) The person receiving the statement must have the power to protect the interest.
       (a) **Example**: While walking past the bank, Marge saw three armed gunmen. She ran to the police station and reported that her neighbour, Bart, was holding up the bank.
       (b) **Note**: The media cannot claim the privilege of protecting the public interest for having published an article defaming a politician. *Reynolds v The Sunday Times* [1999] 4 All ER 609 (HL)
       (c) ***Reynolds* facts**: The House of Lords rejected that the common law should develop political information as a category of information which will always be entitled to qualified privilege, regardless of the circumstances. **Offending statement**: The plaintiff, Albert Reynolds, while Taoiseach, misled the Oireachtas. **Held**: The plaintiff was defamed. Nominal damages were awarded.

5. **Qualified privilege may be lost through**:   **[801]**
  a. **Bad faith;**
    (1) The failure to give the plaintiff's explanation in an article was unfair and not entitled to privilege. *Reynolds*. See [800].

b. **Malice**.
  (1) Onus is on the plaintiff to establish the defendant's malice.
    (a) Whether the plaintiff has shown malice to destroy the defence of qualified immunity is a matter for the jury. *Hynes–O'Sullivan v O'Driscoll* [1988] IR 436 (SC).
  (2) Proof may be intrinsic or extrinsic.
    (a) **Intrinsic proof**: Such as the tone of the communication.
    (b) **Extrinsic proof**: Evidence of the circumstances under which the statement was made.

F. *Offer of amends* [802]

1. **Defamation Act 1961, section 21**
   a. **Defence under certain conditions**: Where the publisher was not aware of the possibility that the plaintiff would be defamed because there was no knowledge either of identification or circumstance by which an innuendo would arise.
     (1) **Section 21(5): Innocent publication**
       (a) The publisher's innocence is dependent on having exercised reasonable care. [803]
2. **Section 21(3)**: An offer to publish a correction and a suitable apology in a manner reasonably suited to *reaching recipients of the original publication* may be a defence, if:
   a. Accepted by the plaintiff. Bars further action.
   b. Rejected by the plaintiff. **Section 21(1)** provides that it is allowed as a defence if the offer was made as soon as possible after the defendant became aware of the potential defamation.

G. *Non-valid defences* [804]

1. **Apology: Defamation Act, section 17**
   a. An offer by the defendant of an apology made before an action is commenced or as soon after as possible is not a defence.
     (1) **Example**: *McDaid v The Examiner* (1999) unrep. (HC). The defendant printed a false article on the front page regarding the plaintiff. The next day, the defendant printed a full apology, admitting the inaccuracy of the front-page article. The plaintiff testified that because of the article he was jostled on a public street and threat-

ened. The plaintiff was awarded damages.
   b. The apology must be genuine and to the plaintiff's satisfaction. *Campbell-Sharp v Magill* (1985) (HC).
   c. However, if the action has commenced, the offer of an apology can be used as evidence in mitigation of damages.
2. **Use of quotation marks** will not provide protection or a defence.   **[805]**
   a. Quotation marks may actually cause more problems.
      (1) The quote may be inaccurate and lead to a defamatory meaning and a suit from the speaker.
      (2) The words quoted may defame another person who could sue the speaker and the media.
3. **Inserting phrases of doubt,** such as 'it is rumoured' or 'it is alleged', does not provide a valid defence in defamation.
4. **Evidence of the bad reputation of the plaintiff**: See [775].

IV. Remedies   **[806]**

A. Damages

1. Are generally the *standard remedy* in defamation.
2. **Compensatory**: The plaintiff is being compensated for the damage to his reputation.
3. **Emotional distress**: Damages may be awarded for anxiety, distress and injury to feelings arising from the publication. *Barrett v Independent Newspapers Ltd* [1986] IR 13.

B. Injunctive relief   **[807]**

1. An injunction may be granted to prevent either the publication or further publication of defamatory material.
   a. Interlocutory injunction: To stop the publication of a libel pending the hearing of the action is only exercised in the clearest case where the court would find that the matter complained of was libellous.
   b. **Example**: *Sinclair v St John Gogarty* [1937] IR 377. An injunction was granted to prevent the publication of a novel which contained clear defamatory material.

V. *Proposals for change* [808]

A. *The Law Reform Commission, Report on Civil Law of Defamation (1991): Recommendations*

1. **The abolition** of the *distinction* between libel and slander.
    a. Replace with the introduction of a single tort of defamation.
2. That *printers* and *distributors* be granted an *immunity* where they are not the original publishers.
3. **LRC 38-91, section 12.32**: The defamed person would retain an entitlement to compel the disclosure of information concerning the publisher and to prevent further publishing.
4. The abolition of the common law presumption of falsity.
    a. **Note:** Currently, the defendant bears the onus of proving that his statement is true.
    b. In all other areas of tort, the plaintiff has the onus of proof.

B. *Legal Advisory Group on Defamation advocated a new statutory defence of reasonable publication (rather than amending qualified privilege).*

C. *United Nations (March 2000)* [809]

1. Abid Hussain, a special UN representative, has recommended that:
    a. Sanctions for libel should be reduced.
       (1) High awards have a 'chilling effect' on free speech.
    b. Onus of proof should be on the plaintiff to prove the falsity of the statement, rather than on the defendant to prove the truth of the statement.
    c. Establishment of an independent press ombudsman.
    d. **Amendment of Broadcasting Act, section 31**
       (1) Currently allows a minister to ban representative of proscribed organisations from being heard on the airwaves.

Chapter 11 Questions

1. Mary is a lecturer in a prestigious university. Mary has information that marks are being altered and inflated to make it appear that the students at the university are doing better than they really are. Mary writes a report concerning the altering of student marks and sends the report to the university's academic council. The council is responsible for maintaining standards at the university. When the

council refuses or fails to take action, one member of the council sends the report to a newspaper in Boston, where the contents appear on the front page of the paper and on the newspaper's website.

(a) Can a university bring an action in defamation?

(b) In her report to the academic council, Mary did not accuse any person of a crime. Is accusation of a crime necessary for a defamation action?

(c) Assume that the report is false. Will Mary be liable in defamation for sending the report to the academic council?

(d) Assume that the report is false. Will Mary be liable in defamation for the report appearing on the front page of the newspaper or on the newspaper's website?

(e) If the university suffers damage because students refuse to attend or withdraw from courses, will the university be able to bring an action in Ireland against the newspaper pursuant to section 5(3) of the Brussels Convention?

(f) Assume that the report is false, but the university does not appear to lose any students or grants, etc. If the university discovers the person that sent the report to the newspaper, can the university maintain a defamation action against the person?

2. Hamish is a food critic. Last week, he visited the hottest new restaurant in town incognito. The following Sunday, in his column he likened the asparagus soup to snot and the steak to shoe leather. Within days of his column appearing in the Sunday paper, no one is eating in the restaurant.

(a) Does Hamish have a valid defence to defamation?

(b) Assume that Hamish also reported that he found the toilet in a filthy condition. Has Hamish exceeded the public aspect of the work?

(c) Assume that Hamish referred in his article to the person that served him as being 'fat'. Can the server sue Hamish for defamation?

(d) Assume that Hamish was once in love with the owner of the restaurant, but the owner rejected Hamish. Could this fact be important?

3. Ricky is a reporter for the *Daily News*. Ricky received a tip from a teller at the local bank that the assistant manager was about to be fired for embezzling. Ricky went to see the assistant manager and told him that he wanted to discuss a delicate matter. Once inside the assistant manager's office, Ricky told him that the news on the street

was that he was an embezzler. The assistant manager strongly denied the allegation. Unknown to both men, Lilly, a trained lip reader, was outside the door to speak to the assistant manager. She knew the content of the conversation because she could see the men through the window in the door, but she could not hear the conversation.

(a) Assume that Ricky accused the wrong assistant manager of embezzlement. Can the man falsely accused bring an action against Ricky for defamation?

(b) Assume that the wrongly accused assistant manager told his secretary of the allegations. Has a publication to a third person taken place?

4. Andrew is the founder of the Anti-Gambling League. Recently, Ricky, the reporter, heard that Andrew was the winner of the first €1 billion lottery pay-out. When Ricky telephoned Andrew to inquire if the rumour was correct, the conversation was overheard by Andrew's secretary, Susan. Susan immediately told Andrew's wife, Winnie, about the conversation. Winnie exclaims, 'That sanctimonious bastard! I hope he doesn't lose his job as president of the Anti-Gambling League if word gets out. All my friends belong to the League.'

(a) Assume that the statement is false. Is the false statement that Andrew won the lottery defamatory in nature?

(b) Assume that the statement is false. Has Susan committed slander?

(c) Assume that the statement is false. Has Winnie committed slander with her outburst to Susan?

(d) If Winnie confronts Andrew and accuses him of being a hypocrite and liar, has Winnie committed slander?

5. During a recess of a high-profile murder case, the judge tells another person via the telephone that the defendant's barrister is 'walking malpractice'.

(a) Can the judge rely on judicial privilege?

(b) What type of defamation, if any, has the judge committed?

(c) Assume that the barrister begins defamation proceedings against the judge, but the barrister suffers a heart attack and dies two days before his case is to be heard. Will his estate be able to maintain the cause of action?

(d) Assume that the judge was speaking to his wife via the telephone. Has he committed defamation?

6. Barney told the lads at work that he is having an affair with Hannah. Yet Barney is *not* having an affair with Hannah. That

night, Fred tells his wife, Wilma, about Barney and Hannah. The following morning, Wilma tells Barney's wife, Betty, about Barney and Hannah. An infuriated Betty drives to Hannah's house and calls Hannah a slapper and makes several statements concerning Hannah's lack of morals.

    (a) Can Hannah sue Barney for defamation? If so, what type of defamation?

    (b) Can Hannah sue Fred for defamation? If so, what type of defamation?

    (c) Can Hannah sue Wilma for defamation? If so, what type of defamation?

    (d) Can Hannah sue Betty for defamation? If so, what type of defamation?

7. Jerome is a gangster rapper of some prominence. Recently, one of his childhood friends told a reporter that Jerome was a sensitive, straight-A student who liked to write poetry in his spare time. Jerome is furious, as he is afraid that this type of statement will ruin his image as a gangster rapper.

    (a) Assume that Jerome, while a decent student, only achieved a B average. Is the false statement concerning his grades a defamation?

    (b) Assume that Jerome's record sales plummet after this statement is made public. Will Jerome be able to maintain a libel action against the magazine printing the statement?

12

PASSING OFF

Chapter synopsis

I.   Historical development
II. Required elements for passing off
III. Further expansion

I. Historical development [810]

A. *The ancient origins of passing off go back to deceit.*

1. The tort of passing off developed as a subset of injurious falsehood.
2. The requirement of fraudulent intent was abandoned as passing off evolved.

B. *Originally, the tort was concerned with the misappropriation of trade names and trademarks for the defendant's profit.*

1. The defendant would make a profit on the success of another business by deceiving consumers.
2. This results in the defendant wrongfully taking a portion of the plaintiff's successful business's share of the market.
   a. **Example**: Dan has a stall at the local market and sells football team jerseys that look exactly like the real football team jerseys. However, because Dan has sourced his 'knock-off' jerseys in India at a fraction of the cost of the real jerseys, he can sell his jerseys for a greatly reduced amount.

C. *Today, the tort of passing off applies when a person is misled as to the origins of goods or the origins of services, and this misleading results in damage to the plaintiff's business.*

II. *Required elements for passing off* [811]

> A. Misrepresentation by the defendant
> B. Made in the course of trading
> C. Made to customers
> D. Calculated to injure
> E. Damage or the likelihood of damage to the plaintiff

A. *Misrepresentation* [812]

1. **Definition**: Some aspects of the plaintiff's business are used to confuse the public into thinking that the defendant's goods or services are the plaintiff's goods or services.

B. *Made in the course of trading* [813]

1. **Commercial**: The misrepresentation must take place in a commercial context.
2. Courts are generally reluctant to find misrepresentation in the absence of compelling evidence due to serious consequences of intervention.
   a. Thus, if the defendant is not making the misrepresentation in a commercial or money-making context, the tort will not arise.
      (1) **Example**: Political parties are not allowed to bring an action.
      (2) **Example**: Charities are allowed to bring actions. *British Diabetic Association v Diabetic Society Ltd* [1995] 4 All ER 812.
      (3) **Example**: *Day v Brownrigg* (1878) 10 Ch D 294. Copying the name of another person's house was held not actionable because it did not have a commercial impact.
   b. The plaintiff must have a commercial reputation associated with the marketing of its product, services, etc. [814]
3. Misrepresentation can be done by the appropriation of the plaintiff's business aspects, such as names of business, products or services, the use of the plaintiff's distinctive packaging or design, and sometimes appropriation occurs in advertising.
4. **Trade association**: *An Bord Trachtala v Waterford Foods plc.* [1994] FSR 316 (HC). Although a trade association is not actively engaged in trade, but rather represents members who are

tradesmen, it could bring an action in passing off against the defendant for falsely claiming to be a member of the association.

C. Made to customers [815]

1. Appropriated business aspects
a. Names of business, product or service.

   (1) **Registered names**: Registration of a trade name provides extensive protection of it to the registered owner.

   (2) **Unregistered names** may develop a specific association, which may easily allow for the confusion of the public by misrepresentation.

      (a) **Example**: *Muckross Park Hotel v Randles* (d/b/a/ Muckross Court Hotel) [1995] 1 IR 130 (SC). The defendant named his hotel a very similar name to the plaintiff's established hotel. The plaintiff believed that the defendant was trading on their reputation and name. The court held that the defendant's hotel was outside the area known as Muckross and this could deceive the public.

      (b) **Example**: *J. Bollinger v Costa Brava Wine Co. Ltd II* [1961] 1 All ER 561. Use of the word 'champagne' in relation to sparkling Spanish wine was held to constitute a misrepresentation regarding the place of origin of the Spanish wine.

b. Packaging [816]

   (1) **Distinctive**: Some packaging is so unique that if a defendant copies it, consumers may be confused and purchase the defendant's product when they intended to buy the plaintiff's.

      (a) **Example**: *Coca-Cola v AG Barr and Co.* [1961] RPC 387. The plaintiff's distinctive bottle shape was held entitled to protection under the tort of passing off.

      (b) **However**: Re *Coca-Cola* [1986] 1 All ER 274. The shape of the bottle was not eligible for registration as a trademark. Like packaging, some designs are so unique and distinctive that if the defendant copies it, consumers may become confused and purchase the defendant's product when they intended to buy the plaintiff's product.

c. **Design**   **[817]**
  (1) **Distinctive**: Like packaging, some designs are so unique
       and distinctive that if the defendant copies it, consumers
       may become confused and purchase the defendant's
       product when they intended to buy the plaintiff's.
       (a) *Adidas Sportschahfabriken Adi Dassler KA v Charles
            O'Neill and Co. Ltd* [1983] ILRM 112. The
            Supreme Court held that the use of three stripes on
            sportswear was the adoption of a fashion trend
            rather than a misrepresentation.
       (b) *Gabbicci v Dunnes Stores* (1991) unrep. (HC). An
            interlocutory injunction was granted for the sale of
            sweaters that were identical to the plaintiff's design.
d. **Advertising**   **[818]**
  (1) **Association**: Businesses spend huge sums of money
       developing unusual and unique advertising to sell their
       goods and services.
       (a) **Examples**: The Budweiser Lizards, the Budweiser
            Clydesdales, Hibernian Insurance's 'Jack and Jill'.
  (2) **Capable of misrepresentation**: If the advertising provides
       the required association with the plaintiff's goods or ser-
       vices and copying of it would lead to consumer confusion.
       (a) *Cadbury-Schweppes v Pub Squash Co.* [1981] 1 All
            ER 213. The action failed because the products
            were clearly distinguishable.
       (b) **Not unique**: *Ragget v Findlater* (1872) LR 17 Eq.
            29. A brewer who customarily placed the phrase
            'nourishing stout' on his label had not created some-
            thing uniquely associated with his product.
  (3) Even the source of advertising can be misleading.
       (a) **Example**: *Associated Newspapers plc. v Insert Media
            Ltd* [1991] 3 All ER 525. The defendant produced
            an advertising flyer and inserted it into the plain-
            tiff's newspapers without the plaintiff's consent. It
            was held that the insertion was a misrepresentation.
            The public would be deceived into thinking that
            the advertisement came from the plaintiff.

D. Calculated to injure   **[819]**

  1. Onus is on the plaintiff to establish that the business aspect
     appropriated is publicly associated with the plaintiff.

2. **Confusion**: The business aspect appropriated has or is likely to deceive the public.
3. The plaintiff is *not* required to prove actual deception of the public, just the likelihood of deception. *An Post v Irish Permanent plc.* [1995] 1 Ir 140.
4. **Must be widespread**: The confusion must be widespread with a general tendency to occur.
   a. *Private Research v Brosman* [1996] ILRM 27. It was held that there was not sufficient proof of a misrepresentation where the plaintiff only showed a similarity between the businesses and that a few customers had mistakenly contacted the defendant instead of the plaintiff.

E. Damage or the likelihood of damage to the plaintiff **[820]**

1. The plaintiff must prove that the misrepresentation has had an adverse impact on the plaintiff's business, or that it is likely that it will have an adverse impact.
2. Actual damages must be shown.
   a. An adverse impact has occurred to the plaintiff's business.
   b. Or that actual damage is imminent to the plaintiff's business.
      (1) **Example**: *Falcon Travel Ltd v Owners Abroad Group plc t/a Falcon Leisure Group* [1991] 1 IR 175. The plaintiff was operating in Ireland and the defendant was operating in England under a similar name. When the defendant opened offices in Ireland, the plaintiff was able to show that the goodwill and reputation of its business was getting mixed with the defendant's. It was held that proof of adverse consequences was not necessary. The court found that the defendant had been acting in good faith and refused to issue an injunction. The measure of damages was based on the cost of advertising the differences between the two businesses.

III. Further expansion   **[821]**

A. Appropriation of the plaintiff's name or likeness

1. Many celebrities make income from endorsing various goods and services.
2. American approach: It is a tort for a defendant for a commercial purpose to use the plaintiff's name or likeness without authorisation.

a. **Celebrity**: The use of the name or likeness of a celebrity has a commercial value.
   (1) Using a celebrity's name or likeness is an invasion of the celebrity's right to sell endorsements for goods or services. *Haelan Labs v Topps Chewing Gum, Inc.*, 202 F.2d 806 (2d Cir.), cert. denied, 346 U.S. 816 (1953).
b. **Non-celebrity**: The unauthorised use of a non-celebrity's name is an invasion of privacy.
   (1) The non-celebrity would have a right to damages for interference with her right to peace. *Fairfield v American Photocopy*, 138 Cal.App.2d 82 (1955).

Chapter 12 Questions

1. During a local speech, Polly, a politician, labelled herself a compassionate democrat. The local democrat party objects to this label, as Polly is clearly a conservative. Can the local democrat party bring an action for passing off?
2. Cajun Country is a popular restaurant in Dublin. Recently, a restaurant named Cajun County opened across town. Many people are confused as to which restaurant received a rave review in the *Times*. Name the economic tort.
3. Tennis racquet designer Bebe Bucks was tired of the standard black, brown or white handgrips on tennis racquets and started using florescent coloured handgrips on his racquets. Within a short time, everyone recognised his racquets because of the unique coloured grips. If other manufacturers begin making different coloured grips, will they be committing passing off?
4. Winona is a wedding planner in Waterford. Just as her business has started doing really well, Suzanne moves into Waterford and sets up a rival business.
   (a) Winona takes Suzanne's business telephone number and posts it on the internet as belonging to a stripper for bachelor parties. Has Winona committed the tort of passing off?
   (b) Winona provides her clients with a scrapbook featuring various aspects of the wedding she planned for them. If Suzanne starts providing similar scrapbooks to her clients, will she commit passing off?
5. Rip Rock is an internationally popular rock star. Recently when he went on tour in Ireland, he discovered that Rip Crisps were using his face on the front of Rip Crisps bags. Have Rip Crisps committed the tort of passing off?

SECTION V:
THE EXAMINATION

13

APPROACHING THE EXAM

Chapter synopsis

I.   Where to concentrate your revision
     Be prepared – early
     Conquering cases
     Answering the exam questions
II. Avoiding common mistakes

I. Where to concentrate your revision

A. Be prepared – early

1. **Step 1**: Make certain that you have all the:
   a. Class notes;
   b. Assigned readings;
   c. Past exam papers.
      (1) **Note**: Past exam papers are useful for answer practice. Do *not* attempt to guess what areas will come up on the exam by reviewing past exam papers.
2. **Step 2**: Assess the materials.
   a. What areas did the lecturer *stress*?
      (1) What areas took up the most amount of time?
      (2) What areas appear year after year on exams?
      (3) What areas did the lecturer state were interesting, unusual, in need of change?
   b. Identify the grey areas, e.g. legal questions that are not resolved or are in need of an update.
      (1) Examiners often ask questions regarding the grey areas.
   c. Identify recent changes in the law:
      (1) Cases, and
      (2) Statutes.

    d. Identify recent recommendations for change:
       (1) Reports of the Law Reform Commission;
       (2) Law review articles;
       (3) Newspaper articles.
    e. Do *not* neglect the settled areas of the law.
       (1) Without a good knowledge of these areas, a student will be unable to make a proper analysis or necessary comparisons.

B. Conquering cases

1. The points that you make in your answers must be backed up with relevant authority.
2. Everyone wrestles with the names of cases.
    a. If you cannot remember the name of a particular case, *briefly* outline enough facts to enable the examiner to know which case you are referring to.
3. For many students, the best way to conquer cases is to test yourself with case flash cards.
    a. Put the name of the case on the front of an index card.
    b. On the back put a brief summary of the facts, holding and the importance of the case.
    c. Look at the name and try to recite the information on the back. If you are correct, put the card in a different stack. Keep going through the cards until you have them correct. Now turn the cards over and try reciting the name from the facts.
    d. Case cards are easier to carry and use than a full set of notes or books.

C. Answering the exam questions

1. **Problem questions**: Test your ability to apply the law to the facts given.
    a. Many students find this type of question the most difficult.
    b. The best way of tackling this type of question is to treat it like a maths problem: *work* your way through it.
       (1) However, unlike a maths problem, there is no one precise correct answer in most law questions.
2. **Planning your answer (problem questions).**
    a. *Read* the question.
    b. *Read* the question again.
    c. **Identify the tort(s).**

  (1) Sometimes this is easy; if you find a question difficult, ask yourself the following questions.

d. **From the facts, which tort(s) may be a possible basis of liability?**

  (1) Remember – the same facts may give rise to numerous torts.

e. **What interest of the plaintiff has been injured?**

  (1) His person?

  (2) His property?

  (3) His reputation? etc.

f. **How has the defendant conducted himself?**

  (1) Performed an intentional act?

  (2) Performed a negligent act?

  (3) Performed no act? (Failed to act?)

g. **Identify the issues.**

  (1) Sometimes this, too, is easy. If not, try asking yourself the following questions.

   (a) **What are the essential elements that the plaintiff must establish as a basis of liability for the tort?**

   (b) **Is each and every essential element present in the facts given?**

   (c) **Consider defences and limitations.**

    i. Does the statute of limitations bar the action?

   (d) **Parties – check the relationship**, if any, between the parties.

    i. Vicarious liability.

    ii. Standard of care issues.

    iii. Publication issues in defamation (spouses).

h. After identifying the issue(s), **select one issue**.

  (1) It is better to take the issues one at a time than to skip back and forth in your answer.

i. **Briefly outline your answer for each issue.**

  (1) Again, check to ensure that you are answering the question asked.

   (a) **Beware** – in exams, it is easy to go off on a tangent.

  (2) All you want are a few basic *phrases*, *words* and *cases* to jog your memory to keep you from going off track or forgetting something.

   (a) Do not spend more than a few minutes outlining your answers.

(3) If you do not like the flow of your proposed answer, just renumber the points quickly.

3. **Writing your problem question answer: Take one issue at a time.**

    a. **The beginning**: The introduction.

        (1) Many students are at a loss where to begin.

        (2) Unless you are instructed otherwise, a good way to begin may be to *define the tort.*

            (a) **Remember** – the examiner is always right, and if the examiner gives you specific instructions concerning the exam, follow them!

        (3) **Example**: A trespass to land is defined as the intentional or negligent entering or remaining or directly causing anything to come into contact with land in the possession of another, without lawful justification.

    b. *Briefly* **discuss the relevant law concerning trespass to land.**

        (1) What is relevant?

            (a) **Example**: It would *not* be relevant to discuss chattels remaining on the land if you are dealing with a trespass by entering the land.

        (2) Remember to cite authority for your points.

            (a) Cases.

            (b) Statutes.

    c. **Apply the *relevant* law to the *facts* given to you in the problem**. Do *not* list every fact; just discuss the facts that are important to your analysis.

    d. **Apply any relevant defences and limitations.** Some students prefer to list all possible defences and eliminate the non-relevant defences quickly.

    e. **Reach a conclusion.**

        (1) Even a wrong conclusion is usually better than no conclusion.

        (2) Some students like to start an answer with 'the answer' (conclusion).

            (a) Just as you would not guess the answer to a maths problem and then work the problem, neither should you guess the answer to a law problem question and then work the problem.

            (b) If you must start the problem with the conclusion, leave space and fill it in after you work the problem.

    f. **Repeat** the above steps until you have covered all the issues presented.

   g. **Reach a final conclusion.**

      (1) Tie up all the issues you have covered.

4. **Negligence problem questions.**

Note: Negligence is the most important area of tort law, and it is the most frequent subject of exam questions. It presents many unique application difficulties.

a. Carefully read through the facts and make certain that you understand the sequence of events!

b. Be methodical and analyse each element of negligence in order.

    (1) For negligence questions, address each element in order. For example, determine if there is an act or omission by the defendant before determining the issue of duty and what duty is owed.

    (2) To determine what duty is owed by the defendant to the plaintiff, look at the relationship between the plaintiff and the defendant. *Never assume that the defendant owes the plaintiff a duty of care.* In most questions, examiners expect you to explain why a duty exists.

    (3) Determine if there was a breach of the duty of care, and then address the issue of causation. Remember that there are two types of causation and both should be addressed.

    (4) Lastly, determine if the facts suggest any defence to the negligence. While most exam questions focus on the issues of duty and causation, you may lose out on valuable marks if you cannot address issues within the question regarding defences and limitations.

---

5. **Essay questions.**

   a. Most students have less difficulty answering essay questions, but they often make the same types of mistakes.

   b. **Read the question.**

   c. **Read the question again.**

   d. **The issue is usually identified for you.**

      (1) Make certain that you answer the question asked.

      (2) If you have prepared essay answers in the hope that the question will come up on the exam, make certain that you *tailor* your prepared essay to answer the question asked.

e. **Take a side.** Because most essay questions ask you to analyse some legal dilemma or problem, at times you will be required to determine which side you want to take, so quickly determine which side you think you can put forth best.
   (1) In doubt? What did your lecturer say about it?
   (2) What do the law commentators write about it?
f. **Ask yourself questions.**
   (1) Why is this true?
   (2) Why is this important?
   (3) How can this be improved?
   (4) How is this issue handled in other jurisdictions?
g. **Outline your answer**.
   (1) Again, if you do not think that it flows well, just renumber the points until you have it the way you like it. Do *not* write out a new outline.
   (2) **Remember** – an instruction in an exam to *discuss, criticise* or *evaluate* does not signify that you should spend three pages stating the posture of the law as it now stands and two paragraphs on analysis. State the law, but *spend* the majority of your time and effort on the critical analysis.
h. **Start writing your answer**.
   (1) Check to make certain you are answering the question asked.
   (2) Cite authorities to back up your points.
   (3) Cite any relevant works, including your textbooks.
i. **Reach a conclusion.**
   (1) The best conclusions tie up many of the points raised in the answer.
   (2) Merely answering the question asked is not the best approach, but it is probably better than just ending abruptly.

II. Avoiding common mistakes

A. Answer the question asked.

1. Many students spend hours revising by writing out answers to what they hope are the exam questions.
   a. One of the problems with this approach is that students often end up writing out their practice answer on the exam and do not answer what has been asked.

   b. If you find it helpful to write out practice answers, make certain that you alter the practice answer to answer the question asked on the exam.

2. Avoid heart-stopping moments. Ever leave an exam hall and learn that you advised the wrong person? Make certain you answer the question asked.

3. **Avoid killing your answer** (and grade).

   a. **Shotgun approach**: Very seldom will you be asked to write everything you know about a particular area of law. Yet many students spend most of their effort and time on writing every single detail they know about the subject in the hope that one or more of the points will hit the target. Blasting away with memorised material, writing pages on the subject and two paragraphs on analysis, is not going to earn you many marks if a question asks you to analyse or criticise, for example.

   b. **Shooting yourself in the foot**: Very few examiners will ask you to write an analysis or critique something in law that is perfectly satisfactory as it stands. *Do not* merely write everything you know about the current status of that area of law and summarise that it does not need to be changed. Write a relevant summary of the status of the law, then:

     (1) Discuss what is right with it.

     (2) Discuss what is wrong with it.

     (3) What has been proposed to make it better?

     (4) Will the proposed changes make it better?

     (5) What would you propose?

4. **Do not jump the gun**.

   a. Many students lead themselves down the primrose path away from higher marks by jumping to a conclusion under the stress of the exam.

   b. This often happens when students only revise limited subjects or areas of the law, if they try to pigeon hole the torts or rely on buzz or key words. **Examples**:

     (1) If a window in your garage is broken, the window is not a chattel but part of the land.

     (2) Just because an animal appears in a question, do not assume that animal liability is the correct issue. If you leave your cat Fluffy with the vet for an operation and Fluffy escapes out the open window, remember that Fluffy is a chattel. Leaving her with the vet created a bailment, so detinue would be a better place to jump, or even professional negligence.

    (3) Every time you see the word 'escape', do not limit your thoughts and answer to *Rylands v Fletcher*.

5. **Time is marks – do not waste it**.
   a. Common time wasters include copying most of the facts given in the exam into the answer. The examiner knows the facts, so just briefly discuss the important or relevant facts in your exam answer.
   b. The use of two or three different colours of ink. The examiner is looking for your knowledge of law, not your knowledge or use of colours. Stick with blue or black ink, and save the time you would waste switching pens.
   c. Over-use of correction fluid.
      (1) There is nothing worse than picking up an exam script and finding the pages stuck together with correction fluid.
      (2) Instead of relying on correction fluid, quickly outline your answer before you begin to write. For those one-page big mistakes, do not waste time trying to paint over it. Cross through the offending page and continue.
   d. Underlining words or phrases.
      (1) Unless you have been instructed otherwise, it is a great waste of time to underline words or phrases.
      (2) Believe it or not, examiners read the answers and do not skim the papers looking for key or buzz words, cases or phrases upon which to award marks. Generally, underlining words or phrases is simply a waste of time.

B. *Do not make reading your exam answers a trial.*
   1. Get the basics right.
      a. **Spelling**: Every year, students make fundamental mistakes with spelling legal and sometimes non-legal words.
      b. If the examiner has any doubts about your ability, it will be removed if you:
         (1) Confuse libel for liable;
         (2) Make the plaintiff into a paintiff;
         (3) Or spell defendant with three Es.
   2. **Sentence structure**: Write in complete sentences, but apply the kiss principle – *keep it short and simple*.
      a. Many students try to emulate the styles of some of the great legal writers of the ages. This is quite understandable after spending a year reading their great works. However, the exam

answers are your work, and you must impress the examiner with your knowledge of the law. To do so you must be able to get your points across.

b. Long, difficult or contorted sentences are not the best way to get your knowledge across to the examiner. If an examiner has to reread a sentence several times to get your meaning, you are not helping your marks.

c. **Warning**: This study aid is in an outline form and many sentences are not complete. Make certain the sentences in your exam answers are complete.

3. **Paragraphs**

a. A paragraph gives the examiner a mental pause before continuing the ascent of your exam answers. Unfortunately, many students fail to see the importance of paragraphs and often write in bullet form or sometimes in a solid block.

(1) Have you ever tried to read a computer printout with words covering the entire page, no margins, no paragraphs, just words and more words? It is not a very pleasurable read.

b. Writing in paragraph form helps you to organise you answer, and allows you to quickly glance over your answer to assess coverage of a topic.

4. **Punctuation**

a. Is not optional – *use it*.

b. Your exam answer is not the time to experiment with new methods of punctuation. Stick to the conventional methods.

5. **Writing in the third person.**

a. Generally, legal writers write in the third person.

b. Yes, judges do often write in the first person, and as one of my law professors told our class, when you become a judge, you, too, can write in the first person.

c. Some lecturers are fanatical about writing in the third person, others are not.

d. Be safe – get in the habit of letting your answer speak for itself.

APPENDIX

ANSWERS TO REVISION QUESTIONS

Introduction Answers

1. The primary function of modern tort law is the protection of interests. See [6].
2. A tort is a private dispute between individuals, with the primary goal being compensation for the harm suffered. A crime is a dispute between an individual and society, with the primary goal being to punish wrongdoers. The plaintiff brings a tort action while the DPP brings a criminal action on behalf of the state. See [9].
3. Under tort law, the duty is fixed by law. Tort duties are owed to others in general, the primary goal being to compensate for harm suffered with unliquidated damages allowed. On the other hand, in contract law the duties are fixed by the parties to the contract and are only owed to the parties. The primary goal in contract law is to enforce the terms of the contract, with damages fixed by the terms of the contract. See [10].
4. Trespass developed first and is criminal in character. It dealt with serious and forcible breaches of the peace resulting in direct injuries, with liability imposed without fault. Trespass on the case developed as a supplement to trespass for injuries caused by some obvious and secondary causes, or in other words, indirect injuries. Unlike trespass on the case, it was not actionable per se. See [3].

Chapter 1 Answers

1. No tort. Mere words are not an assault. See *Tuberville v Savage* [39].
2. Assault. Apprehension is not fear. See [43].
3. No tort. As long as Veronica is free to go where she wants, there is no false imprisonment. See [56].
4. (a) False imprisonment. If Bertha is sitting on Anthony without his consent, she is falsely imprisoning Anthony because he is restrained. See [54].

(b) Battery. If Bertha is sitting on Anthony without his consent, she is committing a battery. See [19].

(c) Possible assault. The facts state that Bertha cornered Anthony. If he was placed in a reasonable apprehension of an immediate battery from Bertha, there may have been an assault. See [35].

5. No battery. Anne consented to the contact. Her consent is not invalidated by Peter's fraud. Peter's fraud did not relate to the nature of the act. See [75].

6. (a) No battery. Battery is the direct application of physical force upon the person of another without consent. There has been no physical force or contact.

(b) Yes. Grainne is not required to risk injury, humiliation or property damage to avail of the tort of false imprisonment. See [55].

7. (a) No. The teacher was in *loco parentis* and is allowed to use reasonable chastisement on a pupil. See [89].

(b) No. In order for an assault to occur, the victim must be in reasonable apprehension of an imminent battery. Because Ralphie's back was turned, he could not have known that the book was raised.

8. (a) No. Sinead's consent to Oliver's spankings is invalidated by his fraud. Oliver's fraud concerned the nature of the acts (spankings). He told Sinead that they were treatment for her whiplash when in fact they were not. See [75] – [76].

(b) Although Ireland has no reported cases of intentional infliction of emotional distress, these facts would probably fall within this tort. See [61] *et seq.*

9. No tort. The elderly gentleman was not acting with voluntary control. He was asleep. See [21].

10. No. Although it was *obiter* in *Walsh v Family Planning Services*, the Supreme Court made it clear that battery will not apply where a doctor exceeds the consent of the patient. Negligence is the proper tort. See [78].

11. No false imprisonment. Liam has not acted, so unless he placed or induced Santa to use the chimney, there has been no false imprisonment of Santa. See [50].

12. (a) (i) Battery. Mike grabbing the handbag. Physical contact extends to any part of the body touched or to anything attached to the body and practically identified with it. See [25].

(ii) Assault. Ken chasing Mike. See [35].

(iii) Battery. Ken caught Mike. See [19].

(iv) Battery. Mike falling on Bob. See [19].
(b) (i) No defences.
    (ii) and (iii) Ken has a valid defence. He can use reasonable force to defend (retrieve) the lady's chattel (handbag). See [99].
    (iv) No battery because Mike's contact was not voluntary. See [21].

13. (a) No. Mrs O'Grady was not placed in reasonable apprehension of receiving a battery. See [35].
    (b) Although Ireland has no reported cases of intentional infliction of emotional distress, these facts would probably fall within this tort. See [61] *et seq.*

14. False imprisonment. Steve may not have intentionally trapped or imprisoned Liz. However, Steve did lock Liz in the pub negligently because he failed to check the toilet stalls. See Street's definition [48].

15. No. Finbar did not place or induce Millie to become imprisoned. See [53].

16. Yes. It is not necessary for Adam to prove that Eve intended to injure or harm Adam. All Adam needs to show is that Eve intended the acts that constitute the battery, i.e. throwing the apple. See [27].

17. (a) Yes.
    (b) Yes. Spencer hit his head on the wheelhouse.
    (c) Yes.
    (d) No. Causation requires that the injury or impact to the plaintiff (Spencer) must be caused by Kate's voluntary act or some force set in motion by Kate's act. See [18].

Chapter 2 Answers

1. Trespass to land. See [113].
2. (a) No, Michael did not act voluntarily. See [108].
   (b) Yes. Tim, by his negligent act (driving), caused Michael to cross the boundary of Fred's land. See [113].
3. (a) Trespass to chattels. Simply moving a chattel from one place to another may be a trespass to chattels. See [161].
   (b) No defences. Note that necessity will not be a valid defence because there is a reasonable alternative. Pauline could ask Naomi to move the bag.
4. (a) Cyril entered under a license with an interest, i.e. he paid consideration to enter. See [130] *et seq.*

     (b) Yes, Cyril's license expired when the film he paid to see ended.

5. (a) Yes, Mai Day committed a trespass when she invaded the airspace with a stone and when the stone hit the ground. See [117]. Note that it was not a trespass to land for the stone to hit the windows for sale. This is because these windows were not attached to the land and hence were not land. See [116].

    (b) No, when Mai Day broke the windows (that were on sale) the windows were chattels. She broke the panes, but generally, broken glass does not destroy the character of the window. Mere damage is not enough for conversion, but it may be enough for trespass to chattels. See [179] *et seq.*

6. Assuming that Toulouse was for breeding purposes, the vet, by wrongfully neutering her, committed a conversion. The character of my pedigree breeding cat has changed. See [179]–[180]. If Toulouse was not for breeding purposes, but was simply a pet or rat warden, the vet has committed a trespass to my chattel by damaging my chattel. See [162].

7. (a) Yes, even though the gentleman does not harm the land, his presence is a trespass. See [109]–[110].

    (b) (i) When the gentleman picked the rose, he severed realty. Assuming that the rose was planted in the garden (and not in a container), it was realty. See [116]. The act of picking it was a severance and hence a conversion. See [190].

        (ii) The picked rose belonged to Miss Marbles. When the gentleman took the rose, that was another act of conversion. See [173]. Remember, a person may act in such a way as to commit several conversions with the same chattel. See [183].

8. It is a trespass to chattels. See [156] *et seq* and Streets comments in [163].

9. (a) Drinking John's tea is a conversion. Consuming something destroys the character of the chattel. John would not want the tea back now, would he? See [179].

    (b) Moving the thermos is a trespass to the chattel. See [161].

10. (a) Acts that are trespass to land include (1) throwing the fire cracker into the sitting room and (2) reaching into the window.

    (b) No. It does not apply to (1), nor does it apply to (2) where Sean caused the greater evil or peril, i.e. the fire. See [140].

    (c) Curtains are generally considered chattels rather than land because they are not permanently attached to the land. Therefore it was a conversion when the curtains caught fire because of Sean's conduct.

11. Assuming that Susan and Michael co-owned their wedding pho-
    tographs, Susan has committed a conversion by burning them. See
    [192].
12. Assuming the stone is an antiquity of importance, the state has the
    best title to it. *Webb v Ireland*. See [197].
13. (a) Bob snapped off a couple of limbs = trespass to chattels.
    (b) Bob entered onto the Scrooge farm = trespass to land.
    (c) Bob chopped down a tree = conversion by severing realty.
    (d) Taking the tree = conversion by taking Scrooge's chattel.
14. (a) Yes, Ziggy entered under authority of law and he later abused
        and exceeded that authority. See [136] *et seq.*
    (b) No. Although Ziggy interfered with Mary's furniture (chattels)
        by moving the furniture, he has two defences: (1) consent (see
        [215]) and (2) lawful authority (see [218]).
    (c) No. Merely opening a drawer is not a conversion. It may be a
        trespass to chattel, but it is not a conversion. However, steal-
        ing Mary's knickers to add to his knicker collection is clearly a
        conversion. See [173].
15. (a) Yes. See [204] *et seq.*
    (b) No. Sean is not required to make a written demand. All that is
        required is that Sean must make a demand for the possession
        of his chattel unless it would be futile to do so. See
        [207]–[208]. When Sean telephoned and learned that his desk
        was destroyed through no fault of ABC, and ABC can prove
        the absence of fault, ABC may escape liability. See [210] *et seq.*
16. First, determine if the six required elements for trespass are present.
    See [107].
    (1) Voluntary act by the defendant? Yes, he walked into the
        premises. See [108].
    (2) Intent or negligence? Yes, he intended to enter the premises.
        See [115].
    (3) Invasion of land? Yes, he was present on the land. See [116].
    (4) Plaintiff in possession (or entitled to possession) of land? Yes.
        See [123].
    (5) Causation? Yes, there is a direct link between the defendant's
        acts and the invasion by entering the land. (Remember, land
        includes buildings!) See [127].
    (6) Any lawful justification for invasion? No. This is the issue of
        the question. Generally, customers are granted a bare license to
        enter business premises. This right of entry does not include
        entry for purposes other than legitimate business. If he did not

have the plan when he entered, his acts in furtherance of his plan (splashing water on the floor) exceeded the bare license, i.e. Supermac's consent for him being on the premises. See [128] and [130].

17. (a) Yes. Under the common law and the Non-Fatal Offences Against the Person Act 1997 and the Criminal Justice (Public Order) Act 1994, a person may use reasonable force to eject a trespasser. If the entry was without force, the occupier must request the trespasser to leave before using force. See [96] *et seq.*

(b) Yes. Trespass protects possession rather than ownership. *Jus tertii* arises where a defendant (Goldilocks) alleges that the plaintiffs (Three Bears) have no right to possession of the land because the right (*jus*) is vested in a third person (*tertii*). So unless Goldilocks was present for Yogi Bear, *jus tertii* is not a valid defence. See [141]. Also, remember that infancy is not a defence in tort law, as it is in criminal law, so the tort of trespass applies to children as well adults.

Chapter 3 Answers

1. No. There was no escape. See [281].
2. (a) Strict liability will only apply to domestic animals where the defendant had knowledge of the dangerous nature of an animal. See [250].

(b) Yes, the act of a stranger defence applies to cattle trespass (see [260]) and the rule in *Rylands v Fletcher* (see [286]).

3. The Accidental Fires Act 1943 provides that no legal action can be initiated by any person who suffers damage because of a fire accidentally occurring in the building of another person. Accidental means without negligence. Irene was negligent in causing the fire and was negligent in failing to control the fire. See [238] *et seq.*

4. Not unless the master instructed Cyril to attack the heifer. See [256].

5. Yes. See [264] *et seq.*

6. (a) No. The owner or keeper of a *ferae naturae* keeps that animal at his peril. See [252].

(b) No, there is no causation between Larry's conduct and Aine's injury. It may have been different if Aine was running from Larry and fell, but she was clearly not in danger from the lion. The owner or keeper of a *ferae naturae* is strictly liable for all damages caused by the animal. See [252].

7. No. Consent will be a complete defence if Michael consented to the risk associated with the dangerous accumulation. Michael did not. He wanted Johnny to remain responsible for building and maintaining the pond. Johnny may have a partial defence. See [289].

8. (a) No. The Act does not apply to repairers. See [302].
   (b) No. The Act does not apply to repairers. See [302].

9. (a) Yes. The Act does not exclude producers of products from outside the EU.
   (b) Yes, under section 2(3), if Schultze's imported the hairdryer. See [301].
   (c) Jane was not contributorily negligent. She did not act unreasonably under the circumstances. See [322].
   (d) No, damage to the product itself is not covered by the Act. See [308].
   (e) No. Jane can recover for the cost of replacing the carpeting minus £350. See [323].
   (f) Yes. The limitation on damages only applies to property damage. See [314].

10. (a) No. Pursuant to section 7, a right of action is barred ten years from the date on which the producer put into circulation the actual product that caused the damage, regardless of whether or not the right of action accrued during the ten years. See [323].
   (b) No. Pursuant to section 5, a defective product is one that fails to provide the safety that a reasonable person is entitled to expect, taking all circumstances into account. Circumstances may include the use to which the product could reasonably be expected to be put. The more unusual or extreme the use, the less likely it could be said to be reasonably expected. It is not usual to use rodent traps as paperweights. See [305].

11. (a) No, the immunity granted in the Act only applies to fires occurring on or in the buildings or lands of another person. See [238].
   (b) Yes, Ms Jewett could bring an action under the Liability for Defective Products Act 1991 and would prevail so long as she could prove (i) a covered injury, (ii) the defect, and (iii) that the injury was caused by the defect in the product that was produced or manufactured by the defendant.
      (i) Covered injury?
         • The ruined clothing is not a covered injury because the value does not exceed £350. See [323].

- The personal injuries are a covered injury, and the injury was caused by a defect in the product that was manufactured by Shock-R-Us.

(ii) The defect?
- Section 5 provides that a defective product is one that fails to provide the safety that a reasonable person is entitled to expect, taking all circumstances into account.
- Circumstances include when the product was put into circulation, the presentation of the product and the use to which the product could reasonably be expected to be used. The defibrillator was apparently used the way it was meant to be used and set the patient's clothing on fire.

(iii) So long as the defibrillator was put into circulation within the last ten years, etc., it seems likely that Ms Jewett should be able to bring a case under the Act for her personal injuries only.

12. (a) The owner – section 21(1) of the Control of Dogs Act 1986 imposes strict liability on the owner or keeper of dogs for damage caused to humans by the dog. See [254].

(b) The woman walking with the owner – unless the woman was a co-owner or keeper of the dogs, she would not be held strictly liable under the Control of Dogs Acts.

(c) School – the occupier of land where the dog attack took place would only be liable under the Control of Dogs Act 1986 if it was the owner or keeper of the dog. It was neither. See [255].

13. (a) Under the common law, the owner or keeper of a *ferae naturae* keeps the wild animal at his or her peril. A camel is not native to Ireland, therefore it is a *ferae naturae* and the circus will be held strictly liable for any damage caused by Saraha. See [252].

(b) Under the Control of Dogs Act 1986, section 21, strict liability is imposed on all dog owners for damage caused by the dog attacking a person or for any damage done to livestock by the dog. The issue here is whether a camel could be considered livestock under the Act. The animals listed in the Act as livestock include traditional farmyard animals and those traditionally used for transportation as well as domesticated deer. It could be argued that camels are also traditionally used for transportation, and belong to the same split-hoofed family as swine, goats, sheep and deer. See [254].

14. A bullock is a *mansuetae naturae*, therefore strict liability will not apply unless it can be proven that Finbar knew of the dangerous propensities of this particular animal to attacking. See [250]. The facts do not indicate how the bullock came to be on the road. Cattle trespass may apply, as the bullock has trespassed onto the chattels of another, i.e. the car. See [257]. However, under the common law, livestock straying onto the public road did not commit cattle trespass. See [257]. Under section 2 of the Animals Act 1985, any person placing animals on land is required to take reasonable care to avoid damage being caused by the animals straying onto the public road. In other words, the Animals Act 1985 does not impose strict liability. Therefore, it seems unlikely that Finbar will be held strictly liable for the damage inflicted by the bullock unless it can be proven that he knew of the dangerous propensities of this particular animal to attacking.

15. • Accumulation of a dangerous or hazardous thing? Yes, trash is accumulated. See [277].
    • Non-natural use of land? Yes, under the special use requirement, a landfill brings increased danger to others. See [279].
    • Escape? Yes, although the accumulation did not escape, its foreseeable dangerous effect or by-product did escape from the defendant's occupation or control. See [281].
    • Damage? Yes, rendering a person's home uninhabitable is certainly an injury. See [282].
    • Causation? Yes, the accumulation of the trash generated the gas that invaded the plaintiff's home, rendering it uninhabitable. Gas and fumes are a foreseeable consequence of decaying trash, and the escape of gas and fumes from a trash landfill is foreseeable. It is doubtful that the issue of remoteness would arise. See [284].
    • Lack of defence? There is nothing to suggest in the facts an act of stranger or an act of God. See [286] and [287]. There is also nothing to indicate consent. See [289].

16. • Accumulation of a dangerous or hazardous Thing? Yes. Remember, plain old water can be a dangerous thing. It was what escaped in *Rylands*. See [277].
    • Non-natural use of land? Yes, under the special use requirement an industry requiring 10,000 gallons of water brings an increased danger to others downhill of the accumulation. See [279].
    • Escape? Yes, the accumulated water escaped. Remember, it is not required that the escape be foreseeable, only that the thing,

if it does escape, could cause damage or mischief if it escapes. See [281].

- Damage? Yes, swamping a house with mud and slime, rendering it uninhabitable, is an injury. See [282].
- Causation? Yes, the accumulation of the water escaped and directly invaded the plaintiff's home, causing extensive damage and rendering it uninhabitable. See [284].
- Lack of defence? Yes. From the facts it does not appear that act of God, act of stranger, consent or contributory negligence apply. See [285] *et seq.*

17. (a) No, the system was put into circulation more than ten years before the injury, therefore under section 7 of the LFDPA 1991 an action is barred. See [323].

   (b) No. Repairers are not covered by the LFDPA 1991. See [302].

Chapter 8 Answers

1. (a) Pure economic loss. See [466] *et seq.*
   (b) Probably. Using the *Ward v McMaster* requirements of (1) proximity between the parties, (2) reasonable foreseeable damages, and (3) no adverse public policy considerations, it would appear that Margaret should recover. See [479] *et seq.*
   (c) Probably not. Applying the *Kelly v Hennessy* principles, Andy suffered harm from exposure to the aftermath, but he cannot recover unless he had a close personal relationship with Nicola. See [494].
   (d) Section 48(1) of the Civil Liability Act 1961. See [505].
   (e) Wrongful death. See [504].
   (f) Section 6(1) of the Statute of Limitations (Amendment) Act 1991 provides that the action must be brought within three years from the date of the death. See [506]. However, now, under the Civil Liability and Courts Acts 2004, if the crash took place after 31 March 2005, Nicola's husband will have two years. See [624].
   (g) No, only one cause of action is allowed under section 48(2) of the Civil Liability Act 1961. See [505].

2. (a) Yes, under the egg shell skull rule. See [581] *et seq.*
   (b) No, negligence is not actionable per se. Paul suffered no physical injury to himself or to his property. There is nothing in the problem to suggest that he suffered nervous shock.
   (c) No. In common law jurisdictions, a person is under no general duty to go to the aid of another in peril. There are two general

exceptions to this rule: (1) if the defendant has a special relationship with the plaintiff, such as between a parent and child, or (2) if the defendant caused or placed the plaintiff in the peril. David was merely a witness to the accident, does not have a special relationship to Mary and did not place her in the peril. Therefore, David did not owe Mary an affirmative duty to help her. See [380] *et seq.*

(d) No. New forces must join with Tony's negligence to injure Shelly. There was no new force. The suitcase was set in motion by Tony's negligence. See [576].

(e) No. Mary has not performed a negligent act that caused Shelly's injuries. See [531].

3. (a) (i) Elmer owed Richard a duty of care.

(ii) Elmer breached the duty of care that he owed to Richard.

(iii) Because Elmer breached the duty of care that he owed to Richard, Richard suffered an injury, loss or damage.

(iv) Richard suffered an injury, loss or damage. See [329].

(b) No. Contributory negligence is concerned with the plaintiff's contribution to his own injuries. It is not concerned with his contribution to the incident that caused his injury. See [586].

(c) (i) But for Elmer leaving his window open, Richard would not have been injured. This statement is not true. There is no actual causation.

(ii) But for Elmer leaving the keys to the gun safe in his home, Richard would not have been injured. This statement is not true. There is no actual causation. Would your answer have been different if the instrumentality causing the death had been a car that Tom stole from Elmer when he found the keys to the car? See Breslin v Corcoran [572].

(iii) But for Tom shooting Richard, Richard would not have been injured. This statement is true. There is actual causation.

(d) No. The cause of Tom's injury is the poor job he performed in cutting off the gun barrel. Did you want to write that Tom was contributorily negligent? This is not the case. To be contributorily negligent means that the defendant (Elmer) had to be negligent. Elmer was not negligent.

4. (a) A dentist must exercise the skills of a reasonable dentist. See [344] *et seq.*

(b) Under *Dunne v National Maternity Hospital,* if there are two or more accepted medical treatments it is well settled that the medical practitioner is protected from liability if he follows one of the accepted procedures. See [363]. In this instance, it would appear that there are two accepted procedures: (1) to send the patient to an oral surgeon, or (2) to remove the impacted wisdom tooth himself. Therefore, the local dentist's decision to remove the tooth himself is not itself a breach of the duty of care owed.

(c) Yes. (1) The defendant had sole control of the incident. (2) The defendant dentist had knowledge denied to the plaintiff. (3) The plaintiff's injuries do not normally happen during a tooth extraction without some element of negligence by the defendant. See [520] *et seq.*

5. (a) Yes. An assault is an act by the defendant that places the plaintiff in reasonable apprehension of an immediate battery. See [35] *et seq.*

(b) No. Under the doctrine of *respondeat superior*, the general rule is that an employer may be liable for the tortious acts committed by her employees within the scope of the employment. Vicarious liability will not apply if the tort is committed outside the scope of the employment. Travel to and from the primary place of employment is outside the scope of employment. See [420] *et seq.*

(c) No. An assault is an intentional tort. The general rule is that an employer may be vicariously liable for the intentional torts committed by her employees within the scope of the employee's employment if the employee's duties involve the use of physical force on others, such as a bodyguard or bouncer, or where the force is used to further the employer's interests. While Daniel may have been acting within the scope of his employment, his duties did not involve the threatened use of physical force on others, nor did the assault he committed further his employer's interest. See [423] *et seq.*

6. (a) No. Under the sixth principle set forth by the Supreme Court in *Kelly v Hennessey*, there are no public policy limits on recovery where the plaintiff establishes sufficient proximity and foreseeability by establishing the five other principles. Thus, membership in a motorcycle gang should have no impact on their ability to pursue an action for nervous shock. See [494].

(b) In addition to the duties of an occupier, the defendant hotel/casino may have owed the same standard as a publican.

Hotel/casinos are not a feature of Ireland, but probably come closest to that of a public house because of the provision of alcohol to patrons. If the hotel/casino is held to the same standard as a public house, then a duty is owed to protect a patron on the premises from a battery by another patron. *Hall and Kennedy v Routledge.* See [428]. More recently, in *Meagher v Shamrock Houses* the High Court held that the owner of a licensed premises owes a duty to patrons to take all reasonable care for his safety while on the premises, which includes ensuring that another patron on the premises does not assault the plaintiff. Thus the questions or issues presented are whether the hotel/casino provided sufficient protection and whether the Hells Angels entering the hotel/casino would be considered 'other patrons on the premises' as they were coming through the doors with weapons.

(c) Not unless the surviving members were 'dependents' of a deceased person or persons killed in the fight. A dependent under the Civil Liability Act 1961 is any member of the family of the deceased suffering injury or mental distress because of the death. See [505].

(d) The defence of *ex turpi* or illegality is based on the public policy objection to allowing a person engaged in an illegal activity from maintaining a lawsuit when injured during the course of the illegal activity. The scope of the defence is not clear in Ireland. Under section 57(1) of the Civil Liability Act 1961, it is not a defence to merely show that the plaintiff was in breach of a civil or criminal law. Under the English approach, *ex turpi* applies to situations where the plaintiff, while engaged in a crime, is negligently injured by the defendant, who was not engaged in the crime. Thus, if this approach is used the plaintiffs were engaged in a crime and even if the defendant hotel/casino was negligent for failing to provide enough security, the defendant hotel/casino was not engaged in the crime. If the English approach is used, the defendant hotel/casino will have a good defence. See [599] *et seq.*

7. (a) A doctor, as a professional, owes a general duty of care to his or her patients to exercise the skills of a reasonable doctor. *Dunne v National Maternity Hospital.* See [345] and [358] *et seq.*

(b) A common law duty of care is owed to persons reasonably foreseen to be injured by the negligence, i.e. foreseeable plaintiffs. See [371]. In this scenario, Dr Quack negligently performed a vasectomy, and of course the patient's spouse or partner is a foreseeable plaintiff because the patient and his spouse/partner are now denied the ability to have children. See also doctors' duties to third parties [411] *et seq.*

8. (a) No. Susan died on 1 August 2003. Under section 48(1) of the Civil Liability Act 1961, an action must be brought within three years from the date of death. See [613]. However, the Civil Liability and Courts Act 2004 provides that any actions for fatal injuries that fell before 31 March 2005 must be brought two years from 31 March 2005 or three years from the relevant date, whichever occurs first. See [615]. The relevant date in this scenario is 1 August 2003. Thus, two years from 31 March 2005 is 31 March 2007, and three years from the relevant date of 1 August 2003 is 1 August 2006. The date occurring first is 1 August 2006, thus Susan's husband has until 1 August 2006 to bring an action.

   (b) Peter died on 3 June 2005 from his injuries incurred on 1 August 2003. Under section 48(1) of the Civil Liability Act 1961, an action must be brought within three years from the date of death. See [613]. However, the Civil Liability and Courts Act 2004 provides that any actions for fatal injuries that fell after 31 March 2005 must be brought within two years from the date of death. See [614]. Thus, as of 24 December 2005, Breda's cause of action for the wrongful death of her son Peter is not statute barred.

   (c) Breda suffered nervous shock when she viewed Peter in the hospital on 1 August 2003 in the aftermath of the car crash. Under section 3 of the Statute of Limitations (Amendment) Act 1991, Breda has three years from the date of her injury to bring a cause of action, i.e. 1 August 2006. See [608]. Thus, as of 24 December 2005, Breda's cause against David for nervous shock is not statute barred.

Chapter 9 Answers

1. No. Georgia is a visitor. See [658]. She is a social guest engaging in recreation, but she is still a visitor.
2. Yes. Premises includes a means of transport. See [653].
3. (a) Visitors, as they entered under a contract. See [658].
   (b) A common law duty in negligence. In other words, the Act requires an occupier to take reasonable care in the

circumstances to ensure that a visitor does not suffer any injury or damages because of any danger or unsafe condition on the premises. See [659].

(c) No. Notices to restrict or exclude liability must be reasonably brought to the attention of the visitor. See [660] *et seq.*

4. (a) Recreational user. See [662].

(b) Generally, the Act imposes a duty on an occupier not to intentionally injure or damage the recreational user's property or to act with reckless disregard for the recreational user's person or property. See [665].

(c) Yes.

(d) No. While structures provided for recreational users must be maintained in a safe condition, there is an exception for entry structures such as gates and stiles. Occupiers are not required to keep entry structures in a safe condition. See [667].

(e) Probably not. Hillary's broken arm was caused by her slipping in cow manure in a field. Generally, the Act imposes a duty on an occupier not to intentionally injure or damage the recreational user's property or to act with reckless disregard for the recreational user's person or property. Obviously, Finbar did not intentionally injure Hillary. With regard to acting with reckless disregard, it must be remembered that the character of the premises is that it is a field where cattle graze. It is doubtful that a failure to remove cow manure from a field, or the failure to place warnings, would be considered to be a reckless disregard. See [673].

5. (a) (i) The court must determine what type of harm the statute was designed to protect.

(ii) Whether the plaintiff is within the class of persons the statute was designed to protect.

(iii) Whether other remedies are available and adequate. See [641] *et seq.*

(b) Yes. The statute wants to keep guns from falling into the hands of criminals to be used in violent crimes.

(c) Perhaps. If Elmer's gun safe was an approved model, he did not breach the statute. If his gun safe was not an approved model, he breached the statute.

(d) Perhaps. It depends on whether Elmer was in breach of the statute and this breach was the cause of the injury to Richard. For example, if Elmer's gun safe was not approved because it is a new superior model, it is doubtful that Richard will prevail.

However, if Elmer's gun safe was not approved because it had a key entry instead of a combination, Richard could argue that the law makers wanted combination locks rather than key entry to avoid the very thing that happened: a person gaining access to the gun by finding the key.

6. (a) Visitor. Jerry is a social guest engaging in recreation, but he is still a visitor. See [658].

  (b) The duty owed to a visitor by an occupier is a common law duty in negligence. In other words, an occupier must take reasonable care in the circumstances to ensure that a visitor does not suffer any injury or damage because of any danger or unsafe condition of the premises. See [659].

  (c) No. The Act is concerned with the occupiers' duty owed to entrants based on the condition of the land or premises. There is nothing to suggest in the facts that the condition of the premises had anything at all to do with Jerry's injury. See [649]–[650].

7. (a) Jerry is a visitor. See [658].

  (b) As an occupier, Home Hospital is required to take reasonable care in the circumstances to ensure that a visitor does not suffer any injury or damage because of any danger or unsafe condition on the premises. See [659].

  (c) Yes, the gap between the lift and the floor is a dangerous or unsafe condition, especially in a hospital.

Chapter 10 Answers

1. (a) No. If the rights interfered with belong to a person as a member of the public, the act or omission is a public nuisance. See [683]. Only the attorney general can bring a civil action for a public nuisance. See [685].

  (b) Yes. A private individual (like Felix) may maintain an action if a special, particular or peculiar damage is suffered. Further, the damage must be more serious than the damage suffered by the general public. A special, particular or peculiar damage may consist of an injury to a person's pecuniary interest where his person or property is damaged or it may include the deprivation of the opportunity to earn a living. Clearly, Felix has suffered a special, particular or peculiar damage that is more serious than the damage, i.e. environmental pollution, suffered by the general public. See [685].

    (c) Yes. Same as (b).

2. (a) Yes, a single act can amount to a nuisance. See [718].

    (b) Yes. There is no requirement that actual injury to land occur. See [713]. A substantial interference with the use and enjoyment of land is enough. See [707]. To determine if the interference was unreasonable, the courts weigh the utility of the defendant's conduct against the gravity of the harm which resulted or is likely to result to the plaintiff. There was no utility for Kevin's conduct. While he did not intentionally cause the stench, etc., he was negligent. The harm that resulted to Clean Jean was against the use and enjoyment of her home. Also, while there was no permanent damage, there may have been a required clean-up due to the brown haze that settled. There was a discomfort of inconvenience for Clean Jean. See [713].

    (c) No, generally parents are not responsible for the torts of their children. See [426]. Also, there are no facts that indicate that Kevin's parents authorised the creation of the nuisance. See [697].

    (d) No. Generally, the interference to Clean Jean's use and enjoyment of her apartment must be something that a reasonable person would take offence at, rather than a mere annoyance. Any reasonable person would take offence at the stench of rotten eggs in their home, particularly since the bomb left a dirty brown haze on everything. Clean Jean is not being unduly sensitive by trying to force her neighbours into accommodating some unusual need that she has. See [711] *et seq.*

3. (a) No. Prescription requires twenty years. See [728].

    (b) No. Coming to the nuisance is not a defence. See [726].

    (c) No. The defence of contributory negligence is not available where it is alleged that the plaintiff came to the nuisance. See [725].

    (d) Perhaps. English authority suggests that planning permission can only be taken as authorising a nuisance if the effect of the permission alters the character of the locale. From the brief facts given in this case, it is not known if the planning permission did alter the character of the locale. See [733].

4. (a) Yes, Ranallo and Jacoby have committed a nuisance.

    (b) Ranallo and Jacoby have committed a private nuisance. While most persons consider a supermarket a public place, it is in fact privately owned. Therefore, an intentional private nuisance has occurred. See [720] and [695] *et seq.* Note that the defendants are liable for all damages and their conduct made one employee physically ill and drove away customers.

(c) No defences will apply.

5. (a) Brenda's removal of the carpeting and the installation of a wooden floor in her apartment may be a private nuisance if it causes inconvenience or interference with Bertie and Cecelia's enjoyment, quiet, freedom or if the noise of overhead steps injuriously affects their senses or nerves. See [707]. The interference with their use and enjoyment of their home by the overhead steps must be something that a reasonable person would take offence at, rather than a mere annoyance. See [711] *et seq.*

(b) The barking dog that Charles is keeping is a private nuisance, particularly because it is keeping Bertie and Cecelia awake. The longer the interference, i.e. barks all night, the more likely the interference will be considered unreasonable. See [718].

(c) While odours may constitute a private nuisance, it seems unlikely that a food that is traditional, such as cabbage, would rise to a private nuisance. It would seem that Bertie and Cecelia may be unduly sensitive in objecting to Carmel cooking cabbage. See [712].

Chapter 11 Answers

1. (a) Yes. A university is a legal person, and legal persons can sue for defamation. See [751].

(b) No. See [757].

(c) Mary will not be liable for libel if her communication falls under the defence of qualified privilege. Mary, as a lecturer, may have a duty to report her statement and the academic council may have a corresponding interest in receiving the statement. So long as the communication was not wider than necessary or motivated by malice, Mary's communication should not amount to libel. See [797].

(d) No. The maker of an alleged defamatory statement will only be liable if she could have reasonably foreseen the particular publication. It is not reasonably foreseeable that sending a report to an internal university council will be sent on to a foreign newspaper. See [760].

(e) No. The newspaper is in the US and the US is not a member of the EU. The convention applies to member states of the EU. See [780].

(f) Yes. The statement is in writing and is thus a libel. Libel is actionable per se. See [779] *et seq.*

2. (a) Hamish's statements may come under the defence of fair comment. See [791].

(b) Probably not. The public has an interest and concern in the cleanliness of eating establishments. See [791].

(c) Probably not. The statement must ruin the person's reputation or good name. A statement merely causing anger or upset is not enough. See [774].

(d) Yes. Malice destroys the defence of fair comment. See [791].

3. (a) No. Defamation requires a publication to a third person. See [758]. Ricky will only be liable if he could have reasonably foreseen the particular publication. See [760]. It is not reasonably foreseeable that when two people retire to a private office that the content of their conversation will be learned by a lip reader peering through a window in the door.

(b) Yes, there was a publication to a third party, but the plaintiff made the publication rather than the defendant. Therefore, the defendant is not responsible.

4. (a) Generally, being falsely accused of winning the lottery would not be a defamatory statement. However, Andrew is the founder and president of the Anti-Gambling League. Such a statement would probably cause a reasonable person to form a negative or adverse view of Andrew's reputation or good name. See [755]. See also innuendo [772].

(b) Perhaps. Susan clearly published the statement to a third person, Winnie. However, slander is not actionable per se, and there is no proof of damages in the problem presented. Because the allegation deals with winning the lottery and not to Andrew's abilities in his place of employment, it is doubtful that the statement is slander per se.

(c) Mere abuse such as name calling is not slander. See [756].

(d) No. Communications between spouses is not defamatory because there is no publication. See [766].

5. (a) No. The privilege generally applies to statements made in the course of the judicial proceedings. This statement was not made in the course of the proceedings, but was made during a recess. See [794].

(b) Slander per se. See [784] *et seq.*

(c) No. Only a living person is able to bring and maintain an action for defamation. See [751].

(d) No. Communications between spouses are not defamatory because there is no publication. See [766]. There must be a publication to a third party.

6. (a) Yes, Barney has published a false statement that Hannah has behaved in an unchaste manner. Telling the lads at work that Hannah is having an affair with Barney is a slander per se. See [784].

(b) No, a communication between spouses is not a publication. See [766].

(c) Yes. Wilma, by telling Betty that Barney is having an affair with Hannah, has committed a slander per se. See [784]. The fact that Betty is Barney's wife is of no consequence. It is not an inter-spousal communication, nor does it attract the defence of qualified privilege. See [797].

(d) No. There has been no publication to a third person. See [758].

7. (a) Probably not. Defamation is the wrongful publication of a false statement about a person which tends to lower that person in the eyes of right-thinking members of society. See [746]. It is doubtful that right-thinking members of society would hold a person obtaining a B average at school up to hatred, ridicule or contempt, or cause that person to be shunned or avoided by right-thinking members of society. *Berry v Irish Times*. See [746]. The statement must be defamatory in nature and cause a reasonable person to form a negative or adverse view of the plaintiff's reputation. See [755].

(b) Since the statement is true in substance, the magazine could probably avail of the defence of justification if it is found to be defamatory. See [787].

Chapter 12 Answers

1. No. Passing off requires that the misrepresentation must take place in a commercial context. See [813]. While a charity may bring an action, political parties are not allowed to.

2. Passing off. The defendant (Cajun County) opened a restaurant with almost the identical name to the plaintiff's business (Cajun Country). Even unregistered names may develop a specific association which may easily allow for the confusion of the public, which is clearly the case in the facts presented. See [815].

3. It depends on a number of factors, including what colours the other manufacturers are using for their handgrips. Do the new

coloured handles confuse the public into thinking that the defendant's goods are Bebe's goods? It would also depend on whether the grips are seen more as a fashion trend rather than a misrepresentation. See *Adidas v O'Neill* [817].

4. (a) No. Some aspect of Suzanne's business must be used to confuse the public into thinking that Winona's services are Suzanne's. In the facts presented, Winona is not trying to confuse the public into thinking that her services are Suzanne's. See [812].

   (b) Perhaps. If the provision of wedding scrapbooks causes the defendant's services to be confused with the plaintiff's services, it may be an appropriation of a business aspect belonging to the plaintiff. See [815].

5. The appropriation of a celebrity's name or likeness for endorsing the defendant's goods or services has been held in other jurisdictions to be passing off. See [821].